A ...
Through the World of
Modern Art

Here is a lively and engaging tour through the realm of modern art which explains how to understand and enjoy it.

Beginning with the 19th century and ending with today's painters, Sarah Newmeyer traces the development of modern art through its various schools, trends and major figures. In vivid, brief biographies of the great artists of the past hundred years, and in 80 reproductions of their work, she illuminates her spirited and sensible comments on art, its methods and techniques and its promise for tomorrow.

Enjoying Modern Art is a wonderful introduction to a deeper appreciation of the rich and challenging world of modern art.

"This is a sensible, mature and readable book."
—*Chicago Tribune*

". . . written to inform, not in a pedantic way but through an entertaining and dramatic presentation . . ."—*Christian Science Monitor*

THIS IS A REPRINT OF THE ORIGINAL HARDCOVER EDITION
PUBLISHED BY THE REINHOLD PUBLISHING CORPORATION

Other MENTOR Books of Special Interest

Enjoying

Modern

Art

by Sarah Newmeyer

A MENTOR BOOK

NEW AMERICAN LIBRARY

TIMES MIRROR

NEW YORK AND SCARBOROUGH, ONTARIO

Published as a MENTOR BOOK
by arrangement with Van Nostrand Reinhold Company,
who have authorized this softcover edition.

 MENTOR TRADEMARK REG. U.S. PAT. OFF. AND FOREIGN COUNTRIES
REGISTERED TRADEMARK—MARCA REGISTRADA
HECHO EN CHICAGO, U.S.A.

SIGNET, SIGNET CLASSICS, SIGNETTE, MENTOR AND PLUME BOOKS
are published *in the United States* by
The New American Library, Inc.,
1301 Avenue of the Americas, New York, New York 10019,
in Canada by The New American Library of Canada Limited,
81 Mack Avenue, Scarborough, 704, Ontario

11 12 13 14 15 16 17 18 19

Contents

1 THE ADVENTURE OF MODERN ART

MODERN ART MAY BE A PICTURE OF A BISON scratched twenty thousand years ago on a wall of the Lascaux caves in southern France. Or it may be a picture painted by Picasso only this morning. The dictionary defines "modern" as being "of the present" or "just now." But the term "modern art" both expands and contracts that definition. It expands it to include the caveman artist lost in the mists of time, but it sharply contracts it to exclude the artist of today who paints pictures his grandfather might have liked sixty years ago.

It is safe to say that practically nobody's grandfather sixty or even fifty years ago liked—and very few even knew—the paintings of Cézanne, van Gogh, Gauguin, Seurat, looked upon today as the Old Masters of modern art. In art, as in many other aspects of life, often what appears to be radically new is indignantly repulsed as an affront to good taste or even to morals by the first generation to meet it, begins to be accepted by the second, is honored as a classic or hugged to the popular breast by the third—and is either ignored or rejected as old hat by the fourth.

Nowhere can this cycle of repulse, acceptance, rejection be more clearly seen than in the work of the expatriate American, James A. McNeill Whistler, who lived most of his mature life in London. Because he developed an individual style and did not paint in the manner taught by the academies—against which all art was measured—his paintings were considered an insult to public taste. Whistler was not a great painter. Much of his work is too delicate, too evanescent, too *twilit*, for greatness. He was sometimes called the "poet of the Thames" and, as Turner had done so differently before him, produced many canvases "revealing the Thames to the people who lived on it but had previously only seen it as a stretch of water." In Turner's paintings the river almost dissolves in a quivering blaze of light; in Whistler's it nearly disappears in dusk or darkness. His quiet, misty night scenes—nocturnes, he called them—and his gentle, haunting portraits, more like memories than living per-

7

sons, so enraged the critics that the most powerful and famous of them, the great John Ruskin, accused him in print of "willful imposture" in presenting his works as art and himself as an artist. It was Whistler's *Nocturne in Black and Gold* that especially aroused Ruskin's wrath. He wrote of it: "I have seen and heard much of cockney impudence before now, but I never expected to hear a coxcomb ask two hundred guineas for flinging a pot of paint in the public's face!" When looking at some of Whistler's darkest "nocturnes," one has a slight feeling of sympathy for Ruskin's bafflement even though his motives were despicable, his manners execrable, and his critical blindness incredible. He did not discriminate when it came to Whistler's paintings. It was enough that they were Whistler's; he damned (or ignored) them all, thereby eventually wrecking his own reputation as an art critic rather than Whistler's as an artist.

Ruskin's vitriolic attack was the climax of the abuse and ridicule heaped on paintings that today seem amazingly inoffensive. Whistler could endure it no longer. He sued Ruskin for libel. To the accompaniment of the world's laughter, the trial was played out to its farcical end—one farthing damages awarded the plaintiff! That half-cent, in American money, cost Whistler dear, for the heavy expense of the suit forced him into bankruptcy and he spent the next decade of his life almost in poverty.

It must be said that in some of his night pictures Whistler was trying to do the impossible—to paint night itself, blackness upon deeper blackness, murk swallowing up form in murk, impenetrable shade emphasized instead of illumined by rocket bursts. But when he abandoned black and lifted his brush out of quagmire grays to produce the beautiful though muted color tonalities of *Old Battersea Bridge: Nocturne in Blue and Gold,* he accomplished the very difficult task he had set for himself—to represent moonlight and mist on canvas. This painting, by the omission or blurring of a few trifling details, is immediately recognizable as an ultramodern abstraction of magnificent design, far more original than the newest canvases seen in avant-garde galleries on New York's Fifty-seventh Street today.

The tide began to turn in Whistler's favor when, in 1892, the French Government bought his *Arrangement in Grey and Black* for eight hundred dollars—and forty years later insured it for half a million when it was sent for exhibition to the United States! Known the world over as "Whistler's Mother," the painting reached the stature of a classic when it entered the collection of the Louvre. It became one of the most popular paintings in the world, with millions upon millions of reproductions sold. But it has lost the spontaneity of its original appeal. We are tired of it. (Pl. III)

Even the greatest paintings and sculpture, if seen too often in reproduction or in imitation by other artists, become unbearably familiar. The Venus de Milo suffers from this. In addition to the countless plaster casts of it in the older museums and art schools and the copies in miniature that have been sold for generations, a photograph of that serene and noble figure was recently used to advertise a brassiere! (Pl. I)

What has all this to do with modern art? A great deal, for modern art is first of all a point of view. The modern artist looks at the world—or that part of it he elects to paint—as though it has been created fresh this morning and he is the first to paint a horse, a face, a landscape. Never having seen these objects before, he must *look* at them. His vision, uncluttered by his own or other artists' previous impressions of a horse, a face, a landscape, and undulled by photographs of these objects, must get its *own* first impression *from the object itself.* A hundred years ago Courbet, artistic rebel of his day, said: "The museums should be closed for twenty years so that today's painters may begin to see the world with their own eyes."

It is this sort of *seeing,* in a very real sense, that distinguishes the modern from the traditional or academic artist. Not all living or contemporary artists are modern. Many artists of today consciously or subconsciously repeat old forms and styles and patterns of art without infusing or renewing them with even a breath of creative originality. On the other hand, a genuine modern artist can take an old style and recreate it in terms of today or of his own individuality, as Matisse has done with Persian art.

The best known—because of the innumerable reproductions of it that have been sold—of all Picasso's paintings is *Woman in White,* a serene, restful portrait done in the classic Greek style. (Pl. I) Yet no one would confuse it with the early Greek sculpture it so plainly resembles, for Picasso has put the stamp of his own art into its every line and brushstroke. Dali, with his pictures of melting watches, women with bouquets for heads, grand pianos shedding their skins, paints with the expert precision of a miniaturist and the finish of a little Dutch Master—but no one could ever mistake him for any but the most modern of modern artists.

In general, the modern artist looks at both the inner world of mind or emotion and the outer world of the senses as though he were the very first person not only to see but to set forth that world in an art form. When he paints a picture of a bird he doesn't try, even subconsciously, to make it look like other paintings or photographs of birds. Perhaps to his fresh vision a bird is not a feathered, winged creature but some quite different visual expression of soaring or freedom. Probably the most famous bird in art is the Rumanian sculptor Brancusi's *Bird in Space*, a slender, irregularly tapered shaft of polished bronze. (Pl. I)

So if a small child shows you a sheet of paper embellished with a squiggle or an angled line, take his word that it is a bird, a fish, or a dog. Perhaps one of those creatures has made exactly that impression on him, and his own free and individual concept has not yet been revised or destroyed by contact with the outer world. Like the child or the savage, the modern artist is free from traditional mental images—at least so far as his art is concerned. Of course with the modern artist this freedom from second-hand images is not instinctive, as with the child or the savage, but is brought about by a conscious effort to free himself so that he may see the world or the inner vision as with newly opened eyes. This does not mean that every modern artist paints "crazy" pictures. Some paintings are exceedingly realistic yet never imitative. Modern art has freshness and individuality.

Cézanne, sometimes called the father of modern painting, saw nature in terms of the cube, the cylinder, the sphere—and he painted it that way Yet his landscapes, his compositions with fruit, his figure paintings, don't appear strange. His fresh, original way of seeing—and painting—has simply added an underlying structural strength that brings three-dimensional solidity to canvas. (Pl. I)

One of the chief qualities of modern art is its infinite diversity. It is a true (sometimes almost painful) reflection of modern life in its bewildering complexities. In its abundant variety there is something for every taste. The works of a single man—Picasso—encompass almost the entire range of modern art, many of the subdivisions of which he originated or renewed in the image of his individual greatness.

But don't try to swallow all of modern art in one cultural gulp. It is sure to give you indigestion. Taste and sample it. Be discriminating. A popular syndicated columnist once wrote that as a young man it distressed him not to like everyone; he thought it indicated that he was anti-social. As he grew older, he found he could love the entire human race without making a bosom friend of every member of it. It's that way with art, especially modern art.

Never be ashamed to admit that you don't like an individual work of art, an artist, or any phase of modern art—but don't arbitrarily bar your mind and taste against it just because it is modern. Give the picture, the artist, and modern art itself a fighting chance to make friends with you.

Pictures are like people. It is only through acquaintance that friendships develop and likes or dislikes are acquired. Of course there are always cases of love (or hate) at first sight, but with both pictures and people instant liking is sometimes merely the attraction of surface qualities, a momentary infatuation that soon results in boredom. Paintings by modern artists which at first startle, annoy, or even repel, often prove on further acquaintance to have such strength and individuality that they take firm root in our affections—if we meet them with an open mind.

To get acquainted with pictures, go where pictures are—to museums, art galleries, or the homes of friends who collect even if only in a small way. If your town has no museum or gallery, the local library is sure to have at least a few art books and magazines carrying fine reproductions. The primary object of a picture is to be *seen*—even in reproduction—rather than heard about in conversation or read about in books.

Yet when the eye of the mind is opened, the outer eye sees more. When the vision is enlarged, enjoyment is greater.

2 ART DICTATOR

AN ARTIST WAS A PROMINENT MEMBER OF THE
Revolutionary Tribunal that in 1793 sentenced Louis XVI to
the guillotine. Jacques Louis David, who had received favors
from the King and was a member of the Royal Academy of
Art, abolished not only the King but the Royal Academy as
well. In its place was set up the *Institut National* in the third
year (1795) of the Republic "to advance the discovery and
perfecting of the Arts and Sciences." (Pl. II)

The following year it was established by law as the *Institut
de France,* a more modern version of the original *Institut de
France* organized in the reign of Louis XIV in 1686. Through
its Academy of Art—a reorganization of the Royal Academy—
it was to hold official sway over the art and the artists of
France well into the twentieth century.

From the time of King Francis I, who brought Leonardo
da Vinci to France in 1516, French royalty and aristocracy
had made much of art. But for almost three centuries before
the Revolution most of the great art in France, with a few
native exceptions, had been imported or looted as spoils of
war, chiefly from Italy and the Low Countries.

French court painters—and they were the only ones who
counted through most of the eighteenth century—created
work that had the glitter of artificiality: exquisite, decorative
and, above all, elegant. Accomplished, highly skilled artists,
their work often had charm, always had polish. Like the
architecture of the period, it was known as the Rococo style
and was characterized by ornamentation that employed short,
broken curves like the convolutions of a shell—hence its name
from the French *rocaille*: shellwork.

Chief among these artists were Watteau, the greatest; Ri-
gaud, portrait painter extraordinary to Louis XIV and XV;
Boucher, arbiter of style in painting and court fashion; Mme.
Vigée-Lebrun, portraitist beloved of Marie Antoinette; and
Fragonard, whose life spanned the old royalty of Louis XV
and XVI, the Revolution, the Republic, the Terror, and the
new royalty created by Napoleon. Fragonard's great-grand-

daughter, Berthe Morisot, was to become one of the first Impressionists, the art movement that three-quarters of a century after the Revolution was to usher in modern art as we know it today.

Except for the work of two genre painters—the sentimentalities of Greuze and the truly distinguished still lifes of Chardin—the art of the eighteenth century was essentially the art of the court painter. It had nothing to do with the harsh or homely realities of life as it was lived by most of the French people. Court paintings either were flattering portraits of royalty and nobility, or dealt in fanciful and ornamental detail with pseudo-shepherds and shepherdesses, nymphs and fauns, gods and goddesses of Greek and Roman mythology.

In court circles there was one curious deviation from this Rococo art. During the petticoat reign of La Pompadour—brilliant and powerful mistress of Louis XV—a craze sprang up for the classic antique in fashion, art and decoration. It was sparked by interest in then-current excavations in Italy that uncovered the ruins of Roman adaptations of ancient Greek architecture and sculpture. Pompadour's architect-brother was one of the leaders in this classic revival. Although limited in scope, it became the rage among ultra-fashionables who wanted to be "different" and who suddenly decided that their clothes must be made, their houses decorated, and their hair dressed "a la Grecque." In 1774, when death released the throne from the tight grip of Louis XV, "la Grecque" style was largely smothered by the towering headdresses and the sham shepherdess simplicity of the court of Marie Antoinette.

But there was one coming into power who remembered. Since his days as a *Prix de Rome* student in Italy, David had favored the Classic style. Before 1775, when he left for Rome, he had completed a large canvas *Minerva's Conquest of War* in slightly simplified court style. It had the regulation Boucher cherub—Boucher was David's first teacher—peeping from the clouds, and the billowy curves both of the feminine figures and flowing garments favored by painters of the Rococo. But the curving lines were longer and less convoluted, the background simpler, and the general aspect of the picture less frothy than the curlicue complexities and butterfly emotions of court paintings.

The first premonitory rumblings of the Revolution freed David to paint as he pleased and in 1784 he produced the stern, rectilinear *Oath of the Horatii*. It received immediate popular acclaim. The King, dimly aware of the tottering state of his throne, bought it as a sign of his closeness to the people, thus reversing in the act of appeasement the former position—through many long reigns—of king and artist.

With the actual ringing up of the curtain on the Revolution, David became the leading painter of the nation. The most famous paintings of the period were, of course, his. The first of these was *Brutus Receiving News of the Death of His Sons,* painted in 1789 before the actual Revolution but after the States General had taken over most of the ruling prerogatives and the royal family had been driven from Versailles and forced to take up residence in the Tuileries under constant surveillance.

The impact of *Brutus* had almost nothing to do with the esthetic values of the painting. It was the subject that roused the frenzied enthusiasm not only of the populace but of the intellectuals as well. Curiously, since the beginning of the Classic revival during the reign of Louis XV, the royal rulers and, later, their Revolutionary supplanters, had taken ancient Rome as their symbol: the royalists as a model of expanding empire under Caesar, the Revolutionaries with Brutus as their hero striking down the Imperator-Dictator.

So great was the furor over the David painting that it influenced the acting of the most popular play of the time, Voltaire's heroic drama *Brutus.* At the play's climax each night the principal actor struck the pose of the figure in the painting and held it in tableau, to the wild acclaim of the audience, all of whom were familiar with the painting. The Brutus theme of patriotic murder for the State so permeated all classes— except mute and hidden royalists—that it was employed both by and against the Revolutionaries. Again and again Charlotte Corday vehemently declared it the inspiration for her assassination of Marat.

Elected to the National Assembly in 1792 through the influence of Marat, Danton, and Robespierre, David became not only the official painter of the Revolution but virtual art dictator of France. He revived the Greco-Roman revival and made Classicism—or, more exactly, *Neo*-Classicism the official art of France. With an iron hand he introduced into all French painting of consequence the simple, cold, formalized style of Greek art as it had filtered down through Roman bas-relief. The Rococo style, which for a century or more had been the pampered, protected darling of all-powerful royalty and aristocracy, did not go through the slow process of lessening favor and decline, as have other styles of painting; it was dead overnight.

As artists, the genre painters were not disturbed; their art was considered of little importance. But every artist of the old regime, every venerable member of the Academy, every youthful student, knew the guillotine yawned for him in a very literal sense if he did not prepare at once to shout on canvas: Rococo is dead! Long live Classicism!

During the ensuing decade, David's fortunes rose and fell with the constantly changing tide of Revolution politics. A week after the execution of his friend and patron, Robespierre, in July 1794, David was imprisoned for five months. He was freed for a short time, then imprisoned again for two months. At the end of the 1795 he was freed in the general amnesty and although no longer officially art dictator and first painter of the Republic, he was still the acknowledged leader of French art.

But Napoleon's rise to power made David's art leadership official again. When Napoleon had himself crowned in 1804, he gave David the title *Premier Peintre de l'Empereur*, and David again became art dictator, originating and virtually ruling fashion in dress, furniture, and interior architectural design. He was chiefly responsible not only for the Directoire style of the Republic but for its development into the Empire style when Napoleon decided to found a new dynasty for the French throne.

Even after Napoleon's exile to Elba in April 1814, the artist still retained his extraordinary luck—or perhaps genius—in avoiding the usual political reprisal by guillotine. The returning Bourbons either overlooked him or did not get around to him before Napoleon's escape from Elba and the final Hundred Days of his power. Then it was that David made his one tactical error: he signed the banishment act against the Bourbons.

Upon Napoleon's final downfall and permanent exile to St. Helena, and the return of Louis XVIII to the throne, David himself was exiled. For the rest of his life, from 1816 to his death in 1825, he lived in Brussels—surely mild retribution for one who had been so active in condemning to the guillotine not only royalty and aristocracy but even his fellow-artists.

Jacques Louis David was a sound and gifted painter who at a stroke, through the influence of his art and the power of his art dictatorship, freed France and the art world in general from the Rococo style of the court painters. He cleared away the rubbishy remnants of a style which had wandered off from the living stream of art to lose itself in the arid wastes of meaningless ornamentation and perpetual self-imitation. He forced the artists of his time to see the clarity and beauty of an uncluttered canvas. In all but his political paintings, David's simple, unadorned backgrounds which focused attention on the important elements, the rhythmic underlying pattern of some of his canvases with their repetition of definite horizontals and verticals, the occasional asymmetrical placement of figure or object all foreshadowed certain phases of modern art, especially some of the "arrangements" by Whistler or even the starkly abstract canvases of Mondrian.

For thirty-two years David ruled French art and artists. Probably no other artist of ancient or modern times has ever had the power held by him. He might have lifted the shackles of the past and given art an impetus to progress never before equalled. Instead he reached back into the past and made old art official, allowing no breath of artistic freedom for any would-be deviator from his own interpretation of the Classic style. He set a pattern for an art tyranny that had not existed before—even the Royal Academy had accepted as members artists who did not conform—and which was to be continued after his death by his most brilliant pupil, Ingres, and other pupils and followers who through the Academy of Art were for nearly a century to hold the power almost of life and death over the art of France and its artists.

3 EARLY REBELS AND THE ACADEMY

AFTER HIS EXILE, DAVID'S CHIEF LIEUTENANT IN France was Antoine-Jean, the Baron Gros. Gros had been a pupil in the large studio-school David had established in 1789, the year of the triumphal exhibition of his *Brutus* canvas. In 1796, through David, the twenty-five-year-old Gros met Napoleon—himself only twenty-seven and already a general—and became attached to his staff as semi-official war artist.

Battle scenes could not, of course, be portrayed in the static, color-subdued style favored and dictated by David. But as these paintings were of and for the great Napoleon, Gros was not affected by the artistic standards set by David but could happily follow the dictates of his own considerable talent, influenced by his passion for Rubens, certainly the most Romantic of the old masters.

With the fall of Napoleon, Gros made his peace with the Bourbons. At the same time, and for many years afterward, he conducted David's school under David's direction from Brussels. So strong was the exiled artist's influence that Gros insisted that even his own pupils force their individual talents into straight-jacket conformity with the rules laid down by David; noble subject, severe line, subdued color, and suppression of emotion. When students protested, Gros insisted upon absolute adherence to the "master's" style, once exclaiming: "It is not I who speak to you. It is David, eternally David!" Similar, though occasional, outbursts like this indicated how tightly Gros had clamped the lid down on his own artistic tendencies.

This desperate little man, so under the authoritarian shadow of the absent David that he denied even his own nature, is sometimes referred to as the herald of Romantic painting. It was not alone the subject matter of his earlier and more representative paintings but the instinctive drive of his talent that demanded the Romantic style. Yet during the nine years of David's exile, until his death in 1825, and for the decade following, Gros fought his own nature to hold the line for

David and Neo-Classicism. It was noted that he grew melancholy. One day in June 1835, he walked to the edge of a shallow tributary of the Seine, removed hat, gloves, and cravat, laid them neatly with his cane on the bank, and drowned himself in a few inches of water.

Gros may have been a herald—a muted one—but he was not a rebel. And, to accomplish a change in art, rebels must dare to cut or, if need be, hack out a new channel for the stream of art. Yet despite his inability to free himself from David and give full reign to his own talent, this artist's paintings—not the artist himself—herald the Romantic movement.

The first real rebel to hoist the flag of Romanticism against the still powerful standard of Neo-Classicism was Théodore Géricault—and he raised this flag almost by accident. A student of Guérin, who was a follower of David, Géricault showed such early promise that when he was only twenty-one he had a picture hung in the Salon of 1812. It was a handsome equestrian portrait, full of action and color. Although it was definitely not of the Davidian school, being more nearly related to the early paintings of Gros and, beyond him, to Rubens, it was generally well received and gave the young artist a healthy start toward a reputation.

Two years later Géricault went to Rome to study and—legend has it—to forget an unhappy love affair. He was again in Paris at the time of the disaster to the transport *Medusa* in 1818. The circumstances arising from this tragedy aroused all France and, in Paris particularly, conversational battles violent with denunciation raged. The *Medusa* had sunk off the African coast, the officers abandoning ship in the lifeboat, leaving the crew of more than one hundred to huddle as best they might on a raft. For a few days the officers had towed the raft, and then had cast it adrift. Weeks later, when most of the crew had died of thirst or madness, a passing vessel sighted the raft and brought it into port with only fifteen survivors.

Fired with indignation, Géricault made the most exact and realistic preparations to reproduce the tragedy on canvas. One of the survivors happened to be the ship's carpenter. Géricault hired him to build a replica of the raft and obtained from him minute descriptions of the placement of the living and dying upon it, and word-pictures of the distress and torment suffered. The artist even went so far as to borrow corpses from a nearby hospital and place them in positions indicated by the carpenter. So much realism finally became distasteful to the senses and sensibilities of the neighbors, and Géricault was obliged to get rid of his involuntary models. But they—plus the power of Géricault's brush and his indignation

—accomplished the artist's purpose. His large and exciting canvas *Raft of the Medusa* was shown in the Salon of 1819. (Pl. II)

It caused a sensation—but not the kind any artist might hope for. The painting was denounced by art officials, critics, dealers, and even by prominent persons who had no connection with art, as utterly inartistic on every count: it lacked dignity, repose, and noble sentiment. Only the public liked it; in those days there were no newsreels of disasters. Even in its depiction of the dying, the painting was fiercely alive, animated, and therefore completely unlike ancient sculpture, still the official ideal of painting.

At first stunned by this storm of adverse criticism—and too intelligent to believe that the public liked his painting for esthetic reasons—Géricault became bitterly resentful. Declaring he would never paint again, he turned his back on his native land and went to England. He took his painting with him and realized a considerable sum from its exhibtion. The public would pay money to see it, but the very publicity which drew crowds blinded art collectors to its merit as a painting. The average art collector is a very sensitive soul who needs guidance and protection by art dealers. Very few collectors have the courage of their own convictions, if, indeed, they have any convictions of their own.

Some years after Géricault's death, the *Raft of the Medusa* was bought by the French Government. It now hangs in the Louvre, the first Romantic painting of the modern school. At this distance of years it is rather difficult for us to make a true estimate of the esthetic value of Romantic painting at its best. We are apt to judge the entire movement by its worst examples for, less than half a century after Géricault painted the great sensation of the 1819 Salon, Romantic painting had degenerated into academic storytelling on canvas. "Romantic" is derived from the French *roman*, tale, and from the beginning such painting always told a story of great and noble deeds, large-scale tragedy, or dramatic event. In every sense— in its esthetic patterns of rhythm, sweeping diagonals, dramatic arrangement of planes or manipulation of perspective, as well as in its pictorial actuality—it was always a little larger than life: richer color, livelier movement, grander emotions; its men always a little more heroic—or, if villains, more formidable—its women more beautiful, in greater danger, or triumphantly virtuous. In short, Romantic painting is bravura realism and the exact opposite o Neo-Classicism. In its beginnings, late in the first quarter of the nineteenth century, it produced some very fine paintings, and it eventually broke the stranglehold of Neo-Classicism.

But to return to Géricault and his vow never to paint again. He found he could keep away neither from art nor from France. During his three-year stay in England he made a series of fascinating animal studies and several paintings of horses, his great passion. His *Cross Country Run* and *Derby at Epsom* clearly foreshadow the style of Degas when the latter painted similar subjects half a century later.

More important than the continuance of his own work in England, however, was Géricault's opportunity there to become acquainted with the work of the rebel English painter, John Constable. Today those peaceful landscapes seem anything but radical. The unexcitable British, instead of reacting violently, as did the French, against a style of painting of which they disapproved, simply punished it by indifference. To paraphrase the chilling remark of their most typical monarch—though it would be almost two decades before Victoria would mount the throne—English critics and public and Royal Academy said of Constable's landscapes, in effect: "We are not interested."

But they greatly excited the young man from France who without doubt also derived a certain personal satisfaction from the paintings of a fellow rebel. When he returned to Paris he told other young artists of the startling departure from tradition of the English painter who actually went to nature for his landscapes, who studied the changing effects of wind and rain and sun and even the light-filled atmosphere on the *appearance* of the natural landscape and strove, successfully, to reproduce these effects on canvas. Up to that time all landscape painting had been studio-contrived, like set pieces for an old-fashioned stage: a tree here, a glade there, a stream or pool placed so as not to violate certain carefully formalized patterns of composition.

Géricault's enthusiasm inspired some of his fellow-artists with the determination to take a trip to England to see for themselves. They did not have to wait for that, however, as the interest and curiosity Géricault stirred up, as well as the pleas he made to the Jury of Selection for the 1824 Salon, resulted in its acceptance for exhibition of three Constable paintings.

Meanwhile Géricault, more subdued and thoughtful than when he had left France, happened to visit a mental institution near Paris. He was profoundly moved by the faces of some of the inmates and painted a series of portraits there. The finest of these, *The Mad Assassin*, must be ranked among the great portraits of the period.

Géricault never saw the Constable landscapes exhibited in the 1824 Salon. Before it opened he was thrown from a horse and killed, at the age of thirty-three. But before the newly raised flag of artistic defiance fell from his hand it was caught up by a younger artist Géricault had befriended at the very beginning of his career and who lived to wave that flag savagely in the face of Neo-Classicism and the Academy for almost forty years.

Eugène Delacroix, who was to become the symbol and standard bearer of Romanticism in art, had from the cradle apparently been prepared for the role. There was even a mystery about his birth. Then followed in quick succession almost miraculous escapes from more than the usual number and form of childhood mishaps. He recovered from several severe illnesses which, however, left him with a frail physique. He almost lost his life in a fire. He was twice rescued from drowning. He mistakenly took poison. He was revived from an accidental hanging. When he was sixteen, after the death of his widowed mother, the family inheritance was lost through a bungled lawsuit. Small wonder that he was an imaginative, restless, introspective youth, never certain of his powers except in painting which—again apparently in accord with the Romantic deity who seemed to rule his life—he casually took up when he was eighteen with the thought that he might gain "a little amateur talent."

Delacroix was twenty-one years old when he saw the *Raft of the Medusa* in the 1819 Salon. Like Géricault, he was a pupil of Guérin and was to veer even more sharply from the Davidian ideals of his teacher. He had posed for one of the figures in the *Medusa* but he was enormously moved by the finished painting and years later wrote in his diary that after seeing it in the Salon he roamed the streets of Paris in a daze, unable to think of anything but the remarkable effects his fellow artist had succeeded in putting on canvas. Three years later, in the Salon of 1822, he himself had a painting. (Pl. III)

It was *The Barque of Dante* and although it complied with the canons of antiquity and nobility of subject which David had laid down, the figures in the painting were alive with drama and struggle, instead of static with the dead serenity of sculpture. The water was turbulent and the sky threatening. Because he was still somewhat inexperienced as an artist, Delacroix had gone to a canvas by Rubens to learn how to paint drops of water running down the writhing bodies of the lost souls struggling to get into the barque.

While not such a sensation as Géricault's canvas three years earlier, this first major painting by Delacroix drew impressive reactions both of praise and of censure. His teacher, Guérin, castigated it almost as severely as he had the *Medusa*. But Gros, a more famous though less powerful personage in the world of art, was delighted. When he saw *The Barque of Dante* he exclaimed: "Rubens has returned!" And because the young artist was too poor to buy a proper frame, Gros himself gave the painting a handsome gilt frame.

And then an odd and dramatic thing happened to the poor young artist. His painting was purchased by the State.

Magnificent though the painting was—and remarkable for so young an artist—its lack of official approval by the Academy would have prevented or certainly long delayed its purchase by the State had it not been for the intervention of an important politician. What made the circumstance doubly odd was that the politician, Thiers by name, knew little about art and apparently cared less. He did not even know Delacroix personally at that time. But from then on, Thiers became the young painter's champion and awarded him important Government commissions on which the artist worked at intervals for many years.

Sometimes, in strange and devious ways, a man's misfortune becomes his fortune. Many a sensitive, talented child—and some not so talented—has secretly imagined himself different from his brothers and sisters, a changeling perhaps. But Delacroix actually *was* different—in appearance, temperament, and natural endowments. His legal father, Charles Delacroix, was a lawyer of mediocre ability who had nevertheless been appointed to a number of rather responsible Government posts. He died when the future artist was a child of seven.

Some of Delacroix's contemporaries and at least one of his biographers thought the artist resembled France's illustrious Minister of Foreign Affairs, the astute and brilliant Talleyrand, who never gave a *direct* hint of any domestic affair with an artistic result. He had, however, sardonically caused a medical paper to be published which referred to a delicate operation Charles Delacroix had had two years before Eugène's birth, an operation which would have made it virtually impossible for him to have become a father again. The summer before the artist's birth near Paris, on April 26, 1798, Charles Delacroix had gone to Batavia as Minister, a post to which Talleyrand had appointed him. The Foreign Minister had for several years been a close friend of the family and continued his friendship with Mme. Delacroix while her husband was away.

There are indications in Eugène Delacroix's diary, published some years after his death, that a sense of insecurity about his kinship with the rest of his family—except his mother, whom he adored—often troubled him. His repeated efforts to establish a likeness between himself and his legal father, as though he were trying constantly to reassure himself, are significant. At the same time, there is no indication that he suspected himself to be the natural son of Talleyrand or had even heard that he was presumed to be. The question of one's legitimacy is not a subject one discusses with friends, and a well-brought-up child would not be likely to bring it up in conversation with his parents.

So what may have seemed to the impoverished young artist a beneficence from Heaven probably appeared to gossips a confirmation of all their suspicions when Delacroix's first exhibited painting was purchased from the Salon of 1822 while Talleyrand, although retired from active government service, was still a power behind the scenes in French politics. Whether or not Thiers bought the painting at Talleyrand's suggestion or request can never be definitely known. For once, however, politics happened to be on the side of the angels. Throughout his career, Delacroix brilliantly vindicated the Government's choice of him as an artist.

But he began to frighten the dictatorial old men of the Academy when, before talk had died down about the amazing State purchase of the young artist's first painting, the Salon of 1824 opened and its sensation proved to be *The Massacre at Chios,* still considered by some critics to be Delacroix's masterpiece.

The painting, a dramatic scene from the Turks' slaughter of 20,000 helpless Greek civilians in April 1822, is a huge picture—nearly fourteen by eleven and a half feet. The Jury of Selection unenthusiastically accepted it for the 1824 Salon. When the Salon opened August 26th the Jury rubbed its collective eyes. *The Massacre at Chios* was undoubtedly the painting they had accepted, but it was strangely unlike the glowing canvas that greeted the dazzled eyes of critics and public that opening day.

What had happened? Delacroix had discovered Constable, and the first step toward modern art as we know it today had been taken.

Two months earlier, as he had neared completion of the *Massacre,* Delacroix one day threw down his brushes and went for a relaxing stroll. On his way he was suddenly transfixed by the sight, in an art dealer's window, of three canvases by the English painter. Their wonderful play of light both enchanted and dismayed Delacroix. He went back to his studio to a painting that now appeared to him drab and lifeless. But he had spent more than a year working toward it and on it. There was no time to produce another painting. So he put on the finishing touches and submitted it.

Four days before the opening of the Salon, Delacroix was

galvanized into action by a wild idea and an even wilder hope. He asked—and amazingly obtained—permission to "retouch" his painting, which had already been hung, as had the Constable canvases. For four days Delacroix alternately studied and frenziedly applied to his own painting the English artist's original technique of bathing a picture in light. *The Massacre at Chios* was still wet when the Salon opened.

Constable's landscapes received much attention, particularly from the younger artists, who studied them with enthusiastic appreciation. The critics complained that they "lacked idealism." They were such ordinary scenes, common to any countryside. They were not "idealized" or even sentimentalized. One painting was actually of a hay wagon. Half a century later the English woke up to the artist their French neighbors—with the exception of the critics and the Academy—had so much admired in 1824, and *The Hay Wain*, Constable's most celebrated painting, is now in the National Gallery, London.

But, after all, Constable was English. The French Academicians, complacent in their belief that France had nothing to fear from British art, felt that painting from such a source could safely be ignored. What really alarmed them was the sensation caused by *The Massacre at Chios* in which Delacroix had heightened the impact of his exciting Romantic style with Constable's method of infusing a canvas with light.

The first trumpet note of the Romantic rebellion had been sounded by Géricault, but the Academicians had soon crushed that young man! Now here was another upstart, one who had not been quelled by their disapproval of his *Barque of Dante* but had topped that first assault by an attack in force, a canvas so shocking in its departure from accepted standards that even Gros turned his back on it and dubbed it *The Massacre of Painting*.

Something must be done, and done quickly, to make sure that power would not be eased or snatched from their guardian hands. The Jury of Selection must be tightened up and instructed to be more severe. "Real" art must be saved. The influence of David, now exiled for eight years, was beginning to wane. His chief lieutenant, Baron Gros, was distrusted as being secretly in love with Romanticism and despised because he did not forthrightly declare himself on one side or the other. A new leader must be found—a staunch Classicist, of course.

The Academicians had not far to look. No farther, in fact, than the Salon of 1824, remarkable in spite of the Academy. But there was one painting in it that met all their requirements. The critics praised it, the public was pleased by it. It was technically skillful and satisfactorily academic. It appealed to both the patriotic and religious sentiments, which were very much to the fore with the restoration of the Bourbons. Moreover, it was by the artist David had considered his most brilliant pupil, Jean Auguste Dominique Ingres, returned to Paris after eighteen years in Italy.

His painting was *The Vow of Louis XIII* and showed that monarch on his knees before the Virgin, offering her his sceptre and crown. In no time at all Ingres was elected to the *Institut de France* and had received the ribbon of the Legion of Honor.

Ingres emerged from the Salon of 1824 the artist of the hour—for the conservatives. He became the rallying point for the frightened Academicians and the following year, when David died, fell heir to his mantle and power. Until his death in 1867 at the age of eighty-seven, Ingres was the acknowledged head of official art in France. (Pl. IV)

Jean Auguste Dominique Ingres was born at Montauban in the south of France in 1780. At sixteen he was sent to Paris to study with David. After working nearly three years in David's studio, Ingres disagreed so strongly with one tenet of his teacher's art credo that they parted and the young artist thereafter had to struggle against the severity and intolerance of David.

Ingres was in no sense a rebel; he wished only to express in his own idiom the Classicism of his master. They both believed that line was the basis of all painting. Color, for them, was negligible. David, however, swore allegiance to the almost mathematical beauty of ancient Graeco-Roman sculpture, Ingres to the "idealized" beauty of the natural form; both of these standards were by their very nature opposed to realism. The figures in David's paintings had to be noble, in Ingres' beautiful; neither artist would ever sully his canvas with life as it really was or as it romantically might be. The Neo-Classicism of David found its dead end in stark sterility; Ingres' in a vapid prettiness that was imitated almost into the twentieth century.

After Ingres as a young artist left David's studio he won the *Prix de Rome*, in 1801, though it was five years more before the funds for his study in Rome were forthcoming. In Rome, where he lived from 1806 to 1820, and in Florence from 1820 to 1824, he supported himself and his family chiefly by the immense number of pencil portraits he did, each for a very modest fee.

Ingres was a superlative craftsman. No other artist of his time, and few of any other time, could equal him in the perfection of drawing. For every picture he painted he made hundreds of study drawings. If he decided to change or rework any part of a painting he preceded it with more pencil studies. His portrait drawings—with no trace of the simpering prettiness that makes many of his canvases distasteful today—are the product of keen observation, masterful delineation, and superb style. His usual method was to make a completely detailed drawing of the face, with high lights and shadows suggesting three-dimensional contour as convincingly as in the best oil portraiture of the period, and then lightly sketch in the figure with a few telling lines. (Pl. IV)

It is significant that when either of these two great champions of Neo-Classicism, Ingres and David, turned to realism—as they felt they must for portraiture—no artist could surpass them. The portraits they produced are admirable when judged by the standards of any period. Yet, like most artists even today, David and Ingres thought of the portraits they painted or drew as minor works. They expected to be, and were, judged by their "studio" paintings.

Now that Ingres, with the death of David in 1825, had become the leading painter of the Academy and was to remain its head for more than forty years, he in turn became intolerant. Partly because of this and partly because the conservative artists had become suddenly aware—through the sensation caused first by Géricault and then by Delacroix—of the vigor of the new movement called Romanticism, the Academy became much more stringent in its dictatorial determination that all artists in France should comply with its standards.

It is human nature, and native to all countries, that the entrenched older generation fights bitterly to perpetuate itself, its customs, ideals, and standards, by crushing down the upstart new generation. Throughout the nineteenth century in France this human instinct—at least so far as it affected the arts—was powerfully reinforced by the despotic official system of the Academy. Art was a ladder at the top of which, if one meekly smothered originality and adhered to all the rules laid down by preceding generations of art, was the multiple prize of honor, wealth, and influence.

The first step up this ladder was the passing of examinations for entrance into the *École des Beaux-Arts*. Then years of uninspired work and study in the *Beaux-Arts* studios, in strict compliance with academic tradition and instruction, prepared the artist for further successive steps: exhibition in the official Salon; honorable mention; third, second, and first class medals; and, for a fortunate few, the *Prix de Rome*. Eventually, if the artist was a conformist and had technical skill, there was the possibility of purchase by the State of one of his works. Still later, perhaps a Government commission.

Some attained the crowning glory: election to the Academy

of Fine Arts of the *Institut de France*. And as the *Institut* through each of its sections—art, literature, music, etc.—held absolute sway over all the arts of France, artists who had conformed each step of the way up to election to the Academy became in their turn the wielders of its power. Completing the vicious circle, the Academy appointed from its own ranks the teachers at the *École des Beaux-Arts*.

Recognition as an artist, upon which the sale of one's paintings chiefly depended, was almost impossible without Academy approval—and the Academy favored its own. Through the juries of selection and award, the Academy governed the acceptance or rejection of paintings for exhibition in the Salon. Through its weighty influence, it largely controlled the purchase of art by the State and the selection of artists for Government commissions. And through granting or withholding recognition of an artist, it opened or closed the purse strings of the buyers of art. It was a brave artist who, by being himself, defied the power of the Academy.

Ingres believed implicitly and didactically in his declared principle that the basis of all good painting was drawing or line. This became the rule and tradition of the *École des Beaux-Arts* and sometimes for years students were permitted only to draw, draw, draw, often the same models or studies again and again and again in exactly the same position or from the same angle. When the time came that they were permitted to paint, many of their canvases were only colored drawings.

Ingres' power, and particularly his theory that line alone made a painter great, was challenged by Eugène Delacroix. Although he had been a student at the *Beaux-Arts* under Guérin—there were no independent art teachers at that time —Delacroix had soon freed himself from the dry, tight tradition of studio teaching and struck out on his own, both in subject matter and technique. In fact, he left Guérin in 1822, immediately after the success of his *Barque of Dante* in the Salon of that year. After that first major work, he tossed aside antique draperies, classical figures, and mythological story subject. Above all, he challenged the importance of line. He let color create form and took as his subjects heroic deeds of contemporary battles, scenes or figures from exotic lands, and historic incidents of the Middle Ages. He painted life, color, action, and passion onto his canvases.

Except in the case of Delacroix, with its strange and never-explained implications, the Government usually bowed to the Academy in the selection of artists for commissions or their works for purchase. The reasons for this are quite understandable: 1) the art preferred by any government, even the most radical, is invariably conservative if not downright reactionary; and 2) governments rose and fell with such frightening rapidity in France until the last quarter of the nineteenth century that the Academy seemed a reassuring stronghold of stability, resting on a secure foundation of tradition.

Had it not been for the almost unprecedented direct purchase by the Government of the young artist's first exhibited painting, two years before Ingres' return to Paris and his sudden rise to power, Delacroix as an artist might never have survived Ingres' intolerance, which was probably all the more bitter just because Delacroix did have direct Government patronage. What made matters worse, in the eyes of the Academy, was that the Government promptly purchased Delacroix's *second* Salon painting and for the unbelievably high price—at that period—of six thousand francs! And this time there was no doubt about Delacroix's art. It was ultra-modern, dangerously radical, and—if allowed to continue and perhaps corrupt other young painters by the contagion of its success—a serious threat to Neo-Classicism and all traditional art.

4 THE GENTLE REBELS

ALL REAL ARTISTS, ACCORDING TO PARIS IN THE first half of the nineteenth century, worked in studios. In fact, to help the pupils of one Paris atelier paint a farm scene, a bull was brought into the studio and chained to the wall, with a countryman in valet attendance.

Here and there an individual artist woke up to the fact that nature in the raw could be caught direct on canvas instead of being captured first in sketches and brought back to the studio for taming. But in those days—it was not until around 1840 that the collapsible tin tube for prepared oil paints was invented by an obscure American artist named Rand—it was far more convenient to perform in the studio the chore of grinding powdered pigments into an oil medium than to lug the necessary materials and paraphernalia, along with easel, canvas, and brushes, on an outdoor painting jaunt. With watercolors it had always been easier. Watercolor kits had long been available, and any artist could easily make his own, as many preferred to do.

In the second quarter of the nineteenth century a group later to be known as the Barbizon painters came loosely into being as, one by one, certain artists picked themselves up from coldly indifferent Paris and withdrew to a small village on the edge of Fontainebleau Forest. There they set up easels in the open air and painted woodland scenes or the rustic landscape, sometimes dotting in a peasant or two—or, preferably, picturesque creatures of their own imaginings—for accent. It was seldom, however, that they did introduce any figure into their pictures, for the Barbizon painters primarily were landscape purists. The natural beauty of their fresh, gentle canvases was scorned as countrified by Salon and Academy and especially by the Parisians, whose watchword in the nineteenth century was Elegance.

The least gentle—in temperament—of these new rebels was Théodore Rousseau (1812-1869), who became leader of the Barbizon group. As an art student at the Academy he was already in rebellion at the age of eighteen against the accepted art and the governing policies of the day. A few years later, in 1834, he had a painting accepted—it seemed almost by accident—by the Salon of that year. But from then until the Revolution of 1848 opened the Salon for a short period to all comers, his work was kept out of exhibitions through Academy intrigue, which found the insurgent young man a perfect target.

Politics could not keep Rousseau from nature. He concerned himself with nothing else in his painting, studying every rock, tree, branch, leaf, and blade of grass in detailed intensity. His landscapes—excellent technically and sometimes beautiful—tended to document the literal reality of field, stream, and woods rather than to suffuse them with revealing light. His painting was strong, somber, had an occasional touch of rugged grandeur, and sometimes seemed actually to escape from the painter to form a picture of evocative rather than documented beauty.

It cost little to live in one of the studio-huts on the edge of Fontainebleau Forest and nothing at all to paint in the nearby woods and the fields of Barbizon. Artists came out for the day, or rented one of the studios for living quarters. After exhibiting in the Salon of 1848, Rousseau enjoyed a little short-lived prosperity, bought a studio-home and settled permanently in Barbizon. He was by far the most articulate and belligerent of the Barbizon School, as the group was finally designated, but his understandable bitterness against Salon and Academy politics and his personal jealousies toward some of the artistically poor but financially prosperous Academic painters severely limited his opportunities.

Of the other outstanding Barbizon painters of the period, most important was Charles Daubigny (1817-1878), whose lyrical landscapes became by far the most popular of the group. In fact, it was Daubigny's painting rather than Rousseau's leadership—for Rousseau the man rather than Rousseau the painter was leader of the group—that one might say "set the style" of Barbizon painting and, two decades after its original artists had been rejected and starved, brought the recognition that began a reign of critical acclaim and world popularity with attendant prosperity that lasted half a century.

There were two painters sometimes classed with the Barbizon School whose connection was more that of friendship and association than of any real artistic identification. The first of these, chronologically, was that gentlest of all rebels: Camille Corot (1796-1875). Never aware of rebelling against anything or anybody, this sweet and childlike soul simply went his own way in the pursuit of art. The son of a Swiss-Parisian mother who had a very successful millinery business, and a French father who even more successfully managed the business, Camille was so bemused a youth that his father soon saw he would never make money in business. In fact, Corot never sold even a picture until he was fifty and had been happily painting—supported by his father—for more than thirty years. Then the tide turned. Before he died, Corot's paintings were bringing in annually many times what his parents' successful business had ever made. And he was awarded the ribbon of the Legion of Honor, to boot! (Pl. V)

Corot began his art life in secret while working—at the behest of his father—as a clerk in a draper's shop in Paris. When he confessed that he could stand it no longer and that he lived only to paint, his father was both wise and kind enough to yield to the one passion of his son's life. He gave Camille a cottage at Ville d'Avray and an allowance sufficient for his very modest wants.

Corot first saw Constable's paintings in the Salon of 1824 and from them drew something in the way of technique but much more in the encouragement of his own instinct to let nature teach him. The following year, supplied with travel money by his indulgent father, he began his art *Wanderjahre*.

It was in Rome that he developed the painting that is now referred to as his "first period." With an underlying structural design almost of the "cones, cylinders, and spheres" that Cézanne half a century later was to make the solid foundation of the modern art of our day, Corot painted Rome and its environs.

He traveled for nearly twenty years, returning for long intervals to his cottage or for sojourns with the Barbizon group, of whom Rousseau, so unlike him in temperament, was his particular friend. But as much as he loved his Barbizon friends—and delighted to help them with private little stratagems to save their pride—Corot preferred his own cottage at Ville d'Avray where, alone but never lonely, he painted his delicate, other-wordly landscapes.

But beneath the translucent veils of his paintings was the sound framework of good drawing, detailed though not obtrusive study, and solid craftsmanship. And then the Victorian Age, with its accent on sentimentality, began to seep across the Channel. Suddenly, Corot was the rage! The demand for his paintings became so great—and Corot, always generous, was so happy to have ample means to ease, in the most delicate manner, the struggles of his artist friends—that he began to turn out painting after painting, hundreds of them, so vaporous that they almost float off the canvas. The buying public loved them and clamored for more.

Few of them knew and none of them cared, at this time, that Corot's talent had a sound and sturdy core which was seldom displayed in the paintings they bought so avidly. But throughout the period when his landscapes were at their most wispy silver-gray, he was quietly producing figure paintings of superb quality—apparently just for his own satisfaction, for he kept these canvases turned to the wall in his studio and seldom showed them even to friends. These solidly constructed, masterfully designed portrait studies are his best and most "modern" paintings. But they did not come into their own until two generations after he died; within another generation they were to bring the highest prices ever paid for his works, even more than his gauzily glamorous landscapes at the height of their popularity.

In his later years "Papa Corot," as he was called by everyone, poured out help in a steady stream to his fellow-artists, in particular his Barbizon friends: heartening encouragement to those flayed by critical obtuseness, academic injustice, public neglect and ridicule; wise counsel in the many problems that beset artists; and gently distributed largesse—often through the anonymous purchase of paintings—that kept many an artist from actual starvation.

Corot continued happily painting until the end. One morning, after a few days of feebleness in bed, he woke without desire for breakfast. Pressed to eat something, he gestured it away.

"It's no use," he said. "Today *le père* Corot breakfasts above."

And he did, probably on a pink cloud. Just before he died, he looked out across the fields to the sky beyond and said: "It seems to me that I have not known how to paint a sky. That out there is much pinker, deeper, more transparent. How I should like to set down for you the grand horizons I see!"

To all but one of the Barbizon painters, landscape was all-important. If humans—or even nymphs—were permitted to intrude, they were minimized, used as tiny accents here and there. The exception was Jean François Millet (1814-1875), a Barbizon painter only by association. To Millet, country-born and a farm laborer from early youth, the landscape and the toiler were interdependent elements. Prettifying neither, he achieved a moving dignity, an earthy grandeur, by the rhythmic interplay of one against the other. (Pl. V)

Millet, deeply intelligent, had little formal education. But he had eyes, and he used them to store up scenes of peasants like himself working on farms, in the forest and quarries. He had ears, and they drank in his grandmother's re-telling of

Bible stories. He had a heart that was to bless on canvas the humble.

Millet was born in a tiny village near Cherbourg. He had almost no access to art but he was filled with a longing to create it. His few attempts to learn something of painting and drawing locally were successful only indirectly. Interest was created in Cherbourg where by public subscription enough was raised to send him to Paris in 1837. He entered the studio of Delaroche, one of the leading teacher-painters of the Academy, but found the instruction worse than useless.

Not being able to paint the pictures dimly struggling within him, he used pencil and brush as work tools to make a living. Nudes were popular, so he imitated the best sellers in that department and sold his results for a few francs. He also produced Biblical subjects, which were in good demand especially when cheap, turned out quick portraits for passersby, and even painted signs for shops.

Whenever he could snatch a few hours from eking out a miserable living for himself and his small but growing family, he went to the Louvre to study the Renaissance masters. But all the while he kept hearing "the cry of the earth," as he told a friend who urged him to "paint like Delacroix."

To his surprise, ten years after he had arrived in Paris, one of his imitative classical paintings, *Oedipus,* was admitted to the Salon of 1847. The next year the Revolution opened the Salon to all comers and Millet exhibited *The Winnower,* one of his real paintings. It was well received, and with that slight encouragement the artist decided to forego potboilers and quit Paris with his wife and three children. He had heard of the Barbizon painters; they were near Paris—and he had very little money. So he bundled his family into an omnibus which took them to Fontainebleau. From there he and his wife, carrying the children, trudged through the rain to the village of Barbizon.

His fellow artists welcomed their poorer fellow and his bedraggled little family. And somehow, through great privation, near-starvation, and never-ending work, Millet managed to maintain his independence as an artist, painting his great pictures of the toilers. He was not an artist who had suddenly discovered nature and embraced her. He returned to the soil as a son to the arms of his mother. This unmistakable kinship shows in all his paintings, in the sculptural strength of his simple figures and their inevitable accord with their surroundings.

Millet continued to send these paintings to the Salon exhibitions, where they were grudgingly exhibited—the Academy was again openly in the ascendant—and received scant attention. The elegants of Paris were not in love with nature unadorned. They had not accepted the Barbizon painters and were only just beginning to appreciate Corot. After all, Corot —even though he did paint direct from nature—had a delicate brush, and his nymphs were quite refined.

But a picture of peasants actually laboring in the fields! Grimy, work-worn, and probably sweaty. Parisians shuddered at the sight and all but held their noses.

These sophisticates could tolerate a painting of a swineherd only if the swineherd were quite plainly the Prodigal Son— definitely a young man of wealth and family who would return to his rich *milieu* as soon as he came to his senses. But a painting by Millet of an ordinary swineherd going about his duties in a rustic setting native to the low fellow—such pictures could not be accepted by people of taste and refinement. Indeed, the Imperial Director of Fine Arts—for within four short years of the Revolution of 1848 Louis Napoleon had made himself Emperor—had said of such pictures: "This is the painting of democrats, of those who don't change their linen, who want to pass themselves off as men of the world; this art displeases and disgusts me."

It was only natural, Parisians supposed, that such uncouth paintings should attract the uncultured Americans. In their near-savage country, Americans had some horrible poet they seemed to think was like Millet—someone named Walt Whitman. Nevertheless, without the help or even the encouragement of French critics and collectors but with the sympathy and sharing of fellow artists almost as poor as himself, the hidden generosity of the gentle Corot, and the occasional purchase of paintings by Americans in Paris, Millet and his ever-growing family managed—just managed, for they were always on the borderline of serious privation—to get along until the big Paris Exposition of 1867.

There he came into his own. First in the way of recognition, then his paintings began to sell—only seven or eight years before he died, but those few years gave him some financial freedom and the sweet satisfaction of public acclaim at last. Within another few years the art world was treated to the sardonic and wryly laughable spectacle of French turn-about when Millet's native land suddenly realized that too many of the best works of her hitherto neglected artist were slipping across the Atlantic to collectors and museums in the United States. France tried to halt the traffic, but was too late to prevent the acquisition of many of Millet's finest works in this country, which today owns outstanding paintings by the artist. One of his most famous, *The Man with the Hoe,* was made even more celebrated by a poem of the same name by the American poet Edwin Markham.

Although serenely sane, unlike the turbulently disturbed younger artist, Millet was the spiritual ancestor of and consciously used model for van Gogh's strong, earthy paintings and drawings of French and Belgian peasants. The monumental simplicity of Millet's figures, his instinctive placement of them in underlying design-tensions and rhythmic movement, foreshadowed the modern art of today.

Millet died with the bittersweet taste of tardy success on his lips, but Daumier was less fortunate. He lived out his life in poverty and neglect, and died without knowing that within a generation or two he would be "discovered" and receive posthumous fame while others gathered the fruits of his labors.

Honoré Daumier (1808-1879) was born in Marseilles, the son of a glazier whose dream was to be a poet. When Honoré was seven the family moved to Paris where they lived in a poor section while M. Daumier sought an audience for his muse and neglected his trade and his family's needs. When young Honoré early decided he wanted to become an artist, he received no encouragement from his impractical father who saw nothing practical in an artist's life. But, after several unbearable jobs and brief attendance at an art class where he quickly tired of endlessly drawing ears, eyes, noses, feet, and other portions of the human anatomy from plaster casts, Honoré suddenly found firm footing. A friend in a lithographer's studio taught him how to transfer crayon drawings to stone, and Honoré found the tool that would make his art a practical means of livelihood. He was soon earning a little at commercial lithography for others and at the same time making his own lithographs. Before he was twenty-one he had published several political cartoons. These so impressed the editor of *La Caricature*, a radical weekly, that he offered the young man a job on his staff. (*La Caricature* was anti-Bourbon, anti-Orléans, and therefore opposed to the current government.)

He worked for *La Caricature* until it succumbed under the government edict of 1835 that forbade political criticism in the press, then became a regular contributor to the daily satirical paper *Le Charivari* which during the following thirteen years published the bulk of his graphic work: great art in the form of social observation and satire and, again, when the ban was lifted for a short time, political commentary. Daumier was no ordinary, nor even an extraordinary, caricaturist or cartoonist. He was an artist. His finest drawings and lithographs are works of art comparable with the drawings of the great Renaissance masters, with Raphael, with

Rubens and Rembrandt, whose works as a boy and a youth he had studied in the Louvre. (Pl. VI)

Largely because of their subject matter, however, neither Daumier nor his contemporaries thought of his drawings as art—and Daumier had started even as a child to become an artist. To him and his world that meant painting. But he had so little time to give to it. Although a vast audience followed his political and social drawings with keen interest, the financial rewards were meagre; he had to turn out hundreds of drawings and lithographs annually even to live. He was in his early fifties before he was able to do much serious work at all. And then no one, except two or three perceptive writers and artists, would accept him as a painter. In 1860, when he was fifty-two, he was dismissed from his post with *Charivari* and suddenly had plenty of time to paint—but no source of income to keep him and his wife alive while he painted. Other newspapers and journals to which he offered his services as a social satirist, political commentator—anything, anything he could draw for them—refused on the grounds that he was out of date.

For three years he and his wife lived in abject poverty, kept alive only by the charity of their friends and a tiny pension certain of them had managed to squeeze out of the government for him. To live more cheaply, the Daumiers left the city for a small house in Valmondois, a village not far from Paris. Daumier settled down to painting but could sell nothing, not even a watercolor for fifty francs. His eyes began to give out. For many years he had abused them, often working through the night to get ahead of his schedule for *Charivari* so that he might have a few hours of daylight for his painting.

Late in 1863 *Charivari* recalled him, and, despite his failing sight, Daumier returned for twelve years more of miserably underpaid labor on its staff. Nearly blind, and for months unable to earn enough to pay his rent, he was about to be evicted from the house in Valmondois on his sixty-fourth birthday when he received a note from a friend:

Dear Old Comrade—

I have acquired a little house at Valmondois near Adam Isle but have been unable to think what to do with it. Then the idea came to hand it over to you. That seemed to me as good an idea as any so I have had the deed recorded in your name.

It is not really for you that I have done this, but simply to annoy your landlord.

Yours,
Corot

So Daumier was assured at least of a roof over his head as long as he lived. But the good Papa Corot died in 1875. Three years later Daubigny, close friend and neighbor of Daumier, followed him. A few months more of darkening eyesight and growing destitution, and then the first great modernist joined their company unhonored and ignored as a painter, and considered—by those who thought of him at all —only a hack artist of innumerable drawings and lithographs as ephemeral as the journals that published them.

There was no money to bury Daumier. One cannot live without money. Equally, it seems, one cannot even die respectably without it. Most of Daumier's close friends had preceded him, or were not near enough at the time of his death to take care of the last obligations. Grudgingly, the state put up twelve francs for a pauper's grave to enclose this great artist of France. The Mayor of Valmondois virtuously refused to requisition even the tiny minimum sum ordinarily supplied to dignify the body of a respectable pauper. Hadn't Daumier been a jailbird (he had been jailed for six months for his political cartoons for *La Caricature*), an agitator through the power of his art, a political caricaturist often on the wrong side? Some newspapers, commending the Mayor, criticized even the expenditure of the twelve francs for the grave.

Once it was known Daumier was in the ground, certain shrewd art dealers came out from Paris and began to sniff around the little house in Valmondois. For literally almost nothing they bought from the distraught widow scores of paintings the great Daumier had slaved to leave in a world that did not want them—then. Years later they were brought out, one by one, from the vaults of dealers who now treated them tenderly, as precious children they had long cherished. And sold them, as the years went by, at high and ever-higher prices.

What did Daumier contribute to the living stream of modern art? Like a few other great artists, he was not directly in or of the main course. Fed underground by waters from the Renaissance, he bubbled up, a fresh spring, beside the stream but not merging with it until years later he was recognized and his influence felt. Far ahead of his time—and contrary to the stand of today's most "advanced" and highly touted artists who hold that, to be modern, art must be amorphous and meaningless—Daumier proved that art as communication is not lessened as art.

Without theories or isms, never arguing art but producing it, Daumier produced works which communicate ideas yet are masterpieces of design, form, and volume, of receding and advancing planes, of underlying rhythmic patterns in the most modern sense. Each picture reaches the viewer with intrinsic meaning and proves that form never need be sacrificed to content, that the most complete art is communication at all levels of response and in all periods of time. Daumier drew and painted the unfortunates of his day and those who were the contributors to their misfortunes. He pierced the mask of respectability and laid bare the hypocrite, the thief, the rascal, the prostitute. Completely of his own time he painted the patient poor, the starving, fiery radical, the bloated *nouveau riche*, the clown, the classic actor, the washwoman, the corrupt judge, the venal attorney—in short, rich man, poor man, beggarman, thief, doctor, lawyer, merchant, chief—of his day. And how we recognize them today, as of our day!

5 TWO ARTISTS OF SPAIN

TWO ARTISTS OF SPAIN MUST BE HERE INCLUDED who do not follow in the direct line of chronological progression but who entered the mainstream of modern art as contributory influences. (Pl. X, XI)

Later in time but earlier in influence, Francisco de Goya (1746-1828) was exactly contemporary with David and his exact opposite except that both these painters managed—David in France by cold calculation, Goya in Spain by impudent daring—to keep their official status as premier painters in the midst of violent changes of government. Both died in exile from their native lands—David an exile by royal edict, in Brussels; Goya by choice, in Bordeaux.

Goya was a peasant, born in the poverty-ridden mountain village of Fuendetodos, Aragon. Like all the village children he labored from daylight to dark in the fields. Yet somehow he found time for his passion for drawing—with burnt ends of sticks on stones or rocks when he had nothing else. The persistence, the very evident talent, and no doubt the audacious personality of the overworked little urchin made a stir in the tiny village and he was given the opportunity to paint an altar curtain which, if good enough, would be hung in the village church. Sixty years later, when Goya revisited his birthplace, the curtain was still the altar-hanging.

He had been twelve when he made this first attempt at professional painting. Two years later he was sent by a wealthy patron to nearby Saragossa, capital of Aragon, to study with a court painter. Here, at the age of fourteen, Goya began the violent, lusty, unfettered life that was to express itself in art of extraordinary vitality.

Painting by day, carousing by night, engaging in bull-fighting Sundays and holidays—with singing, dancing, and sword play thrown in for good measure—Goya reached his first serious crisis at nineteen when the gang of which he was leader tangled with a rival gang and several were killed. Goya fled to Madrid where he again mixed violence with art, becoming better known for the former than for the latter. Picked up one night from the gutter with a dagger in his back, he was spirited to the coast by bull-fighter friends, who got him on a ship to Italy. In Rome, on the fringes of the French art colony, he painted potboiling scenes of Spanish life which he sold for a few liras—enough for him to engage in the really serious business of roistering. He became the hero of low-life adventurings, a ruffianly international playboy whose legendary exploits gladdened the hearts of gossips. He also spent some time in Parma, where apparently he gave more serious attention to painting for he won an Academy prize there in 1771.

After a few years in Italy he felt homesick for his family and Spain. He returned to Aragon and at the age of twenty-nine settled down long enough to marry the sister of a well-known painter.

Soon after his marriage, and probably through the influence of his brother-in-law, Goya received an appointment as a designer in the royal tapestry factory. During the next four years his dashing impudence as a man and his ripening genius as an artist merged, and he became famous through his series of tapestry designs in which he flouted the prevailing French style of the followers of Rubens and struck out boldly on his own. Instead of nymphs and goddesses meandering through the high-life doings of mythology, Goya's cartoons for the tapestries were wonderfully designed pictures of contemporary Spanish life in its everyday activities. And instead of the conventional line and form-blocking, Goya achieved his startlingly new effects by a cunning mixture of mass and silhouette.

With this, Goya arrived as an artist. He received all kinds of commissions—portraits, murals, altar-pieces—and executed them with remarkable speed and bravura. He moved to Madrid and soon became an inseparable friend of the King's brother. The King himself, Charles III, frowned on his brother's roistering pal and refused to appoint him to a court job. But Goya by now was not dependent on royal favor. He was the acknowledged genius of the day. Once his art was recognized, his picaresque reputation fanned rather than dimmed the flame of popular adulation. In spite of professional jealousy and political maneuvering, he was made president of the Academy. Great ladies threw themselves at him and wealthy noblemen insisted upon being portrayed by him. Charles III died and Goya's boon companion ascended the throne and lost no time in making Goya a court painter.

Then came the painter's great years of art and scandal. Spain was fearfully corrupt and Goya had lived on all its levels: the grinding poverty of its masses; the gang warfare and snatched, violent pleasures of its under-privileged youth;

the quick, sharp gayeties of its half-world; and now the shameless libertinism of court and aristocracy. Goya joined in their revels and painted their portraits, glossing nothing over, leaving nothing out. Magnificently designed in patterns of light and mass and silhouette, with patches of broken color (long before the Impressionists) adding excitement, his group portrait *Family of Charles IV*—dominated by its licentious, incredibly ugly Queen and its florid-faced, bourgeois King—is a devastating annihilation of royalty as royal.

But the more Goya insulted his patrons in paint, the more extravagantly they praised and paid him, particularly the ladies. One of the world's most spicy scandals of all time is Goya's blatant, long-lasting affair with the Duchess of Alba, reigning beauty of Spain and member of one of its oldest families. It has always been believed—and, from the beginning, always feebly denied—that she was the model for his two most seductively beautiful paintings: *Maja Nude* and *Maja Clothed*. *Maja* may be roughly or, one might say, loosely translated "gay lady." Although sixteen years his senior, the Duchess was a close and familiar friend of the painter, often dropping in at his studio—not always for sittings. (Pl. XI)

It was on one of his escapades with the Duchess—making a hasty trip through the mountains—that Goya came down with a chill which affected his ears, leaving him totally deaf. In his world of silence, though as popular and sought-after as ever, Goya took up the etcher's needle and produced his first great series of aquatints, *Los Caprichos,* castigating with ferocious ridicule his whole disorderly world of the flesh and the devil.

In 1808 the French came. The slaughter began and, with it, Goya's great series of aquatints *Disasters of War;* later, a group of paintings known as *The Horrors of War*. These etchings and paintings are the first examples of genuine art—probably of art in any degree—not to glorify war or romanticize carnage. (Pl. X)

There was neither glory nor gallantry in Goya's heaped-up corpses, each twisted into its separate agony of death; in his groups of wretched civilians facing a firing squad. Nothing related to death was beautiful or glorious to Goya. Yet every one of these awful portrayals has a violent vitality—life arrested in its last uninhibited upsurge. Every thrusting line and even the powerful, dramatic interplay of light against dark masses is instinct with the final frantic push of life against the moment of death. It is the tremendous vitality of these pictures, less of war itself than of the results and by-products of war, that has given them their great and lasting impact and has made them the most renowned of all Goya's works.

After a few months of long-distance political jockeying—playing Goya's friend Charles IV against his son Ferdinand, who detested the painter—Napoleon in Paris threw them both over and placed his brother Joseph on the throne. This was just too much for the Spaniards, and a sudden and spontaneous uprising took place all over Spain. To put down the insurrection, Napoleon himself invaded the country with an army of 180,000 men.

Through it all Goya continued to paint. He even managed to retain his court position under Joseph Bonaparte, who gave him a decoration in spite of the anti-French propaganda implicit in the artist's war paintings and etchings. With the fall of Napoleon and the restoration of the Bourbons, Ferdinand ascended the throne in Spain and Goya had to take the current loyalty oath and prove he had never been on the opponent's side. He offered as evidence the fact that although he had received a decoration from Bonaparte, he had never *worn* it.

The new King, Ferdinand VII, looked on him with jaundiced eye—very evident in the grim and covertly comical State portrait of him by Goya—and grudgingly permitted him to take the oath of allegiance, sourly remarking: "You deserve exile. You deserve hanging. But you are an artist. Therefore I will forget everything." And he actually permitted Goya to retain his post as premier court painter.

But Goya no longer had a taste for court life. He left Madrid for Seville, where he decorated the Cathedral, slipping in as celestial beings the faces and forms of two well-known ladies of easy virtue. When he returned to Madrid he kept much to himself in his home on the outskirts of the capital. On the walls of this house, which he bought in 1819, he painted in oil his last great pictures almost in surrealist vein, particularly the gigantic *Saturn Devouring His Sons* and *The Witches' Sabbath*.

In his seventy-eighth year, a rheumatic old man, deaf, half-blind, Goya arrived in Paris still eager for life. He visited the studios of the younger artists, unerringly selecting those—among them Géricault and Delacroix—destined to make their mark in the long history of art. He then went to Bordeaux where, after one short return trip to Madrid, he died in his eighty-third year.

Goya has been described as a Romantic, a Realist, an Expressionist and even, occasionally, as an Impressionist and a Surrealist. But he cannot be circumscribed within any or even all of those labels, most of which were affixed to artists well after Goya's time. The great Spanish artist was above all an individualist, though many of the elements now attributed to the modern school can be found in his work. Its supreme quality is vitality. Even in the portrayal of physical death—as in his war pictures and, amazingly, in his still-life paintings of game during his last years in Bordeaux—all of his work pulses with life.

Goya was a forerunner of modern art more than an influence or direct contributor to its development. But in his blithe willingness to smash old forms or break with polite artistic conventions if they interfered with the expression of his genius, he is completely in the spirit of modern art. He once remarked: "The professors are always talking about lines and never about masses. But where does one see lines? I find that neither lines nor colors exist in nature—only light and shade." In this acute and remarkable observation about the non-existence of color except in terms of light, Goya was a century ahead of the modern science of the chemistry of light and many years in advance of the science of optics which was so to excite the Impressionists forty years after his death.

In the year 1541, or thereabouts, Domenicos Theotocopoulos was born on the Island of Crete, then a possession of Venice, queen city-state of the Adriatic. Proudly a Greek, a people he never hesitated to proclaim greater than the Italians and the Spanish, Theotocopoulos in adolescence learned the richly colored, stylized design of the Byzantine art of the icon. In early manhood he went to Venice where in the studios of Titian and Tintoretto he absorbed the technique of Renaissance painting and portraiture.

After four intensive years of steeping himself in the tradition and techniques of these masters, he proceeded to Rome, where he was accepted as a full-fledged artist of the Venetian School.

Then he moved on to Spain where, about the year 1577, he settled in Toledo, remaining there until he died nearly four decades later. In Venice and Rome he had been casually referred to as "Il Greco." In Toledo "El Greco" was permanently fastened on him by the Spaniards.

From the beginning of his life in Spain, El Greco was arrogant and often quarrelsome, disliked by the King and unpopular with the masses. But he was known from the first as an artist of the Venetian School and that carried great weight in Spain, as it did in the rest of the civilized world. He was kept busy from his arrival with commissions both for portraits and for religious works. His financial success enabled him to live extravagantly in the elegance of twenty-four sumptuous rooms, to which he brought musicians from Venice to entertain him at mealtimes. He deliberately set out to enjoy all the pleasures of the senses and took great pride in his intellectual delights. He scorned personal piety and convention; apparently he never married the mother of his one acknowledged child, though Doña Jeronima lived for many years in his household as his wife and their son was his sole heir. Paradoxically, every El Greco painting that has come down to us, with the exception of two or three portraits, shows a spiritual longing, even a striving, to transcend the flesh.

El Greco's early work in Spain, particularly the *Assumption of the Virgin,* done in 1577 and now owned by the Art Institute of Chicago, shows clearly the Renaissance influence. But his style began to change. In 1588 he painted the enormous crowded canvas—approximately sixteen by twelve feet—entitled *Burial of Count Orgaz.* Designated by the artist "my sublime work," this painting is a tightly organized synthesis of rich Byzantine design combined with the upward sweep and elevation of Tintoretto. The lower third of the painting is separated from the upper portion by a mosaic of Spanish laces fringed with white ruffs and bordered by the black of the costumes below and the darkness of the background just above the heads. A similar mosaic, but fainter and more colorful, appears in the crowding together of saints in the extreme upper right of the canvas. Rising from the limp, dull-armored body of the Count held by the resplendently robed Saints Stephen and Augustine in the lower foreground of the painting, a cloud-embryo soul soars upward through a vortex of heavenly figures to the apex of the triangle, the white-clad figure of Christ. (Pl. XI)

Landscape even as a very surbordinate background, such as the one in *Saint Martin and the Beggar* (National Gallery, Washington), has very little part in El Greco's paintings. His portraits are placed against a neutral blankness or a simple interior Most of his other paintings, celestial or terrestrial, usually are so crowded with figures as to leave little room for anything but clouds. His most elaborate scenic backgrounds are the walls of the Temple with a distant view of Jerusalem seen through an arch in *Cleansing of the Temple,* the weird stage-set cloud-and-hill effects of *Christ on the Mount of Olives* (both in the National Gallery, London) and the far view of the city in *The Laocoön* (National Gallery, Washington). Yet again the paradox: El Greco's one pure landscape *View of Toledo* is probably the greatest landscape in the entire history of art. Fortunately for Americans, it is owned by the Metropolitan Museum of Art and is on almost continuous view there (Pl X)

The brooding magnificence of this unforgettable painting

holds one enthralled. At first glance only the ominous sky seems threatening. Heavy clouds rent by flashes of light crush downward over the symbols of man's power, the proud cathedral and the massive castle which stand on the highest eminence of the hill and dominate the upward surge of the gray-blue buildings and bridges of the town. Then the inner eye becomes aware of movement beneath the seemingly static earth: the yellow-green meadows and the black-green trees, the motionless stream which seems just on the verge of reversing its natural flow to push upward with all the earth to meet the down-pressing heavens in a mighty apocalyptic clash that will burst open the universe.

But why include an artist of four centuries ago in a book on modern art? Because, by warrant of discovery and right of perceptive appreciation, the moderns have made El Greco their own. After thirty-seven years of fame and success in his adopted country, El Greco died in 1614 and his paintings, unlighted by the corruscating spotlight of his personality, were neglected and ignored through three forgetful centuries. The moderns—first the artists, then the writers on art, the dealers, and finally the art-conscious public—rescued him from obscurity.

At the beginning of the last half of the nineteenth century the avant-garde Realists, sparked by the earlier interest of the Romantic painters in lands of the sun—but spurning what they considered their elders' romantic twaddle in paint—were still subconsciously influenced by the exotic pull of the South. They chose Spain as the land of their inspiration and Velázquez as their hero of Realism—which of course he was not, except in their imaginations. They overlooked El Greco.

But when the next generation of avant-gardists rose to ascendancy and, near the end of the nineteenth century, Realism fell, taking with it the false idol of Velázquez, the artistic eye was still trained on Spain and some of the new radicals began to be aware of El Greco. A few, Cézanne in particular, understood his work and were influenced by it. Later, even newer radicals, happy to have an old master to fling in the face of their critics in the artistically turbulent early years of the twentieth century, joyfully pointed out parallels between their own often meaningless distortions and the purposeful elongations of El Greco. Astute art dealers, quick to follow a lucrative lead, began quietly to search out obscurely placed paintings by the master. The noted German art critic and scholar, Meier-Graefe, who was later to perform a similar service for van Gogh, went to Spain to renew his studies of Velázquez but returned to write a glowing book on El Greco, acclaiming him the great master of that country.

Forty years have passed since the publications of Meier-Graefe's book and one published about the same time by a Spanish scholar, Manuel B. Cossio. Today the early excitement of rediscovery has long since died down, but El Greco is still the darling of the moderns. And with greater reason than most of the moderns suspect: *before* he expressed the individuality of his genius by breaking orthodox rules—and it is the breaking of those rules that most endears him to the modern artist—El Greco was a superb painter thoroughly grounded in not one but two of the world's greatest traditions of art: Renaissance painting and Byzantine design. He had a masterly technique and a fundamental understanding of anatomy even though he often deliberately chose to distort certain of its aspects. The paint quality of his canvases is as richly fresh today as it was three centuries ago.

El Greco had not been long in Spain before his individual genius began to transcend the technique and tradition he had mastered. By 1600 the slight elongation that had already appeared in the delicate, tapering hands and high-domed heads of his paintings became pronounced in the disproportionate lengthening of nearly all his figures—physical symbol of the spirit's effort to rise above and beyond the fetters of the flesh. Subtle distortions in perspective, particularly in the placement of figures, and the occasional unnaturalistic representation of certain natural objects such as hills and clouds, brought about pattern tensions and, by breaking up expected rhythms, created visual excitement. He anticipated Cézanne and the moderns in drawing directly with the brush, creating planes with area and volumes of color rather than defining them with lines.

There is one element in El Greco's paintings that has been largely ignored by modern commentators, yet perhaps more than any other single quality it subconsciously has the greatest effect in pleasing the modern eye. It is his almost invariable use of what can only be called "sophisticated" colors. The Renaissance masters, especially Raphael, used richly harmonious colors and color combinations that are immediately and universally appealing. But for that very reason they quickly begin to pall on the visual appetite. Too steady a diet of deep or clear reds, madonna and cerulean blues, sunny or delicate yellows, instantly satisfying greens, and lusciously glowing purples tend to surfeit the modern taste, and the eyes turn with fresh interest to a more subtle and unusual color range. El Greco seldom employs a simple green or yellow; in a skillful interplay of light and shadow each is always tinctured with the other. His reds and pinks are muted by an admixture of blue or made harsh with orange, the resulting tonalities sometimes juxtaposed in oddly satisfying combinations. His flesh tones are frequently an ashy-gray highlighted with a luminous pale yellow—in one case to show the aging process of a dissolute old man; in another, a high attenuation of spirituality.

El Greco is never guilty, however, of handling color in unusual ways for mere shock value or in a strained effort to be "different." As with his elongated forms, there is always a definite artistic purpose behind his unorthodox methods—both purpose and methods abundantly justified in works of genius.

But modern art and artists have a valid claim on El Greco and have done him and the world an invaluable service. Without them, he would still be forgotten. For several generations their rejection of Academic formulas and their breaking of rules sacred to each preceding generation prepared the way for appreciation of Spain's greatest painter, in many ways today's most modern of modern artists.

6 M. GUSTAVE COURBET, REALIST

RETURNING TO THE MAINSTREAM OF MODERN ART
as it flowed turbulently through France in the mid-nineteenth
century, we find a new and mighty figure joining the ranks
against the Academy and, at the same time, starting a one-
man war against the Romantics, his double-edged progress
pouring a surge of new vitality into the forward movement
of art. This hearty, high-humored giant from the village of
Ornans, near the Swiss-French border, was the black-bearded,
life-loving Gustave Courbet (1819-1877), the country boy
who made good in the big city by remaining a country boy.

He grew up in the midst of a happy, warm-hearted family,
his father a fairly prosperous farmer. From the beginning,
young Gustave hated schoolbooks but took delight in his
earliest teacher's lessons in sketching nature on field trips.
He continued his fight against book-learning when his father
sent him, against his will, to the Collège Royal at Besançon,
where he spent most of his time in the Beaux-Arts classes
taught by a minor pupil of David. In 1839 the young man
was sent to Paris to study law. Enlisting the aid of a famous
attorney there who happened also to be a relative on his
mother's side of the family, Courbet returned to Ornans and
declared his determination to become a painter. Convinced at
last, his father capitulated. He did more. He promised to
stake his son to an art career—even, if need be, to "sell my
last field to help you." In his turn, before an approving family
council, Courbet pledged to "make a name for myself in
Paris" within a decade.

To this end, returning to Paris in 1840, he threw his super-
abundant energy and strength, his native intelligence, and
his considerable talent into the task. Quickly dissatisfied with
Academic teaching, he turned to the masterworks in the
Louvre as his guide, copying paintings by Rembrandt and
Frans Hals, and *Dante's Barque* by Delacroix. In the Studio
Suisse, which had no teacher, he worked from living models.

The Salon of 1844 hung the first painting Courbet submitted
for exhibition, his *Courbet with a Black Dog*. Then there

was a series of rejections until the Revolution of 1848 when, the power of the Academy temporarily diminished, the Salon was open to all artists. In the Salon of 1849 Courbet showed several paintings, among them the superb semi-self-portrait *Man with Leather Belt* and the finely atmospheric *After Dinner at Ornans*, in its subject matter Realistic but certainly in its style Romantic.

Happily, *After Dinner at Ornans* pleased both public and critics and won a "second place" medal. This modest victory accomplished two very desirable results: in justifying Courbet's chosen career it delighted the artist's family and friends at home; more important to that career, it made unnecessary future submission of his paintings for the approval of a Salon jury. This was indeed fortunate, as in the Salon of 1850 Courbet entered an enormous canvas—more than ten by twenty-one feet—which would probably have been rejected by the jury. But the jury could do nothing about it, and when the Salon opened the painting was there to shock the critics and rock Parisian society.

The canvas was *Funeral at Ornans*, a pageantlike stretch of figures—priests, acolytes, townsmen, mourners—spread out across the wide canvas, its center of focus a husky, red-cheeked gravedigger in shirtsleeves kneeling at the edge of the open grave and obviously impatient for the priest to finish the service. At the other side of the grave a white dog supplies a secondary accent against the dark-clothed mourners. There is no heavy pathos, no dramatic lighting, no tragic glamorizing. Everything in the painting—the serious faces of the townspeople, their still postures and somber dress, the mist-gray of the sky, the crucifix held high by a white-robed acolyte—is convincingly, quietly natural. These are real people at a real funeral.

That is what enraged Paris. *Real* people—worse, people of the lower order—painted on a canvas so large it should have been reserved only for a "noble" subject classically portrayed. Here was vulgarity in painting. Here was *socialism!* For the Academy was back in power; painting, if it could not be classic or ideal, must at least be refined.

To us today, accustomed to grim documents on the seamy side of life which modern Realists have presented as the only Realism, these paintings which caused such an uproar a century ago seem gently Romantic. Courbet did not tell a story on canvas or highlight a dramatic incident, as the true Romantics did, but at this distance of time the painting techniques seem very similar and only the subject matter noticeably different. The Romantics felt that the emotion evoked both in and by the painting was the important thing. The Realists considered the recording of reality basic and all that was necessary. As Courbet once stated, he confined himself to "finding the most complete expression of an existing object, but never imagining or creating the object." Both schools of painting, however, were blackballed whenever possible by the Academicians, still in control of all official art, art commissions, and Salon exhibitions.

Every new picture Courbet painted stirred fresh controversy. Young and old painters, writers who, like Zola, were to become famous novelists, poets, and one affluent art collector who became a patron of Courbet, gathered around him, applauding his independence even when some of them did not altogether like his paintings. He was a storm center who thoroughly enjoyed the storms he aroused even though he was sometimes astounded—as we are today—by their violence. At times the virulence of the attacks hurt and bewildered him with their impenetrable stupidity. But nothing could long affect his vigorous optimism.

The industrial age was gaining momentum. In 1855, under the patronage of Napoleon III, a giant world's fair, the great *Exposition Universelle,* was organized in Paris. As a cultural part of it, leading painters of twenty-eight nations were invited to submit works for a huge exhibition to be held in the *Palais des Arts.* Inevitably, the jury of selection was composed of Academicians. Just as inevitably, they excluded Courbet's paintings.

Furiously indignant, the fighting son of Ornans built at his own expense—and very close to the *Palais des Arts*—a *Pavillon du Réalisme* and filled it with his own paintings. He put up a sign at the entrance announcing:

REALISM: EXHIBIT AND SALE
of 40 pictures and 4 drawings by M. Gustave Courbet
Admission 1 Franc

Unfortunately, there was so much more than art going on in the great Exposition that Courbet's self-supported solo exhibition drew comparatively few customers in spite of the fact that his *chef d'oeuvre* caused a sensation. It was entitled *The Painter's Studio; a true-allegory showing a phase of seven years of my artistic life.* Nearly twelve by twenty feet, it is a unique composition—a huge, shadowy-ceilinged studio with a group of people at each end, while in the center sits the painter putting finishing touches on the large and beautifully executed landscape on his easel. Standing behind the painter, her attention concentrated on his brush strokes, is a tall, vigorously built nude model. At the other side of the artist stands a little boy, raptly watching him paint. Again, as in *Funeral at Ornans,* there is a white accent center foreground, in this case a playful cat. The group at the left, all men, is made up of models and friends Courbet had used in some of his paintings during the preceding seven years. Even a hunting dog, the violin in *After Dinner at Ornans,* and other props are shown. On the right of the canvas the group is composed of various literary and social friends of the artist, the most conspicuous being the poet Baudelaire, bending over a book, the open pages of which give a secondary accent of white. (Pl. VII)

The canvas is really three paintings in one, coordinated by the theme of seven years in the artist's studio. There are several fully worked-up portraits, including the self-portrait of the artist. The central group—artist, model, small boy, cat, and landscape—is not only the climax and highlight of the canvas but a very arresting composition in itself.

Despite official disdain and obstruction, the savage ridicule of most of the critics, and the marked disapproval of Parisian society—the Emperor once cut his whip across a Courbet canvas of nude bathers while the Empress Eugénie inquired with haughty contempt if the robust women were Percheron mares—Courbet's paintings sold at good prices in France and abroad and his work was praised by discerning men of letters and the arts not only in France but elsewhere in Europe.

Announcing Realism as a "democratic" art, Courbet charged up and down France and through Holland, Belgium, Switzerland, and Germany, organizing exhibitions of his work and proclaiming his doctrine.

It is no exaggeration to say that, beginning with the furious retort of his *Pavillon du Réalisme* to the Academicans who excluded him from the Exposition of 1855, Courbet became the world's best-known living artist, somewhat as Picasso is today. The tide of Realism rose with its founder's fame to the high point, in 1867, of another Paris World's Exposition in which Courbet had 130 paintings and a number of sculptures. Two years later he had the immense satisfaction of loudly rejecting the Emperor's offer of the Cross of the Legion of Honor.

The following year the Emperor surrendered at Sedan, and the Second Empire fell apart, more from internal weakness than from the assaults of the oncoming Prussians. The new Republican government made Courbet Director of Fine Arts, with general supervision over all national museums. He acted with dispatch, removing the art treasures of France from danger of bombardment. At the same time, with native wholeheartedness, he wrote an open letter to all German artists proposing a goal of general disarmament, fraternization between nations, and a United States of Europe.

But the Germans bombarded, besieged, and marched into Paris, and the Republican government fell. Then the Commune of Paris formed a government and in March 1871 Courbet was made president of the Artists Federation during the short and rioting regime of the Commune. Then, after a week of bloody contests, the conservatives took over and formed still another government. The Academicians were immediately back in power. And what a target they had!

Now Courbet's fame became his misfortune. Forgotten was his service to France in the protection of its art treasures from German bombardment. Overlooked was the fact that he had resigned from the presidency of the Artists Federation four days before the column in the Place Vendôme was torn down by zealots determined to destroy every monument that reminded of the monarchy. Even though it was later proved that he opposed such destruction, Courbet was accused as responsible for this act of vandalism and sentenced to six months imprisonment, plus a heavy fine. After his release he went to Ornans. There he met his most bitter reversal. His fellow citizens repudiated him.

And then the government decided to reopen the case against Courbet. Fearing he might again lose his liberty, the artist went into exile in Switzerland. He was tried *in absentia,* and the entire cost of rebuilding the Vendôme Column was levied against him. His property and possessions, including all his unsold paintings, were confiscated.

Grief-stricken and broken in health, Courbet continued to paint in exile—some of his canvases from this last period are very fine, though others are too hurriedly executed—and to sell to foreign collectors. He died in Switzerland the last day of December 1877. In 1919, on the centenary of his birth, his ashes were removed to the cemetery of Ornans, scene of his first great painting. Twenty years later, just before the beginning of World War II, his natal village made posthumous amends by unveiling a bust of the artist and proclaiming him "the most glorious of the sons of Ornans."

Although he had great virtuosity and masterly technique, Courbet was a thoughtful painter, as is shown by his fine portraits and—perhaps more unusual among painters—in his landscapes with figures, in which the figures are often genuine portrait studies. Later in his career he became artistically aware of the sea off the coast of Normandy and produced some magnificent seascapes.

In contrast to the stiff or classically posed, two-dimensional paintings of David, Courbet puts the movement and color of life and nature on his canvases. Unlike the soft and slightly sickening nudes of Ingres, Courbet's are robust, healthy young women, full-bodied like the nudes of Rubens but with less fat and more wholesome strength—less blubber and more beauty.

Rejecting the drama (often the melodrama) of the Romantics, Courbet brought art down to the good solid earth. He established the right of the art'st to paint what he *saw* without being bound by tradition or held in line by schools or the art fashion of the hour. Most of all, he raised the standard of the artist as an independent individual with freedom of esthetic choice.

7 MANET AND THE CAFÉS OF PARIS

IT WAS WITH ENRAGED DISGUST THAT THE refined and delicate Parisians greeted a painting by one of their own social standing who, they felt, had let them down—the elegant, witty, wealthy man-about-Paris, Édouard Manet (1832-1883). Not that Manet painted pictures of swineherds. Far from it. He offended by breaking the rules of polite art in another way even though he had studied under a prominent Academician and had been honored by having two paintings hung in the Salon of 1861. Lately he had fallen in with some irresponsible fellows who wasted their time away from l'École des Beaux-Arts to spend it, against the advice and warnings of the Academicians, in an independent studio and in cafés and restaurants talking art instead of creating it.

It was only the dilettante, however, the painter who wanted the life without the work of an artist, who talked art and did not create it. The serious artists—Courbet, Manet, occasionally even Daumier, and the group of young painters who a decade or so later were to launch Impressionism—put in long hours, like honest workmen, at their easels, meeting at night for lively and sometimes raucous discussions of their new theories of art, or to fulminate against the blindly stupid power of the Academy, or even to compare notes on the delightful follies of women. There were many to listen when Courbet roared out his hearty defiances of bourgeois critics and Academy rejections, and there was much to enjoy in the clashes of wit and ideas between artists and the writers, famous or soon-to-be-famous, who also frequented the several cafés which were the centers and breeding grounds of new and vital expressions in art and literature.

This was the period when the cult of Bohemianism of the Left Bank and the Latin Quarter began to flourish. Henri Murger had named it in his "Scènes de la Vie de Boheme" in which Murger immortalized the Café Momus where Courbet, Baudelaire, Gautier, Champfleury and the de Goncourt brothers were often seen—and especially heard—of a night. Another café, the Guerbois, became the gathering place of the young Impressionists. Then, as now, most of the artists who made the Left Bank cafés their clubs were young and their antics were simply vagrant sparks struck off from the serious revolt against fixed ideas and crushing tradition.

Probably as an antidote to the poison of freedom being sniffed and sometimes swallowed by these younger artists, the Jury for the 1863 Salon was unusually severe. More than 4,000 paintings were rejected, among them canvases by Whistler, Cézanne, Pissarro, and Manet. The creators of the 4,000 paintings raised an outcry so great that Emperor Napoleon III decreed a *Salon des Refusés* (to be held in the same building as the official Salon) in which all the rejected pictures were to be shown unless withheld by the artists themselves. As it was considered the reverse of an honor to appear with the *Refusés*, more than six hundred paintings were withdrawn.

Nevertheless, all Paris went to the "Exhibition of Rejected Painters," as Whistler called it, to see and to ridicule but not to recognize as masterpieces paintings that later became known as great works of art. One of these was Whistler's *The White Girl*, now in the National Gallery of Art at Washington, D. C. But the picture that caused the greatest sensation was Manet's woodland scene of a picnic, *Luncheon on the Grass*. The simplified brushwork, with areas of opposing color instead of lines defining contour; the trees and stream of the background suggested rather than carefully painted in, were considered artistically offensive. But what really constituted the outrage to public taste was the fact that although the two gentlemen in the picture were fully and even fashionably dressed in morning clothes, one of the ladies, kneeling beside a stream in the background, was clad only in a chemise, while the other lady, boldly in the foreground, and the focus of interest, was simply clad in nothing at all. (Pl. VII)

Paris was shocked. The Emperor himself openly declared the painting immodest, and all Paris rushed to see it. Yet in the nearby official Salon was another stark naked lady that Paris acclaimed and the Emperor bought. It was a *Venus* by the Academic painter Cabanel which, although much more suggestive—in fact, the Manet was not at all suggestive—was held to be entirely inoffensive. Though "wanton and lascivious," one critic wrote, the *Venus* was "not in the least indecent."

That was because she was Venus. In the opinion of the bourgeois society which composed the powerful upper circles in the France of Napoleon III, it was considered thoroughly proper to paint gods and goddesses, nymphs and fauns, in the nude and quite evidently up to no good. That was only to be expected of such delightful creatures. But not ordinary mortals—no, never!

Two years later the official Salon itself, by some strange reversal or perhaps oversight, exhibited another nude by Manet, his most famous painting, *Olympia*. Here again the scene and the two figures were of contemporary Paris: A grave-eyed young girl, nude except for a slipper on her toe, a bow in her hair, and a ribbon round her neck, reclines on her bed while a Negro maid shows her a bouquet, doubtless from an admirer.

Olympia caused such a violent outburst of public rage that the Minister of Fine Arts stationed a special guard before it to protect it from possible mutilation or destruction by self-appointed monitors of public morals. Actually, the painting was in the tradition of the nude reclining figure—and the French have never been noted for their objection either to tradition or to nudes—that began its long descent through the centuries before the Renaissance. She adorns medieval tapestries in the guise of a goddess or a legendary Dido. Titian painted her, Rubens, the French Court artists, Goya, and innumerable lesser artists. She will continue to be painted, with variations, until the end of time. But *Olympia,* naked and unashamed, stared gravely out of the painting into the curtained chambers of the French bourgeois soul; she was the woman everyone knew about but nobody talked about. So the public had to be protected, not from her folly but from her frankness.

In 1890, a quarter of a century later and seven years after the death of Manet, his Impressionist friends raised 20,000 francs to buy *Olympia* and present it to the Government. It now hangs in the Louvre.

Manet occupies a curious position in the progression of art. Early in his career he was classed with Courbet as a Realist and adhered even more closely to the latter's creed of emotionless objectively than did Courbet himself. Courbet was of a far more emotional, not to say explosive, temperament, and some of that temperament inevitably seeped into his paintings, giving them emotional overtones and a flavor of Romanticism of which the artist was unaware. Manet's emotions were reserved for his private life. He was no country boy, but an urbane, polished Parisian, extremely serious about his painting but able to regard his subject with cool and knowledgeable detachment.

He was born in Paris, the son of well-to-do parents, his father a magistrate. From boyhood he wanted to be an artist. When he was sixteen, he threatened to run off to sea unless he were given an education in art. His parents let him ship to Rio de Janeiro, working his round-trip passage. They hoped it would cure him of both sea and art, but he returned with a greater love for both and years later combined the two in lyrical watercolor sketches and etchings. At eighteen his parents gave him the opportunity to study under Couture.

Six years of this Academic training, though it equipped him expertly with the tools and techniques of art, pleased neither master nor pupil, and Manet launched out on a self-conducted study of Louvre masterpieces. Still an eager student, he traveled to Germany and the Low Countries, where the works of Frans Hals interested him most. A trip to Italy acquainted him at first hand with the masterpieces of that country, and there he saw paintings by Velázquez, who was to become his greatest influence.

After the storm created by *Olympia* Manet again left Paris for a while and went to Spain, where he renewed and greatly enlarged his knowledge of Goya's paintings. When he returned to Paris he produced a number of "Spanish" paintings, some of them almost identical with Goya paintings in subject but otherwise showing only a superficial influence.

There was another influence, which came about almost by accident, that at this period affected not only Manet but many of the young painters, the American Whistler among them. It was the sudden craze for Japanese prints. Japan had been opened to the West in 1853 by Commodore Perry of the U. S. Navy. Three years later a small shipment of Japanese porcelain reached Paris, with prints by the master artist Hokusai used as part of the packing material. These caused such interest, even excitement, among the artists, that an assortment of prints was ordered by another Paris shop frequented by painters and writers. These prints finally arrived in 1862. Five years later, in the World's Fair held in Paris, an entire section was devoted to Japanese wares: porcelain, prints, costumes, etc. Many artists—Manet, Whistler, Degas, van Gogh, Monet, Gauguin, Toulouse-Lautrec—became enthusiasts for things Japanese, incorporating fans, prints, porcelain, hangings, and even costumes into their paintings as decorative accents. A few were seriously influenced by the flat-patterned, boldly colored, two-dimensional technique of Japanese prints. Though never slavishly copied, this influence is evident in some of Manet's paintings.

Edouard Manet was a Realist in his objectivity, but he was not naturalistic, as Courbet always was. Nor did he develop one consistent style of painting. With his intellectual keenness, he was an experimenter. He would virtually *taste* the technique of an artist or a style that interested him, then for a period adapt or assimilate into his own work what he found good. He painted many brilliant pictures and although they all are unmistakably his, their variations in style show how richly complex was his talent, what technical skill he commanded.

As he was never really a follower of Courbet, though at first classified with him as a Realist, so he was never the leader of the Impressionists although he was their hero and friend and for several years worked with them in their endless experiments and efforts to reproduce as exactly as possible on their canvases the actual illumination of light. Manet evolved his own technique—very different from the Impressionists'—for approximating the effect of light. Instead of preparing his canvas with a dark underpainting, which was the custom, and then adding highlights, he reversed the process. He gave his canvases an underpainting of clear, light brilliance —called *Peinture claire*—then worked in the darker tones while the underpainting was still wet. Going even farther, he began to light most of his forms and faces from the front, without reference to any light source in the picture. This further reduced shadowed areas, flattened out or practically eliminated modeling, and made light appear to come *from* the canvas rather than to lie on its surface.

Although Constable and Turner had bathed their pictures in light, that light was the natural illumination of sun and sky. Manet's lighting—except during the comparatively few years he worked with the Impressionists—was arbitrary, an effect of art, not nature. This was an amazing departure for any painter of the period but particularly for one classed as a follower of Courbet, whose canvases always had a dark base.

But it was not his technique that drew the young rebels to Manet. It was the uproar caused first by the exhibition of his *Luncheon on the Grass* and the even louder roar that his *Olympia* brought forth. At the Café Guerbois they gathered around him, happy to be dominated by his wit, his knowledge of the world and of art. They were all as yet unknown—Monet, Pissarro, Renoir, Degas, Cézanne—but he was an acknowledged artist cast down and almost literally spat upon, his works reviled. Manet was warmed by their admiration and partisanship. A firm friendship grew up among them which held through the years even though Manet frequently left them to paint in his own fashion and live his own life along the boulevards and in the more elegant cafés, at the opera or the races, all of which he recorded in paintings that today give us keenly observed and esthetically enjoyable views of fashionable life in Paris a century ago.

Often classed with the Impressionists, Manet was not so much one of that group of painters artistically as he was their forerunner and friend. Although he painted a few canvases that can be labeled Impressionist and more that might fall loosely into that category, he did not once show paintings in their group exhibitions or join with them in group sales and auctions of their work. It was his independent point of view that allied him with the Impressionists in friendship, his willingness to experiment with new techniques that made him their forerunner in painting. And it was his financial aid in desperate moments that kept Monet, leader of the Impressionists, from actual starvation.

He was only fifty-one years old, when he died on April 20, 1883. A brilliant but not a superficial painter, Manet never quite found his place in art, his theme, his style. Artistically, he was continually in a state of flux, not because he was uncertain but because he was always seeking—yet never for a constant goal. With him, art was forever in transit. He was the bridge between Realism and Impressionism.

8 FREEDOM OF COLOR:

THE IMPRESSIONISTS

For the Government to accept such filth there would have to be a great moral slackening.

THAT WAS THE OUTCRY RAISED IN 1893—NEARLY twenty years after the group of painters known as the Impressionists had held their first exhibition in Paris—to embarrass the Government of France and prevent it from accepting a magnificent bequest.

Of what did this "filth"—or magnificence—consist? It was a collection of sixty-five works by the leading painters classified as Impressionists: Monet, Pissarro, Sisley, Renoir, Manet, Degas, Cézanne. Renoir was executor of the will made by his friend Caillebotte, himself a minor Impressionist and one of the earliest collectors of his fellow artists' paintings.

With mouselike courage the French Government finally, and with noticeable reluctance, accepted not quite three-fifths of the bequest. It rejected two of the paintings by Cézanne, one by Manet, eight by Monet, eleven by Pissarro, two by Renoir, and three by Sisley. These twenty-seven rejected paintings would today, at the most conservative estimate, bring a price of at least half a million dollars. This loss to the State and the French people was another, even though partial, victory racked up by the Academicians.

During most of the nineteenth century the fundamental rule laid down by the Academy was the supreme importance of "line." Color was secondary and subservient. Line formed the painting; color only filled it in. Manet, following in the footsteps of the older Delacroix he so much admired, had completely disregarded this dictum. More than Delacroix, he painted forms with color areas, contrasts, and juxtapositions. Like Courbet, he rejected the Academicians' insistence on Biblical, mythological, or classical subjects, and the Romanticists' passion for the dramatic that often verged upon the melodramatic and their interest, as well, in literary allusion on canvas. He casually ignored Courbet's obsession with naturalism and the familiar incident. Manet found his subjects in the passing scene of the Parisian life of which he was so much a part—the race track, the opera bar, the boudoir or the *fêtes champêtres*.

The Impressionists took the next step forward. They abolished line completely, not even suggesting it by juxtaposed areas of color, and tried as nearly and as spontaneously as possible to produce by means of paint on canvas the immediate sensory reaction made on the optic nerve by the quick glimpse of an object or a scene. This impression, the newly discovered and much-discussed law of optics told them, is made solely through light reflected from the object to the optic nerve. The Impressionists therefore attempted to record on canvas not what they knew was form but what they *saw* as light. A friend of Renoir's described this type of painting as "treating a subject in terms of the tone and not of the subject itself."

The actual method was a development of the technique Constable had been the first to use consciously and had described to Delacroix and which Delacroix, in that invaluable Journal of his, had so brilliantly set down and analyzed. In short, it was to apply the paint in tiny strokes—some critics called them daubs—of pure, unmixed color which resembled the iridescent play of light upon a surface. By breaking up the surface of the canvas with this shimmer of prismatic tones, the artist produced the impression of form, distance, depth, and shadow. This was such a significant departure from all previous methods of painting that it can be called the *beginning* of modern art as we know it today. It is not today's modern art. In fact, much of Impressionism looks slightly old-fashioned to us today; and the followers of it, who have stayed in the same groove and technique as the leaders of seventy-five years ago, are simply today's academicians and imitators, no matter how young they may be. For *followers* are never modern artists in any period. Nevertheless Impressionism, ridiculed and rejected seventy-five and even sixty years ago, was the great point of departure from which modern art was to take off—in all directions at once, some critics still seem to feel.

In his last years Titian, by observing the effect of light in breaking up a surface into patches of color, had become aware of the principle on which Impressionism is based. A century later Velázquez, though reducing his colors almost to a range of gray tonalities, manipulated lighter and darker shades somewhat in the manner of Impressionism and enveloped his figures in a tonal atmosphere.

But it was the group called Impressionists who scientifically analyzed, formulated, developed, and almost standardized a technique of painting in conformity with the laws of optics, the physics of light, and the chemistry of paint. Shadows were no longer black or muddy brown. On the snow, for example, they became blue or lavender or violet—as they actually are. One of the simpler manifestations of imitative Impressionism is the blue-shadowed snow landscape that will probably haunt us forever. Impressionism must also be held at least indirectly responsible—though its founders were never guilty of it and certainly never foresaw it—for the arbitrary, hit-or-miss placement of red, purple, or green facial shadows by certain modern artists.

One of their discoveries that most delighted the Impressionists was the use of complementary colors juxtaposed as shadows against so-called primary colors; i.e., red opposed by green (which is a combination of the two other primary colors, blue and yellow); blue opposed by orange (red plus yellow); yellow opposed by violet (red plus blue). These juxtapositions bring out the greatest and most dazzling intensities of each color.

But the Impressionists went one step further: they split or *divided* (and for this reason the technique in its final form as developed by Seurat was called *divisionist*) even the complementary colors into their two primary components. Instead of red being opposed by green (out of a tube or mixed on the palette), the two colors that compose green—blue and yellow —were laid on the canvas in tiny strokes so close together that the eye of the viewer *saw* them as green unless he came so near the canvas as to see only the strokes and lose the picture as a whole. Even then, so dazzling was the effect, the optic nerve could hold the colors separate for only a moment; the eye inevitably blended them.

Thus was born the "rainbow" palette of the Impressionists, sometimes called the prismatic or spectrum palette. Instead of being mixed on the actual palette of the artist, however, the tiny strokes of pure color used both for shadowed and light areas on Impressionist canvases were merged by the eye of the observer. Constable had been the first to use this method but never so completely or analytically as the Impressionists.

Another important result of this revolution in art was that its use necessarily forced abandonment of the "concealed" brush stroke. Up to this time, and for Academic artists and conservatives during many years to come, one of the highest marks of perfection was the skill with which each stroke of the brush was so deftly blended with the next that the painting appeared to have bloomed complete and perfect on the canvas without the aid of brush or hand. It is true that Frans Hals in Holland and Salvator Rosa in Italy, as well as certain painters of the late Renaissance, had added a visible brush stroke as an accentuation or sort of bravura touch. In the nineteenth century a few painters developed this into a minor style, using a brush heavily loaded with paint to accent an outline or pattern in the composition in order to give it dash and an appearance of spontaneity—even though such effect was always carefully planned. In the last quarter of the nineteenth century this bravura brush stroke became a distinguishing mark of the fashionable portrait painter, particularly Boldini, Chase, and Sargent.

But until Impressionism this visible brush stroke—except possibly with Frans Hals—was an added flourish or at least a finishing touch to the picture. It was not basic, as it was with the Impressionists; in fact, an Impressionist picture could be painted in no other way than by use of the visible brush stroke. From this developed an interest in the *appearance* of the brush stroke itself as an esthetic element in painting. Some artists even today use it to bring up their paintings almost to bas-relief proportions on the canvas. Others abandon the brush altogether and lay on the paint in heavy impasto with a palette knife. Courbet on occasion used the palette knife to give a rugged accent. Beginning with Impressionism, however, the visible brush stroke, heavy or light, was not used to define contours or areas, as in the earlier days. It was an integral part of the all-over *texture* of the painting. One of the most obvious examp es of the later development of this use of the brush stroke is in the work of van Gogh.

The rainbow palette was only a part—though the larger part—of the Impressionist revolution. The other basic tenet of their revolt was their insistence on transferring to canvas the spontaneity of the immediate visual impression without the interposition of conscious thought or arrangement. They tried to insist that the painter's hand register on canvas the instant of optical sensation as impartially as the camera—still a new and exciting pictorial instrument—registered on the sensitized plate the light reflected from the object or scene before the lens But this very striving to catch the immediacy of visual sensation on canvas, regardless of the subject, freed the painter forever from the tyranny of subject. Now a painting could be a picture of anything. Or of nothing, although this ultimate freedom was not to reach its zenith until the middle of the twentieth century.

Who were the heroes of this revolution? They were unknown young artists who never thought of themselves as playing stellar roles. They were not even aware of themselves as Impressionists until an art critic gave them the name in ridicule.

Let us see how the art stage was set when they received their entrance cues and came on, one by one, unnoticed extras. It was in 1855 that the great *Exposition Universelle* opened in Paris. This big world's fair was organized to exhibit the wonders of the rapidly developing industrial age, and was the first to devote a large section to art. It included works from the leading artists of twenty-eight nations, though it excluded France's most widely known and vociferous artist Gustave Courbet.

As though all this were not excitement enough for any young art student beginning his study in Paris, all the living great of French artists—and that meant the greatest contemporary art in the world—were shown. France's two foremost painters, still bitter rivals, were amply represented: Ingres, now seventy-five years old, with forty paintings and innumerable drawings in a special gallery; Delacroix, fifty-six years old, and because of Ingres' implacable enmity not even yet a member of the Academy, reigned in the huge central gallery with thirty-five paintings. Although not officially of the elect, he was known and honored as leader of the Romantic movement which was now, because of its large number of adherents, generally respected. In this exhibition Delacroix once again showed his originality: he had selected the thirty-five paintings from the full range of his works, showing his development as an artist step by step through various phases. This was, in effect, the first retrospective one-man show ever held.

Corot, at the age of fifty-nine just becoming known, showed six of his gentle and poetic landscapes. Daubigny, only thirty-eight and destined to become the most popular of the Barbizon painters, was represented by three or four canvases. Millet, barely able to continue his crushing economic struggle at the age of forty-one, had only a single painting among the five thousand and more in the huge exhibition. Daumier had none.

Manet, who was to become the big brother of the yet unfledged Impressionists, was still an art student under Couture, from whom he was to break away in rebellion before another year had passed. Couture was well represented in the exhibition but, as a leading teacher and Academician, he haughtily refused the first-class medal awarded him; he had expected a higher honor.

Entirely unnoticed among the throngs that crowded the exhibition, a thoughtful young man of twenty-five from the West Indies wandered through the enormous galleries where the paintings were hung one above another up to the ceiling in endless rows, frame jammed against frame. Out of the thousands of paintings, he chose six that most appealed to him —the landscapes by Corot.

The young man was Camille Pissarro (1830-1903), born in St. Thomas, capital of the Danish West Indies. He was the son of a French father and a Creole mother. His father kept a general store in St. Thomas where Pissarro began clerking in 1847, after a few years schooling in Paris. Every moment of his spare time and some of his working hours, however, he spent sketching the life and scenery around him. But he longed to devote himself to painting. After five years of frustration he ran away, taking ship to Venezuela with a painter from Copenhagen with whom he had become acquainted while sketching on the docks where shipments for his father's store were unloaded.

This decisive act made his parents realize they could no longer deny him the career of a painter. So they sent him to Paris to prepare for it. For a year or two he worked at one studio and another, once even taking instruction from a pupil of Ingres; but in the 1855 Exposition he found the one master most akin to his own temperament. He diffidently went to see Corot who, kindly as always, encouraged him. But Corot himself, still largely unrecognized, took no regular pupils although he had "followers" to whom he generously opened his studio, giving advice and encouragement to his young disciples. Pissarro was by temperament and artistic inclination particularly fitted to benefit from his guidance. Oddly, he was also influenced by Courbet, almost the direct antithesis of Corot except that both painters loved nature—but how differently!—and this influence underlies some of Pissarro's most poetic landscapes. (Pl. VIII)

He continued to work at various studios, occasionally at the *Académie Suisse*. There he met Claude Monet, son of a Le Havre grocer. Monet was only nineteen, ten years younger than Pissarro, but the two were drawn together by their unorthodox pleasure in painting out of doors, as Monet had learned to do a year or two before coming to Paris. (Pl. VIII)

From his early schooldays, Monet's skill at sketching had shown itself in the caricatures he drew on the margins of his lesson books. By the time he was fifteen his reputation as a "caricature-portraitist" had spread through the town and he was besieged with orders to make them at 20 francs each. To his delight, some of these were displayed in a window of Le Havre's only art supply and framing shop. But it hurt the talented lad's vanity to find that in the same window were also exhibited—above his own caricatures—a row of marines, pictures actually painted in the open, as though the artist were too poor or too unprofessional to do his painting in a studio!

The marines were by Eugène Boudin, an excellent though not highly regarded painter who had been the original owner of the framing shop. Day-to-day contact with artists to whom he sold frames and supplies—Millet, Couture, Troyon, and others who spent summers in or near the seacoast town—had served to embolden and partially instruct Boudin's native talent. He left the shop to the care of an associate and went to Paris, where he copied paintings in the Louvre. Then, largely through the influence and recommendations of artist friends, he received a three-year art fellowship from the city of Le Havre. But he took his love of open-air painting with him to Paris—and brought it back with him, little the worse or the better for his somewhat reluctant study at the *Beaux-Arts*.

When Boudin expressed a generous interest in the youthful caricaturist, Monet at first—with the arrogance of the extremely young who have too early received a pat on the head—avoided the painter of the despised marines. But Boudin's gentle appreciation of the youth's evident talent began to win him over. Boudin urged him really to perceive the beauties of nature and to make on-the-spot transcriptions of them on paper or canvas. But the cocksure young man—he was only seventeen—balked. "Finally," he later wrote, "I could no longer make valid excuses. Weary of resisting, I gave in at last and Boudin, with untiring kindness, undertook my education. My eyes were finally opened—I understood nature and at the same time learned to love it."

Like Boudin before him, Monet took with him the love of nature and open-air painting when he went to Paris in 1859. But the following year he had to leave for his term of military service. He was sent to Algiers, where the intensity of light and color deeply impressed him. Long afterward he wrote that, although he did not realize it at the time, these impressions "contained the germ of my future researches."

Early in 1861, while Monet was still away on military service, Pissarro became acquainted with an abnormally shy young man from the south of France—dark, romantically intense in a quiet, withdrawn fashion, and almost painfully unsure of himself despite a mute, tenacious holding to his own ideas. He was Paul Cézanne and he worked regularly at the *Académie Suisse,* presumably to prepare himself for the entrance examinations to *l'École des Beaux-Arts*. His father, a banker of Aix-en-Provence, had reluctantly permitted him to follow a school friend, Émile Zola, to Paris. But even at the age of twenty-two, and with such a lively, out-going companion as willing guide, Cézanne was a solitary spirit. (Pl. XII)

Here he was—a young man in Paris in the Spring! Even more, he was financially free on an allowance from his father to follow that most fictionally fascinating of all careers, the life of an artist, or at least an art student. But Cézanne always managed to carry with him, wherever he went, his heaviness of spirit. The young Zola, writing to a friend, reported that his fellow-townsman, although "the kindest fellow in the world," was generally moody, often subject to attacks of discouragement, and always obstinate.

"To convince him of anything," Zola wrote, "is like trying to persuade the towers of Notre Dame to dance a quadrille." And he added the penetrating observation, which supplies one key to the artist's subsequent career, that "in spite of the rather exaggerated contempt he pretends to feel for glory, I can see that he would like to make a big success."

But no despair is so great as the despair of youth. Within the year Cézanne had become so discouraged by what he considered his slow progress that, gloomily deaf to Zola's urgent pleas that he remain and work on, he renounced Paris, art (half a century later he was to be called the father of modern art), and his dreams of success. He returned to Aix to clerk in his father's bank.

Given time to evaporate, however, youthful despair often lifts like a morning mist. The following year Cézanne returned to Paris, again on a generous allowance from his father, determined to make art his life. He never again wavered from that determination through a long lifetime of frustration and lack of recognition.

That same year, Monet also returned—first to Le Havre to recuperate from a serious illness contracted in Algiers, then to Paris in the fall of 1862, where he entered the studio of Academician Marc-Gabriel Gleyre, who upheld the classical antique as the model for students to follow, but who supplied living models for them to paint from. He instructed his pupils always to improve upon the attributes Nature had given or failed to give the model. His first criticism of Monet's work was that he had painted the model—a short, thickset man with large feet—as a short, thickset man with large feet! "All that is very ugly," he told Monet. "When one executes a figure, one should always think of the antique. Nature is all right as an element of study, but it offers no interest."

Monet was thoroughly disgusted with such advice and remained in Gleyre's studio only because his father had warned him that his meagre allowance would be stopped if he did not pursue his study of art seriously under a recognized master. So he stayed on, somewhat cheered by the companionship of his fellow-student Bazille who, also under strict parental orders, had to divide his time between the pursuit of art and the study of medicine. Bazille was supported on a very ample allowance from his wealthy father in Montpellier.

Another of the thirty or forty students at Gleyre's was also free from immediate financial worries—Alfred Sisley, a young Englishman who had been born in France and had spent most of his twenty-three years in Paris, where his father had a prosperous business. There was a fourth young man at Gleyre's who with these other three and Pissarro—introduced to the group by Monet—was to start a revolution in art a dozen years later.

This young man was Pierre Auguste Renoir. Born in Limoges February 24, 1841, he had gone to school in Paris, to which his family moved when he was four. His father was a tailor and at fourteen the young Renoir—having already shown considerable skill in drawing and a decided talent with colors—was apprenticed in a china factory. There he learned to paint on china plates, cupids and nymphs, flowers, fruits, and dainty scenes in imitation of Boucher and Watteau. But the age of the machine was developing fast and soon it replaced the hand even in china painting. Renoir had already attained such skill and speed, however, that when the factory closed he transferred his talents and industry to the painting of fans, screens, and other objects that required the light and elegant—and exceedingly dexterous—Boucher touch.

By the time he was twenty-one, Renoir had saved enough from his wages to leave commercial painting and embark on the full-time pursuit of fine art as a career. He entered Gleyre's studio, continuing as well his habit of studying the old masters in the Louvre. Of the four young men at Gleyre's who soon formed a close and lasting friendship, Renoir came equipped with greater technical skill than the others and a more instinctive love of painting. Slight of build, charming in personality and appearance, gaily companionable, Auguste Renoir was filled with *joie de vivre*, asking nothing more of life than to be allowed to paint it in all its color, brightness and beauty—in its abundance of pretty girls, luscious fruit, rainbow flowers. From beginning to end, painting was an exercise in pure joy. (Pl. VIII)

Soon after he had entered Gleyre's studio the master paused one day to look at his canvas. Seeing nothing of the "classical antique" there, he remarked sarcastically: "No doubt you paint for pleasure?"

"Naturally," Renoir replied. "If it weren't a pleasure, believe me, I wouldn't paint."

None of the four young art students had met Manet; in 1862 they had probably never heard of him. Nor did they know Degas. But it was about this time that the latter two, one day in the Louvre, became acquainted. Degas was copying a Velázquez and Manet, an even greater admirer of the Spanish master, stopped to comment. From this casual contact a friendship developed that was, all unknowingly, to draw Degas into close association with the four young art students at Gleyre's and with the two—Pissarro and Cézanne—who had met a year earlier at the *Académie Suisse*. And neither of the two young Parisians who had met so casually that day in the Louvre dreamed that two young women, one in France and one at that time in far-off America, were to join them within a few years and be forever after artistically associated with them.

And now that the cast of characters is on stage—or hovering close in the wings—the play builds up to its first climax, the Salon of 1863 and its infinitely more important alter ego, the *Salon des Refusés*. The former opened May 1st, the excitement generated by the *Salon des Refusés* and its storm center, Manet's *Luncheon on the Grass*, had diminished, a once-leading character made his exit. On August 13, 1863, Delacroix died.

Throughout his artistic life this valiant painter—first to force a new channel where the stream of art could flow more abundantly than between the narrow confines of Academic tradition—was frustrated and denied honors by Ingres and his colleagues. The battle between the two painters and their rival camps ended only with the death of Delacroix. He was much nearer in age to Ingres than the latter had been to David; the struggle between the two was therefore much longer and the younger man died four years before his older rival. In spite of the blockade by officialdom, Delacroix was a strong influence upon painters of the succeeding generation, who admired his work and revered the artist himself.

Now he was gone and Manet, quite unwittingly, had taken his place as the rallying point for the rebellious younger generation. That was something Manet had not intended at all. He was a hero in spite of himself.

The year after the *Salon des Refusés*, Gleyre closed his studio and Monet, whose rebellion against the ideas of Gleyre and all Academic teaching made him the leader of his small group, persuaded his friends to go with him for outdoor painting to the village of Chailly, on the outskirts of Fontainebleau Forest. There they became acquainted with the older group of Barbizon painters whose names—though still in 1864 no guarantee of sales—were now synonymous with landscapes painted in the open.

It was in the Salon of 1865 that Manet received such vilification for his *Olympia*. Again the younger men rallied round.

Cézanne, who had never received anything but rejections, was so incensed by the treatment accorded Manet by both public and critics, that he brought his friend Zola to see the painting. Happy to be indignant in such a good cause, Zola listened to Cézanne's accounts of Salon politics and corruption, and later wrote a series of articles attacking a system that placed mediocrity on a pedestal and declaring that Manet was assured of a place in the Louvre. Enraged, Salon officialdom and the Academicians complained so effectively to the owner of the paper that he abruptly terminated the series.

Monet fared well in both the Salon of 1865 and that of 1866, particularly in the latter where he exhibited *Camille*, one of his paintings of the beautiful woman who later became his wife. Renoir, now living with Bazille in the latter's Paris studio—a hospitality which Monet had enjoyed the previous year—was rejected by the Salon of 1866, but Bazille was accepted for the first time, as was Sisley. Both Pissarro and Berthe Morisot had paintings hung, while Cézanne as usual was rejected. Edgar de Gas—he was to change the spelling of his old and distinguished family name a few years later—had his first oil accepted, a scene at the rack trace; he had had a pastel hung the year before in the Salon of 1865.

Born in 1834, Degas was expected by his rich banking family to turn either to banking or to the law. But he wanted to become a painter. His family frowned on this foolish notion but when he proved his determination by leaving home to live and paint in a garret, his father supplied the funds for him to study at the *École des Beaux-Arts* and at a private studio under an Ingres pupil. The endless hours spent drawing were no frustration to him but a joy. He was a lover of the classics—as a boy in school he had been an avid student of Greek and Latin—and he loved the classic line in art. Ingres was his great idol and he never forgot the advice the old Academician gave him when he was taken to Ingres' studio by a friend: "Lines, young man, draw many lines from memory or from nature, and you will become a good artist!" (Pl. IX)

At the time of the 1866 Salon Degas was not in any way connected with the group of young painters—Monet, Bazille, Renoir, Sisley—who had studied at Gleyre's, or with Pissarro and Cézanne, who had met at the *Académie Suisse*. He had met Manet in the Louvre four years earlier and their similar backgrounds, wealth, and worldly position, as well as their admiration for Velázquez, had drawn them all together. Manet himself met Zola, Cézanne, and Monet only after he had been excluded from the Salon of 1866. Berthe Morisot knew none of them, but in the 1867 Salon Manet admired her painting, *View of Paris*, and the following year they met. They became

well acquainted—in 1874 she married his brother Eugène—
and she posed for one of his important paintings, *The Balcony*,
which was exhibited in the 1869 Salon.

In July of 1870, the Franco-Prussian War was declared.
Six weeks later Emperor Napoleon III surrendered at Sedan
and the Third Republic was proclaimed. Manet served as an
officer in the National Guard, Renoir was drafted, Bazille enlisted and was killed in action a few months later. This very
tall, bearded, generous young man of twenty-nine was just at
the beginning of his career, but he had already produced paintings that indicated his potential stature as one of the important
painters of France had he lived out a normal life span. The few
works he left are now chiefly in the Louvre and other leading
museums of France, England, and the United States.

Pissarro fled from Louveciennes, a small town near Paris,
just ahead of the advancing Prussians, leaving his studio
crammed with paintings. He managed to get his family to
the farm in Brittany where in brighter days he had painted,
then escaped with them to England, where his mother was
living. The Prussians turned his studio into a butcher shop
and, so the story goes, used his paintings—and some left with
him by Monet for safe-keeping—to wrap around meat; others
of his canvases served to carpet the dirt floor of the studio.
When he returned a year later he was able to recover only
about forty of the fifteen hundred he had left behind him.

A few months later Monet, in Le Havre, decided to cross
the Channel, as did a number of other artists, including two
of the Barbizon painters, Diaz and Daubigny. Sisley was already in England.

Pissarro lived with his mother and a half-sister, who had
settled in a London suburb. He and Monet were delighted to
discover each other by chance. They worked at their painting
separately, Monet in London parks and Pissarro in his suburb.
Together they visited museums, studying particularly the
works of Constable and Turner. The two French painters, in
their scientific experiments with light in terms of color, had
already advanced in sureness of effect beyond their great British predecessors, but for that very reason they were better
able to appreciate and understand their works. Monet, however, confided to a friend that Turner was too exuberantly
romantic for his taste. Pissarro's reaction was more thoughtful.

"Turner and Constable," he later stated, "while they taught
us something, showed us in their works that they had no understanding of the analysis of shadow, which in Turner's
painting is used simply as an effect, a mere absence of light.
So far as tone division is concerned, Turner proved the value

of this as a method, among methods, although he did not apply it correctly and naturally."

A very acute analysis of the difference between instinctive painting and painting directed by conscious design!

Although he had escaped the Prussians by crossing the Channel, Monet was relentlessly followed to England by his most persistent enemy, poverty. At lowest ebb, however, his old Barbizon friend, Daubigny, ran into him and held out a helping hand. He did more than succour him physically. He introduced him to his Paris art dealer, Paul Durand-Ruel, who had managed to get not only himself but most of the paintings in his gallery across to England and who had recently opened a gallery in London. He had been the first dealer to recognize and befriend the Barbizon painters, and now his artistic perception and courage was beginning to pay off. Daubigny was even then painting scenes along the Thames which were hardly dry before they were snatched up by London collectors.

Monet was naturally very happy to meet the distinguished art dealer and even happier—and perhaps momentarily dazed with surprise—to learn that Durand-Ruel was already familiar not only with his paintings but also with those of Sisley, Renoir, and Degas, as well. And not only knew their works but admired them and considered them important! He even championed the work of Manet. All this was more than meat and drink to Monet. And to make it even better, Durand-Ruel bought two small paintings by Pissarro and gave Monet some financial aid.

The war was over, the Prussians had gone, Paris streets were cleansed of the blood shed by the Versaillists in their savage overthrow of the Commune. At last the Republicans had taken over and were uniting and rebuilding the country. It had paid a terrible price for the corruption and weakness of Napoleon III's regime. It was still paying, though with remarkable speed, the heavy reparations demanded by the Prussians. But the new government was both stable and progressive. A spirit of confidence swept France.

Again artists began to gather in and around Paris. Even Cézanne, who had evaded the draft simply by staying on his father's estate in the south of France where he always painted for half the year, had taken a small apartment in Paris for himself and the woman who subsequently became his wife. There his son was born. Hortense Fiquet, the mother, was a patient woman. She had to be. It was fourteen years—only a few months before the death of Cézanne's father freed the artist from his ever-present dread of parental disapproval—before Cézanne legitimized the union. Hortense then spent the rest of her life posing with monumental calm for the many studies and portraits her husband made of her.

Degas, who had enlisted (in his army examination it was discovered that he was almost blind in one eye), now found on his return to Paris his great field of art backstage at the Opera, where he endlessly observed and sketched the ballet girls in their exercises and rehearsals. In the fall of 1872 Degas went for several months to New Orleans to visit his two brothers who conducted a branch of the family bank in that city. While there, Degas painted portraits of several members of his brothers' families and one splendidly original group composition *The Cotton Market in New Orleans*. At first glance it seems almost like an unposed photograph—and then as the eye travels from the foreground figure back into the architechtonic spatial arrangement, it is plain that not even the most modern camera technique could achieve such convincing three-dimensional quality. Only a master hand could compose the pictorial elements in a design of such underlying strength, such outward casualness.

Degas, as a matter of fact, was greatly interested in photography but it is a mistake to assume that his knowledge of camera technique was responsible for the unusual angles, dramatic perspectives, tilting of planes, partially cut closeups, and the "shooting" or focusing of a picture noticeably above or below eye-level. In his day the camera was a very clumsy, almost immobile instrument. Except for its ability instantly to record a scene exactly as at the moment of clicking the shutter—and no camera of the period could equal the *appearance* of spontaneity or instantaneity achieved by Degas' brush or crayon—the young science of photography had little to suggest to the art of Degas. On the contrary, it took the camera almost half a century to catch up with Degas.

Back in France after the war, Durand-Ruel bought paintings from others of the group—particularly Degas and Sisley, whom he met through Monet and Pissarro. He was a rare dealer who loved not only art but the artist as well, reinforcing his professional belief in an artist with financial aid, often long before he had been able to sell any of the artist's paintings.

By 1873 works of the group were beginning slowly—very slowly—to sell, and Monet advanced the suggestion of a group show. Pissarro strongly seconded the idea. But it was still only an idea when, early in 1874, the business boom France had been enjoying since the war suddenly yielded to a depression and there was scarcely any market for paintings, particularly for paintings by little-known artists. Durand-Ruel, overstocked with unsaleable works by these younger painters, had to sacrifice major works by his Barbizon artists even to keep his gallery open. He could no longer—at least for the time—continue to purchase works from members of the group or help any of them financially. In fact, merely to be known as their dealer was a risk. It shook the confidence of his wealthy clients in his taste and artistic judgment.

At the very beginning of 1874, however, several of the group—Monet, Pissarro, Sisley, and Degas—had a bit of luck. Paintings of theirs brought comparatively high prices in an auction held in a Paris department store. It was not unusual for works of art to be sold at reputable art auctions; the public seemed more willing to take a chance on such purchases if they could have the satisfaction of competitive bidding.

This unexpected encouragement was taken as an indication that even if Durand-Ruel's patrons scorned works by the group, perhaps a wider public might be induced to buy. After further persuasion by Monet and Pissarro, this time joined by Degas, the entire group—still unnamed and still held loosely together only by friendship and a common but vaguely defined goal—decided to hold the proposed exhibition not only to make themselves better known but in the hope of attracting buyers.

Manet alone of the group opposed the plan, as did the writer Théodore Duret, friendly with several of the painters, especially Pissarro. Duret pointed out that they had only a small nucleus of friends and friends of friends, a perceptive critic or two, a few art lovers, and no patrons of real financial standing on whom they could rely. He was afraid that the general public would not accept paintings so new and so shockingl different from accepted standards. He urged them to give up the idea of a group exhibition and try for Salon recognition which alone, he felt, would reach the wider public they needed. And he almost begged them to submit to the Salon Jury their most conventional paintings, above all paintings with *subjects*—not vagrant scenes built out of shattered rainbows, or iridescent landscapes that might be glimpses from a moving train in dazzling sunlight. In other words, he advised them to give up—for Salon prestige which, of course, meant sales —all they had struggled to attain.

Manet's argument was similar and was, furthermore, reinforced by his recent personal triumph. In the Salon of the previous year, 1873, he had at last achieved resounding success. He had shown *Le Bon Bock,* a Dutch-masterish painting of a comfortable burgher smoking a pipe, his left hand caressing a glass of bock beer. It was praised by the critics, popular with the public—and embarrassing to his artist-friends. Competently painted, it was plainly imitative and fell far below Manet's standard of originality and distinction. But he had waited so long for Salon recognition—which in spite of his bitter disappointments he felt was essential to sound success for any painter—that he had probably deceived himself as to the picture's merits both while painting it and certainly after it was finished and receiving the plaudits of the crowd and the approval of the Salon. So sure was he that this tardy accolade had at long last proved his contention that the Salon was the road to success, that, even after the decision had been made to hold the group exhibition, he tried to dissuade Monet, Renoir, Degas, and Berthe Morisot from showing in it.

But they all turned a deaf ear to him and to Duret, refusing to compromise their artistic integrity as they felt Manet had. They found a centrally located gallery in the studio of the photographer Nadar, who was just moving out of it. Then they had to decide upon a name for their group presentation, in which they decided to include other painters as well. Both Degas and Renoir were strongly opposed to a definite title. Renoir in particular wanted to avoid the inference that they were launching a new "school" of painting. Finally they decided on the innocuous designation *Société anonyme des artistes peintres sculpteurs, graveurs*.

Then the active members of the group—Monet, Pissarro, Sisley, Renoir, Degas, Berthe Morisot—set out to invite other exhibitors. Pissarro succeeded in having Cézanne included although there was some opposition from Monet and Degas who felt that his canvases were so strange and unattractive, even ugly, that they would meet with a hostile reception from the public. But he was accepted at last a roster of thirty exhibitors was completed and their 165 works hung, with the arrangement committee lazily leaving most of the arranging to be done by Renoir.

The exhibition opened April 15, 1874, and it made history —though not the immediate history the hopeful artists longed for.

The critics came, but they came to excoriate or ridicule. The public came, and laughed uproariously. And the unnamed little group that had struggled so long and so gallantly suddenly had a name, given in derision but finally worn in honor.

Monet was the inadvertent cause of the name. One of the five paintings he had entered in the exhibition was innocently titled: *Impression, Sunrise*. Ten days after the exhibition opened an article appeared in *Charivari* in which the writer, Louis Leroy, obviously impressed by his own devastating sense of humor, took his cue from the first word in the picture's title and sarcastically rang all possible changes on it: impress, impressed, impressing, impression—and called his article

"Exhibition of the Impressionists." He lampooned the paintings and pilloried the painters.

Years of work, years of deprivation, and then a little success and a venturing hope—all shattered by the laughter that now shrilled through Paris. Verily, saith the preacher, "The laughter of fools is as the crackling of thorns under a flowerpot."

But the end is not yet. At this lowest ebb of fortune, there were tiny ripples just beginning to tremble in the opposite direction—an almost imperceptible turning of the tide whose flow would be scarcely visible for several years to come. At the exhibition Cézanne made one of his first sales, a now-famous landscape from the three canvases he showed. Two or three collectors and a dealer or two jotted down notes for possible future acquisitions. Several perceptive critics and writers—though they were certainly in the minority at that exhibition—seriously studied the work of the group and became aware that something new was happening in art. Zola, now causing a stir—usually of disapproval—as a writer, brought his publisher Charpentier and Mme. Charpentier, both of whom were to figure largely in the life and career of Renoir. And Pissarro, anti-capitalist and poorest of them all, brought a wealthy stockbroker, by name Gauguin.

The roster of the Impressionists' second exhibition, held in 1876 at Durand-Ruel's, decreased from thirty to nineteen exhibitors. Cézanne did not show, but Caillebotte was a newcomer and entered one canvas, which is now in the Louvre. The public was not hostile, although the leading critics again castigated the paintings. But now other critics began to raise their voices in favor of Impressionism. A few pictures were sold at very modest prices.

In April 1877 came the third Impressionist Exhibition—a very large one. An undertone of hostility was felt, but nothing came of it. Then in June it broke into a storm of ugly abuse when Renoir, Pissarro, and Caillebotte put up forty-five pictures at auction in the Hotel Druot. As at a previous auction in the same place after the first exhibition two years before, noisy groups shouted down each painting as it was put up. Bidding dropped heavily. One of Renoir's canvases went for forty-five francs and Pissarro's brought only between 100 and 200 francs.

The cause? It was clear. The label "Communard!" This painting was different, therefore it was dangerous. Worse, it was gaining adherents—that was its real crime!

To go back a few years. After the Versaillists had taken over the government by bloody means, they were defeated when the people of France realized they were plotting to place royalty again on the throne. France was having no more of that. The Liberal Republicans quickly came into power, the Constitution was adopted, and the Third Republic took the form France more or less retains to this day. But Royalist plotting still went on, very much undercover at first, then more boldly. Combining with the extreme Right and with the Bonapartists, they called themselves the Party of Order and began to advance the idea that there was little difference between Liberal Republicans and *Le Spectre Rouge* or Red Terror. They fastened the label "Communard" wherever they thought it would stick, hoping through fear to stampede the country to their side and restoration of the Throne.

Their campaign of terror and confusion reached its height in the spring of 1877, at the time of the third Impressionist exhibition. The Impressionists were easy to label, as few people had any knowledge of them. Although better known, Manet could still be called a Communard through association with the labeled and libeled Impressionists; and because of the still-remembered scandals aroused by his *Luncheon on the Grass* in 1863 and *Olympia* in 1865, he could also be called a painter of "degenerate" art.

This crushing blow against the helpless Impressionists had been followed by another. Durand-Ruel, who had risked so much financially and annoyed his rich patrons esthetically by supporting the Impressionists, could take no more. In an understandable panic he put away all his Impressionist paintings and hung his gallery with "safe" pictures—Corot, Millet, and the Barbizon group, respectable now they were dead— till the storm should pass. It did pass. The country voted down the Royalists and returned the Republicans with a substantial majority. By December the country was stable again under a Liberal Republican prime minister and a Liberal Republican president.

But the mischief had been done. The miasma of calumny and suspicion lifted slowly. The Salon refused to show any pictures by Manet. Timid dealers and wavering collectors sold off their Impressionist paintings at cut-rate prices, and it was almost impossible for any member of the group to sell. Pissarro was so desperate he thought of giving up painting to do anything, anything at all to bring in a little money to support himself and his family. In despair he asked: "Is art necessary? Is it edible? No! Well, then."

At last, in 1879, the political atmosphere changed, there was less fear, and the Liberal Republicans seemed more firmly in power. The group decided to hold its fourth exhibition this time without Renoir, Sisley, and Cézanne, all of whom were hoping for Salon acceptance that year, which would certainly be denied them if they at the same time identified themselves with the Salon-despised Impressionists.

Degas, however, stayed with the group, although only on condition that the terms "Impressionist" and "Impressionism" be omitted from their posters and advertisements. He brought in as a new exhibitor the young American, Mary Cassatt of Philadelphia, whose work he guided though he refused to accept her—or anyone—as a pupil.

The fourth Impressionist exhibition opened April 10, 1879. The public came in great numbers, each paying a franc, and all seemed to enjoy—with appreciative smiles instead of ribald laughter—what they saw. The critics again served up adverse notices, but the public continued to come and enjoy, a few sales were made, and when the exhibition closed a month later there was enough money from admissions, over expenses, to give each exhibitor 439 francs. Mary Cassatt promptly spent her share on the purchase of a painting by Monet and one by Degas.

9 IMPRESSIONISM—AND BEYOND

THE ART MOVEMENT CALLED IMPRESSIONISM had both centripetal and centrifugal action. Of the group of painters originally associated with it, three were drawn ever closer into its center—were from the beginning, in fact, its central force. These were Monet, Pissarro, Sisley. The others of the original group—Renoir, Cézanne, Degas—swung out from Impressionism into their individual orbits. These three, for whom Impressionism acted as a catapult to greatness, were by far the more important artists.

Then there were those—fine artists but not forces in art —on the periphery of the movement: Bazille, of the original group, killed before Impressionism actually took form; Morisot, friend and fellow-traveler with the Impressionists, who became Manet's sister-in-law; Caillebotte, first important collector of Impressionism, amateur painter who reached museum stature, and zealous promoter of works by the group; and Mary Cassatt, that American woman of remarkable artistic insight brought into the movement by Degas, whose works she so admired. And of course there was the brilliant Manet, bridge between dark-toned, detailed Realism and the bright-hued shimmer of the momentary glance, who for a short time was with the Impressionists as a painter as he was always their friend.

Other artists, lesser but excellent, were drawn into the movement, as their works in European and American museums attest. After impressionism became established toward the end of the nineteenth century as the forward movement in art—and in becoming established ceased being the forward movement—there was a horde of followers. Most of their canvases were, perhaps unconsciously, imitative or—to use the politer but no less derogatory adjective which so often occurs in today's art criticism—"derivative."

There were several important artists, however, whose relation to Impressionism must be fixed to round out an account of the movement. The most important and certainly the most amazing of these was Seurat (1859-1891) who developed

Impressionism to the nth degree of color separation in the form of tiny dots of pure color covering an entire canvas and sometimes even extending over its surrounding frame. This came to be known as Pointillism or Divisionism.

Although the turning of the tide was definitely perceptible with the Impressionists' fourth exhibition in 1879, it did not draw the group closer together. In fact, for several years a somewhat disintegrating action was apparent. Renoir, who had not shown in the fourth exhibition, had a resounding success in the Salon of 1879 with his large portrait group *Mme. Charpentier and Her Daughters,* success no doubt due as much to the prominence of the lady portrayed as to the generally pleasing qualities of the painting. But one does not argue with success, and Monet began to waver—with the result that the following year he himself, heretofore the strong man of Impressionism, submitted two paintings to the 1880 Salon instead of showing in the fifth Impressionist exhibition of that same year. Degas despised him as a renegade. In fact, with Monet, Renoir, Sisley and Cézanne not represented, the only ones of the original group who showed were Degas himself and Pissarro, flanked by Berthe Morisot and Caillebotte, with Guillamin, Mary Cassatt and other latecomers also present. For the first time, Gauguin exhibited with them.

Monet, haughtily resenting being labeled a renegade, took revenge in referring to the newcomers as "daubers," which did not heal the breach. Renoir, Sisley and Cézanne also felt the sting of Degas' contempt. Caillebotte, now the most active in organizing the Impressionist exhibitions, felt that Degas with his neurotic temperament and holier-than-thou criticism was the divisive influence that was breaking up the group. In a long letter to Pissarro he proposed that together they organize a sixth exhibition excluding Degas and the painter-friends he had brought in. Then, Caillebotte hoped, the other four might be persuaded to return. But Pissarro refused to abandon Degas, "a terrible man," he admitted, "but frank and loyal." So Caillebotte withdrew, and the sixth exhibition, held in April 1881, was indeed slim.

Caillebotte tried again early in 1882 to organize a seventh group show, but was meeting with dismal failure when Durand-Ruel, disturbed by the disputes that were wrecking the unity of the artists he handled exclusively, stepped in and took command. He obtained the consent of the dissident artists to organize an exhibition at least of those works of theirs he himself owned. This dissolved the deadlock and the result was an exhibition, opening March 1, 1882, brilliant with a lavish display of the finest works of the original Impressionists. There were only two left out: Degas, who refused to show because

his followers were not asked to exhibit; and Cézanne, un-
invited because his works had not yet begun to interest Durand-
Ruel, who had not only organized the exhibition but paid for
the rented premises in which it was held. But Cézanne was
happy—for the first time in his life he had a painting in the
Salon! It had been admitted solely because a friend of his
was on the jury and insisted that the work of his "pupil" be
hung. Mary Cassatt, out of loyalty to Degas, also refused to
show in this seventh Impressionist exhibition.

The exhibition was moderately successful, but misfortune
had not yet parted for good with the Impressionists. The year
of the exhibition was the year of the 1882 crash, with its ac-
companying rash of bankruptcies. Durand-Ruel's chief patron
and friend was ruined and the art dealer insisted on refunding
the advances his patron had made on future purchases of Impressionist art. Once more Durand-Ruel was scarcely able
to keep afloat and the painters could no longer rely on regular
payments from him toward the purchase of new paintings.

Then followed nearly three years of financial difficulties for
Monet, Sisley and Pissarro—not as desperate as before, but
exceedingly discouraging; hope continually deferred "maketh
the heart sick." In the fall of 1885, invited by the American
Art Association to bring a large exhibition to New York,
Durand-Ruel desperately got together a show of 300 paintings; it seemed his last chance to save his foundering business.

With scant belief that paintings Paris was unwilling to buy
could be sold in the United States, the Impressionists set about
organizing their eighth—and what was to be their last—exhibition. Pissarro suggested inviting as exhibitors two young
artists he had recently met: Paul Signac, a great admirer of
Monet's work, and Georges Seurat, in whose exact theories of
color separation and significance Pissarro had become deeply
interested.

Most open-minded and humble of all the Impressionists,
Pissarro could also be very firm—or stubborn—and he was
determined to have admitted to the eighth exhibition these two
young artists whose strange new methods of painting he not
only championed but had wholeheartedly adopted into his own
work. Early in 1886, when the proposed eighth exhibition
was under violent discussion among the entire group of Impressionists, he had written his son Lucien that "Seurat has
something new to contribute. . . . I am personally convinced
of the progressive character of his art and certain that in time
it will yield extraordinary results."

The patriarchal Pissarro—though now only fifty-six he had
been benignly bald for years and had worn, perhaps as com-
pensation for his baldness, a luxuriant long white beard—won

out. Seurat and Signac were admitted but their works were hung in a separate room with those in the new style by Pissarro and his son, also a follower of Seurat. It was a strange anomaly that Pissarro, long considered the "elder statesman" of the Impressionists and from the beginning at the center of the movement, should in this last exhibition be banished to the outer fringes with unknown young artists never ranked even as followers of Impressionism.

What Pissarro did not at first realize was the uniquely individual quality of Pointillism. He had set about learning its technique from Seurat and worked in it for nearly four years, first with the enthusiasm of a boy, then with a growing awareness that it was not for him. He finally confided to a friend that it "inhibits me and hinders the development of spontaneity of sensation." With a sensible about-face, he destroyed some of his Pointillist canvases and reworked others. Happily, he did not lose what he had learned. Although his later canvases regained free play of light and spontaneity, they have a purer color and a structural strength greater and more defined than before his sortie into Pointillism.

Still painting with youthful enthusiasm, Pissarro now began slowly to attain recognition, with resultant sales at better prices. In 1892 Durand-Ruel gave him a big retrospective exhibition, which enlarged his reputation. In November 1903, he died in Paris at the age of seventy-three. Of all the Impressionists, Pissarro had the greatest influence on other artists, particularly those painters whose art was to succeed and transcend Impressionism—Cézanne, Gauguin, van Gogh. At once the teacher and the most teachable of the original group, Pissarro's perceptive faith in a fellow artist's work, his generous sharing of his own knowledge and experience, his genuine sweetness and childlike humility, made it possible for even the tightly inhibited Cézanne to learn from him. The two painted side by side in Pontoise in 1872 and again in 1877. It was then that Cézanne turned strongly to nature, lightening his palette and adopting for a time Pissarro's technique of the short stroke. Translating into his own artistic idiom Pissarro's freedom yet strength of color, Cézanne laid the groundwork for his use of color rather than modeling as the structural element of his paintings. Years later he spoke of "the humble and colossal Pissarro" and in warm remembrance signed one of his paintings "pupil of Pissarro."

Monet, the most complete and undeviating Impressionist of them all, lived the longest and therefore garnered the greatest financial rewards and highest honors. With his wealth, many years before he died in 1926 at the age of eighty-seven, he built a fabulous garden at his home in Giverney, near Paris.

The garden was both studio and combined canvas, brush, and palette, for he not only painted in it but with it, creating beautiful arrangements in trees, shrubs, flowers, with pond and stream mirroring light and color. This was a far cry from that early morning of despair in 1879 when, after an all-night vigil, Monet had knelt beside his wife's body and against his will noted the changing colors of Camille's beautiful face as the light grew stronger and the death pallor—the gray and blue tonalities, the waxy yellow—deepened. Struck with horror by his obsession with visual experience "even in the midst of personal tragedy," he realized that he was a prisoner of the fascination of light and color.

Though sorrow and despair were now far behind him, Monet was still obsessed by the alchemy of light and still experimenting with it in terms of color. In 1890 he began his most famous series of paintings, carrying the theories of Impressionism to their ultimate peak in an hour-by-hour recording of the changing effect of light on a given object. He began the first of the experimental series by planting himself, his easel, and a stack of blank canvases before a haystack early one morning. As the sun rose to its zenith and then moved into its descending arc, he replaced each canvas on his easel with a fresh one at hourly intervals, ending the day with eight or ten canvases, on each of which he had worked for an hour or so. The following day, seating himself in the same position before the haystack, he took up the canvases one by one in the same order and continued work on each approximately at the same hour as the day before. And so on, day after day, until the entire series was finished. In this way, as no artist has done before or since, he transferred from nature to canvas an hour-by-hour record of the artistry of light.

Later, and even more successfully, he repeated the experiment with a series of canvases of the façade of the Cathedral at Rouen, in which the solid masonry seems to quiver in the sunlight. Next came his series of poplar trees and finally the greatest and most difficult of all—waterlilies floating on a pond in Giverney. The crowning achievement of his waterlilies paintings is a series of large panels called *The Nympheas*. Permanently installed in the Orangerie, at the entrance to the gardens of the Tuileries, these beautiful paintings become the walls of the large oval gallery devoted to them. As the spectator enters, the whole gallery seems afloat with lovely forms of light and color—a fitting memorial to the great artist of Impressionism. As Cézanne once said: "Monet is only an eye —but what an eye!"

Renoir was for years so closely associated with Monet that it is impossible to separate the contributions of the two artists to the early development of Impressionism. Renoir is usually given credit for the "rainbow palette" but a comparison of the canvases the two friends painted side by side in 1869 in Bougival and at the nearby bathing beach La Grenoillière, and in Argenteuil during the summers of 1873 and 1874, shows an almost interchangeable progression of technique and innovation. Renoir was always more interested in painting people; Monet inclined toward pure landscape. As the years went on, they drifted artistically apart, each tending more and more in his own direction. Figures, usually incidental to his landscapes, finally disappeared from Monet's paintings. With Renoir, landscape became only a background or an enchanting atmosphere for his figures.

Renoir arrived both artistically—so far as the critics were concerned—and financially, with the success of his canvas *Mme. Charpentier and Her Daughters* in the 1879 Salon. His new-found prosperity enabled him to travel. More than any others of the group, he had always been a student of the masters in the Louvre. Now he went to Italy. He saw the Raphaels and the splendors of the Doges' palace and the Grand Canal. But he wrote Mme. Charpentier that, save for a certain painting by Tiepolo, he could see as great masterpieces in the Louvre, and he preferred the Seine to the waterways of Venice. He returned to Paris and his garden studio in Montmartre and married one of the plumply pretty girls in his famous *Luncheon of the Boating Party* (now in the Phillips Memorial Gallery, Washington). In April 1883 Durand-Ruel gave him a one-man show of seventy canvases which included many of his finest Impressionist paintings.

Renoir was now forty-two and could have continued the rest of his life painting in the same manner. But he began to be assailed by self-doubt, entering what is variously called his "dry," "hard" or "sour" period. For about five years he worked in a somewhat classical manner, giving his figures definite outlines and firm contours instead of letting them emerge softly from the shimmering brightness of his Impressionist canvases. His color was still ascendant but in these paintings it is more a single unifying tonality—though composed of infinite gradations—than his former broken, rainbow strokes. His modeling became much stronger and his design more pronounced. Late in the 1880's he returned somewhat to his earlier style but alternated it with his newer manner. His palette changed and instead of the iridescent rosy pinks, cerulean blues, and tones of pearl, we find earth colors of brown and orange-red.

In 1899 Renoir was severely attacked by the arthritis which progressively crippled him during the remaining twenty years of his life. Instead of diminishing his art, however, it spurred him in a new direction. The figures on his canvases became monumental in proportions and powerfully modeled. Neither they nor the earth-warm colors of his palette have the immediate appeal of the humming-bird brightness and lyric charm of his earlier canvases. They offer, instead, the simplified strength and satisfying substantiality of sculpture—large, generous woman-forms, Juno and Ceres, the fruitfulness of harvest time, the mellow glow of late summer. It was in this period also that the painter turned to sculpture, his figures very like those of his canvases.

World-famous, Renoir spent the last few years of his life in his home near Cagnes. His legs were entirely crippled but on every day that the sun shone he was lifted from the bed where he had suffered through the night, placed gently in his chair, and wheeled into the garden, where he forgot pain and age in his eternal delight in painting. His favorite model was Gabrielle, the young cousin of his wife who had become part of the household as a nurse for his three sons. Jean, the second son who is now a famous motion picture director, was with his father the last years of Renoir's life.

It is to Jean that we owe the debunking of a legend that continues to bob up in everything written about Renoir—the myth that his hands were so crippled that he could paint only with the brush strapped to his wrist or attached between his fingers. One recent book, the memoirs of a lady whom Renoir painted several times, even claims that rubber bands were used to affix the brush to Renoir's fingers. This is obviously impossible as, to hold the brush in place, it would have been necessary to make the bands so tight they would have stopped circulation and cut into the flesh. Probably the elastics were sometimes used to hold lightly in place the protecting linen described by Jean Renoir in an article published in *Life* Magazine May 19, 1952, and quoted here by permission:

> During the last 20 years of his life a strange and persistent rheumatism deprived my father of the use of his legs, crippled his hands. There is even a legend that his model had to tie the brush to his impotent fingers. The truth is that his deformed hands were still strong enough to hold a brush and were still as precise as a compass. But the rubbing of the handle irritated his parchmentlike skin, and he had to protect it with a piece of white linen.

And it is to Jean Renoir, in the same *Life* article, that we owe two revealing glimpses of the last years of the great painter who fixed on canvas so much beauty:

*In 1910, nine years before he died, my father painted his
last self-portrait using two large mirrors. One day I broke
one of the mirrors and, before I could replace it, the daylight was gone. Since father never worked in artificial
light, he left the portrait as it was, saying he would much
rather paint the opposite sex. To the very end father remained eager about life and beauty. People called on
him all the time and he questioned them about everything that was going on. Yet he was so weak and thin
you had a feeling that you were being confronted by little
more than a soul. But he kept right on painting. A few
days before he died he asked the chauffeur to bring him
a bowl of anemones. As he dipped into his colors to paint
the flowers he said he hoped his little picture would be a
suitable card to introduce himself to the great painters
of heaven.*

Degas was the first of the Impressionist group to acquire
a reputation and achieve substantial sales. As the years went
by, pictures he had sold earlier were resold for many times
their original prices. Although he did not need money, this
enraged him, particularly when in 1912 a painting of his
went at auction for 19,000 pounds (almost $100,000), still
the highest sum ever paid for a work by any living artist.
His early pictures are in oil. To get a more delicate effect—
particularly for his ballet pictures—and to reduce the gloss
inevitable to the surface of oil paintings, he began to thin his
oils with a good deal of turpentine, giving his work nearly the
mat finish of gouache. He always blocked out his forms in
charcoal before applying the color in oil or gouache and developed his own broken-color technique—irregular overlays
of color, cross-hatching, dabs and strokes—that gave his pictures a filmy iridescence or wonderfully rich color vibrations.
He combined oil and gouache; oil, tempera, gouache, and
pastel; then for a time settled on gouache and pastel. Finally,
in 1890, he began to work entirely in pastel, steaming the
sticks until they became as soft and workable as oil on brush
and obtaining textures quite unlike the hard dryness of ordinary pastel. Graphic, diaphanous as a dancer's skirt, apparently spontaneously as a joyous jeté, this final medium was
ideal for his choice of subjects.

In the eighth Impressionist exhibition Degas showed fifteen
pastels, including a new series of ten nudes not posed in the
immemorial fashion of a lady (chaste or wanton) without
any clothes, but showing women engaged in the ordinary rou-
tines of bathing—for bodily cleanliness rather than artistic appreciation—drying themselves, combing their hair, and so on;

as though, Degas explained, the artist saw them unaware in the privacy of bathtub or boudoir, "through a keyhole."

A chronic hypochondriac, Degas constantly examined himself for real or imaginary ills. He traveled restlessly over Europe from spa to spa, taking the "cure." When in Paris he would often close his doors to friends and refuse their invitations, only to take long, lonely walks about the city. He had little liking for flowers, women, or children, and sometimes he hated even himself. His eyesight declined and for the last few years of his life he was almost blind. He lived like a hermit, leaving the sad seclusion of his apartment only to wander aimlessly about Paris, unrecognized and unrecognizing. He died in 1917, at the age of eighty-three. Yet this lonely introvert, subject to fits of depression, hypochondria, and quarrelsomeness, poured forth a shining galaxy of pictures. No painter has ever equaled Degas in catching the drama of a woman's body in motion—the airy grace of a dancer, the arresting lift of a black-gloved hand, the tired force of the laundress as she presses the iron down, the vital twist of a torso as a woman towels herself, the perk of a girl's head as she tries on a hat. There, by the hand of the Impressionist who was a master Realist, is Woman.

While the eighth Impressionist exhibition was on in Paris, May 15-June 15, 1886, Durand-Ruel was concluding the successful showing he had taken to New York as "Works in Oil and Pastel by the Impressionists of Paris," in which he had included a number of drawings and an oil by Seurat, as well as some works by Academic painters. But New York did not need these examples of Academism to bolster its faith in the esthetic standards of the Durand-Ruel collection. One of their own countrywomen had paved the way for an understanding of the new art. Mary Cassatt's untiring efforts to interest her compatriots not only to look at but actually to buy the works of the Impressionists had borne fruit. New Yorkers welcomed the Durand-Ruel exhibition and turned to Impressionism without prejudice, eager to appreciate it.

With the advance guard of the new generation just beginning to appear above the horizon, Impressionism had at last arrived. Soon it would be admired, then respected, then cast aside in the forward movement of art. As always happens, however, those at the core of the struggle did not realize that the battle was over. Almost imperceptibly the opposition had been lessening and the forces on both sides disintegrating. For some time the group had no longer existed as a group. The seventh exhibition, organized by Durand-Ruel in 1882, had been the brilliant culmination of its achievement. The eighth served not so much to present the group as to signal its break-up. Monet, Renoir, Sisley, even Caillebotte, and of course Cézanne, declined to exhibit. Pissarro was artistically quarantined with newcomers of less than half his age and one-tenth his painting experience. Among those exhibiting were Berthe Morisot, Gauguin, Mary Cassatt, and a newcomer slated for subsequent fame—Odilon Rédon, who had been one of the youthful leaders in organizing the first *Salon des Indépendants* two years earlier.

Seurat and the lesser Signac were not followers. They were originators. Paul Signac (1863-1935) painted many lyrical canvases that partook both of Impressionism and Pointillism but his chief service to art was his book "From Eugène Delacroix to Neo-Impressionism" in which he set forth in great detail the color theories of the "scientific" method of painting first called neo-Impressionism, contrasting it with—and thereby damning, at least by implication—the old or "romantic" Impressionism.

Georges Seurat (1859-1891) was born into a Parisian family comfortably well-off though not wealthy. Seurat received a good schooling ending with two years at the *École des Beaux-Arts*, which he entered at the age of nineteen. He was a reserved youth, with a classical turn of mind well suited to study under Lehman, leading teacher in the Ingres tradition and a pupil of that master.

The exact rules and exacting practice of classical instruction did not weary or annoy Seurat but deeply satisfied his extraordinarily methodical nature. He went even further, augmenting his *Beaux-Arts* teaching with constant trips to the Louvre and an intensive study of painting methods and color theories in the art school library. After a year of military training at Brest he returned to Paris and plunged even more deeply into his art research, making extensive notes on a number of paintings by Delacroix and the writings of French and American scientists on the theories of optics and the chemistry of color. At the same time, he continued making meticulous drawings, developing a personal style as precise as the classical but highly individual. His conte crayon drawings are unique masterpieces, and he was only twenty-three when he had one hung in the Salon of 1883. But when he transferred the technique of his drawings to his first major oil painting, *The Bathers,* the Salon of 1884 promptly rejected it. A few months later it was shown in the first *Indépendants'* show, of which Seurat was one of the organizers and through which he first met Signac.

As could only be expected, the *Indépendants*—an open exhibition organized by painters who had been excluded from the official Salon year after year by the unbending Academism of its juries—was received with a blast from the critics and ridicule from the public, although one important critic, Félix Fénéon, perceived the extraordinary quality of Seurat's work and did not hesitate to champion it then and always. Two years later, at the eighth Impressionist exhibition, Seurat showed his huge *Sunday Afternoon on the Island of La Grande Jatte* which was eventually to be acknowledged a landmark in the history of painting. It is now one of the treasures of the Art Institute of Chicago. (Pl. IX)

The result of two years intensive work and seventy or more preliminary drawings and oil sketches—which Seurat called *croquetons—Sunday Afternoon on the Island of La Grande Jatte* was the complete expression of Seurat's individual style and unique genius. For the remaining years of his short life he never deviated from the perfection of his method. He worked very slowly but with great intensity and incredible patience, night and day. It was unnecessary for him to finish a daylight painting in the daylight. Gaslight served just as well, for in his preliminary oil sketches he had worked out such precise color relationships according to exact formulas that he could almost have completed his paintings in the dark.

He was not concerned with the problems of color alone. The other half of his absorption was with three-dimensional depth. This was something the Impressionists had totally disregarded, although of course it inevitably came into the picture, even if sketchily, as a by-product of light and shade. Seurat, however, calculated to a fractional degree the placement of each tiny spot of color in determining the position and relation of every figure and object in his spatial arrangements. He constantly strove to "hollow out the canvas" by leading the eye deeper and deeper into the scene through recessively three-dimensional treatment of each figure and object as it disappeared in the distance. His foreground figures had the cylindrical roundness of sculpture.

Seurat thus restored to painting the substantiality which the Impressionists had all but lost through their insistence on the flat impression of the fleeting glance. Without dulling a single hue, he replaced the ephemeral quality of the Impressionist canvas with the three-dimensional solidity which a little later Cézanne in his own way—and very differently—was to give to painting. Without destroying, but rather enhancing, the pictorial aspect of a painting, he produced a breaking up of forms into elements of color that two decades hence new artists were to claim as a departure toward Cubism.

Yet with this magnificently advanced and never-equalled technique, Seurat at the same time brought the color theories of the Impressionists to their culmination. With miraculously disciplined brush and completely calculated effect, he actually practiced what they had preached but never had tried fully to achieve. His tiny dots of pure color—variously called color pellets, lozenges, points and even, sarcastically, "petit point" —gave his paintings a luminous quality that seemed to emanate from the canvas itself yet heightened the structural form that the Impressionists had almost dazzled out of existence. He was diametrically opposed to their theory of spontaneity, which he considered appropriate only for sketches. He "arranged" his paintings on a fundamental design pattern in which every element was as perfectly related to the whole as each note in a symphonic composition.

Pursuing the pleasures of analytical exactitude to the ultimate, Seurat separated the emotional impact of a painting into color divisions and lineal directions. He drew up the following esthetic chart:

> *Gaiety is induced by light or warm colors, with lines rising from the horizontal. Calmness by a balance between warm and cool tones, and the horizontal line. Sadness by dark and cold colors, with lines descending from the horizontal.*

At the *Salon des Indépendants* in 1886 Seurat exhibited *La Grande Jatte* for the second time. The following year he showed it with *Les Vingts*, a newly formed group of European artists in Brussels. It was greeted there with laughter that echoed its Paris reception, yet it deeply impressed some of the younger artists. Hurt by the laughter and disappointed because the unrecognized masterpiece was returned to him unsold (half a century later the Chicago Art Institute refused nearly half a million dollars for it), Seurat became increasingly reserved and painted longer hours and more incessantly than ever. He carried his little note pads wherever he went and jotted down notes as well as sketches for later development. He went particularly to places animated by people and movement, such as ports, fairs, and circuses, being especially fond of the little boats on the Seine and the life and activity on and around its islands. He did many canvases and color sketches of these scenes and his last painting was an elaborate one of the circus—the only major work by Seurat now in France— presented to the Louvre by an American!

In March 1891, three months after his thirty-first birthday, Seurat died from an attack of quinsy aggravated by constant overwork at his easel and a final feverish week devoted to arranging the seventh *Salon des Indépendants* exhibition.

Curiously, just as Degas' off-center angles and device of the "cropped" picture and closeup long antedated their use in modern photography, Seurat's confetti-dot method anticipated the half-tone screen process used in printing to reproduce pictures. Both the mechanical means and Seurat's painting method create form through extraodinarily fine variations of light and shade by a system of larger or smaller, denser or more widely spaced, dots. Under a microscope these groupings of dots show up plainly. In neither system are there any lines or masses of shade or color; these are simulated by closer arrangements of dots. Exactly the same system was used later to transmit pictures electrically by wire and, still later, by electronic impulse via radio beam. Now it is the basis for color television.

Seurat's critics complained that his method, with its exactly calculated arrangements of color, line, and form, excluded all emotion. It did—for those artists who tried to follow him. No one could imitate Seurat for no one else was Seurat. In the most complete sense the style was the man himself. But Seurat's genius transcended both method and style. His paintings have a profound effect on those who look into and not merely at them. Behind the transparent screen of tiny dots like lightly falling snow, the carnival figures of *La Parade* are forever suspended in luminous time and space, while the strolling or somnolent Parisians in the sunlight and shadows of *Sunday Afternoon on the Island of La Grande Jatte* are held timeless and ageless in the still ambience of eternity.

Degas had many followers but only two disciples: Mary Cassatt and Henri de Toulouse-Lautrec. Two more dissimilar disciples could not be imagined—the prim American spinster and the dissolute young Frenchman. The first, Degas acknowledged as a friend and helped as an artist, even permitting her to use the designation: "pupil of M. Degas." With Toulouse-Lautrec he had the merest nodding acquaintance even though that misshapen and brilliant young man took a studio in the same block and showed his admiration for the older artist by painting very similar subjects in a style that might have been imitative had it not been for Lautrec's irrepressible originality and mordant sense of humor.

Mary Cassatt, still America's foremost woman painter, was born near Pittsburgh, Pa., in 1845, daughter of a wealthy and conservative family. For five years, from the little girl's seventh to her twelfth year, they lived in Paris. Upon their return to the United States, Mary Cassatt completed her formal education in private schools and then attended the

Pennsylvania Academy of Fine Arts in Phildelphia to study painting. When she was twenty-four she returned to Paris, which was to be her home until her death in 1926, when she was in her eighty-second year. (Pl. XIV)

Before settling down to the further study of art in Paris, Miss Cassatt went purposefully to the museums of Italy, Spain, and Holland. In her reserved, intelligent fashion, she examined the great art of those countries, then returned to Paris to work in the atelier of Chaplin, a leading teacher of the day. The Salon of 1874 showed one of her paintings. Degas noticed it and remarked: "Ah, there is one who sees as I do." He was not then acquainted with her, and she knew him only through his paintings, which she was beginning to admire with those of Courbet and Manet.

In 1877 a friend brought Degas to her studio. He looked at her canvases and invited her to exhibit with the Impressionists. She accepted with delight, later declaring: "At last I could work in complete independence, without bothering about the eventual judgment of a jury. I had already recognized who were my true masters. I admired Manet, Courbet, Degas. I hated conventional art. Now I began to live."

And so this reserved, wealthy, and keenly perceptive spinster from Pittsburgh, Pa., cast her lot with the most despised and ridiculed group of artists in Paris. She was quietly but intensely loyal to them, not only exhibiting with them but buying their paintings and bringing affluent friends to their studios to see, to understand, and to buy for themselves this radically new modern art. She did more than any other American to make her countrymen conscious of the finest and most progressive painting not only of her time but of great art that was still purchasable in Europe. The magnificent Havemeyer Collection now in the Metropolitan Museum of Art in New York had its beginning in Mary Cassatt's girlhood friendship with Mrs. Horace Havemeyer, whose judgment in art she helped form and many of whose purchases she suggested.

But in her own right as an artist this lady from Pennsylvania is to be admired and tremendously respected. In that Victorian period of lush sentimentality she accomplished the incredible feat of painting the most sentimentally dangerous of all subjects—mother and child—without an ounce of sentimentality, yet with a tender realism as strong and practical as mother love. She sometimes used the short but never the divided strokes of Impressionism, and her freedom in handling color and achieving luminosity is Impressionistc. Her paintings are more substantial, however, with an underlying strength of design absorbed from her study of Japanese prints. Although Whistler, Manet, Degas, and Lautrec seem more obviously influenced by Japanese prints, it was perhaps Mary Cassatt who most completely assimilated their purity of line, translating it into her individual idiom, especially in her beautiful series of color etchings.

No artist has more completely expressed his life in his work than Henri de Toulouse-Lautrec. His art is quintessence and climax of the Bohemia which was named and romanticized in Henri Murger's novels of mid-nineteenth century Paris—a Bohemia that rose to its peak as the century drew to its close. Intensely in it and of it, Lautrec recorded it with lightning line and mordant color.

For a short time, at the beginning of his career, he tried the technique of the Impressionists, although he was completely out of sympathy with their fondness for nature and their passion for the out-of-doors. He thought anyone an imbecile who could fix his gaze on an unpeopled landscape, and a thick-skinned dolt who could endure the raw light of day. It was the bright lights and the night life for Lautrec. And his avid passion was for people, people, people! Not for the dressed-up portrait, the softer mood, the respectable façade of life lived properly—or at least discreetly. He sought out and painted people stripped of their protective masks by the excitement of dissipation, the frenetic gaiety of drink or drugs, the abandonment to sensual pleasure, the unveiled face of a life ill-lived. He was neither moralist nor muckraker. He simply had to *see*, and what he saw he painted.

Lautrec had early shown a talent that promised great things. One of his first canvases *Young Rorty*, a portrait in oil, is amazing for a boy of eighteen, not only in its skillfully original adaptation of the Impressionist technique but in its foreshadowing of the artist's ability to probe the personality of his subject. Five years later the portrait of his mother makes even greater use of the Impressionist short-stroke, misty technique, though the sitter is solidly worked in. Within another two years, however, Lautrec had dropped the Impressionist style for a much closer approximation of Degas' technique and subject matter. At times he seemed even to challenge the older artist in paintings so like his in subject and treatment that comparison was almost compulsory. This is especially the case with Lautrec's *À La Mie*, painted in 1891, which was certainly inspired by Degas' famous *Absinthe* of 1876.

Like Degas, Lautrec was much impressed by Japanese prints—the formal arrangement, foreshortening of planes, bringing forward and off-center placement of important pictorial elements. Whether he absorbed these influences chiefly first hand from Japanese prints or second hand from Degas, it is hard to tell. But he integrated them completely with his own highly original sense of design and consummate draftsmanship, which is expressed most brilliantly in his incomparable posters and lithographs. Color lithography was his greatest medium. He worked out new methods in it which gave such striking effects that he led a rejuvenated movement in color lithography that greatly influenced the young artists of the period. No one has surpassed Lautrec in this art or equalled his influence in it.

Yet it was this superb talent, plus the compelling demand of his temperament for quick, flashing results, that prevented Lautrec from becoming the great painter he might have been. By the time he was twenty-seven—in 1892—he had produced many of his best paintings, including the masterpiece *At the Moulin Rouge* owned by the Art Institute of Chicago. Four years earlier his *At the Cirque Fernando: Equestrienne* (also owned by the Art Institute), though not so richly painted, is a *tour de force* of rhythm and movement and has the dash and speed and instant characterization of his drawings. The nervous, quick lines of the hatching he used in many of his oils gave them the immediacy of on-the-spot sketches.

The lightning line of Lautrec's brush and pencil ran away with him. His art and his life were concentrated on a limited range of interest so intense that, like a burning glass, it destroyed him. As in his short life—from the compressed haste with which he lived it, he seemed to know intuitively that it would be brief—his art crowded in upon itself. Both life and art gained momentum as his years rushed to their close. In the decade between his twenty-fifth and thirty-fifth years—the period of his artistic maturity—he produced an enormous number of drawings, lithographs, and paintings.

Degas' line was motion, Lautrec's emotion. All of the movement in Degas' work—and he was a master of movement—is the expression of nothing more than physical motion. With Lautrec, movements are *acts*. Degas was detached from his subjects and they were detached from emotion. Lautrec's people are always *inside* their movements, back of their faces —suffering, sinning, enjoying, mocking, sizing up situation or client, humorously or cynically awaiting an expected end. There is more art in Degas' work, more life in Lautrec's.

Lautrec was an associate but not a member of a group of young artists that came into being in 1889. Calling themselves the "Nabis"—a Hebrew word meaning prophets or illuminated ones—the artists forming the group were composed partly of painters who had been among the early followers of Gauguin. Drawn together synthetically, more by theories than through organic growth of artistic kinship, as in the case of the Impressionists, the Nabis declared themselves in theory, though they often deviated in practice, for the color simplification propounded by Gauguin. They also proclaimed at their monthly dinners and other meetings the ascendancy of art over nature and the inner idea over the outer aspect; in the same breath they announced art to be primarily decoration.

Opposed to the Impressionist theory of the immediate, fleeting glimpse, the Nabis sought to bring a patterned though somewhat surface order to their painting and to produce cohesive compositions which were seldom, however, organically structural.

The Nabis were not an important group. They are worthy of mention as a group chiefly because they mark a definite step away from Impressionism and a return to organized form. They were influential in and influenced by the immensely popular revival of lithography, particularly for book illustration. And they were active in demanding—and successful in getting—walls to paint on, not so much in mural technique but in the form of decorative wall panels.

Paradoxically, although the Nabis declared themselves anti-Impressionists, by far the most important artist of the group, Pierre Bonnard, can only be ranked with Impressionism; in fact, he was the last great Impressionist. Second only to Bonnard in importance among the Nabis was Vuillard, much of whose work shows the influence of Impressionism and who was an admirer of several of the great Impressionists. (Pl. XIV)

Born in 1868 in Cuiseaux, France, Édouard Vuillard was the son of a mother who devoted the forty-five years of her widowhood to him. The family moved to Paris when Édouard was nine years old. When the boy was fifteen his father, nearly thirty years older than his mother, died. To supplement the family income—Édouard had an older brother and sister— the mother opened a dressmaking shop. She was a native Parisian whose father and brother were textile designers, the brother being responsible for many of the elaborate, small-patterned designs of the cashmere and Paisley shawls so fashionable during the period.

Édouard's close school friends were two who were later to be members of the Nabi group: Maurice Denis and K-X Roussel, already interested in art. No doubt influenced by them, he began to attend classes with them at the *École des Beaux-Arts* in 1886. After two years, dissatisfied with Academic teaching, the three joined a rebel group at the *Acadé-*

mie Julian. A year later, in 1889, the group organized formally as the Nabis.

Vuillard was inclined to leave Nabi theorizing to his friends while he painted. His work met with almost instant success. Greatly admiring Degas, he was nevertheless influenced in the early years of his career more by Gauguin, particularly by the latter's well-known exhortation to reduce the palette to strong primary colors, and his oft-quoted advice: "How does that tree look to you? Green? Then use green, the greenest green on your palette. And that shadow? A little bluish? Don't be afraid. Paint it as blue as you can."

But it was not long before Vuillard enlarged the range of his colors, muting them in more subtle gradations. Not much later he abandoned the flat-patterned style of Gauguin with its large and simplified detail for the tightly organized, tiny-patterned "intimate" paintings for which he is famous.

Perhaps as an inheritance from his mother's textile-designing family, Vuillard became obsessed with the desire to put on canvas or board the intricately figured designs characteristic of late-Victorian wallpapers and textiles. Although his paintings have a structural base not found in true Impressionism, the multitude of tiny strokes that cover his canvases give a superficial effect similar to that of Impressionism's broken-color technique. But with this difference: the short strokes of the Impressionists were applied without specific reference to the object itself but only to the light that played upon it and the atmosphere that surrounded it. Vuillard's tiny strokes are specific representations of the pattern of the wallpaper, rugs, upholstery, dresses, and curtains in the interiors he was so fond of putting on canvas or board. He seemed to like nothing better than to lose himself in a welter of wallpaper. In one painting only 12½ by 14⅜ inches he shows the wall of a room, a hallway, and a farther room, the individual, intricately patterned wallpaper of each juxtaposed to form the entire background of the tiny painting, while in the foreground stands a woman in a dress with an all-over pattern of white dots on dark material. In his comparatively few outdoor scenes, he managed to give a sense of enclosure. He found tiny patterns everywhere—in flowers, leaves, bricks, lattice-work. Even clouds gave his brush a closely patterned design to play with.

Most of his interiors are painted on small boards or canvases on which so much intricate detail is compressed that, in viewing them, it is as though one had stepped into a fussily arranged late-Victorian room overcrowded with furniture and overwhelmed with pattern. The people he painted into these interiors—and Vuillard seldom did interiors without figures

Venus
de Milo

Cézanne:
Mme. Cézanne
in the
Conservatory,
1890

COLLECTION, STEPHEN C. CLARK

LOUVRE

Brancusi: Bird in Space, *1919*

MUSEUM OF MODERN ART

Picasso: Woman in White, *1923*

METROPOLITAN MUSEUM OF ART

PLATE I

David: The Death of Socrates, *1787*

LOUVRE

Géricault: Raft of the Medusa, *1819*

LOUVRE

PLATE II

LOUVRE

Whistler: Arrangement in Grey and Black, *1871*

LOUVRE

Delacroix: The Barque of Dante, *1822*

PLATE III

Ingres: Le Bain Turc, *1862*

Ingres: Madame Destouche, *1816*

PLATE IV

Corot: Pond at Avray

Millet: The Gleaners, *1856*

PLATE V

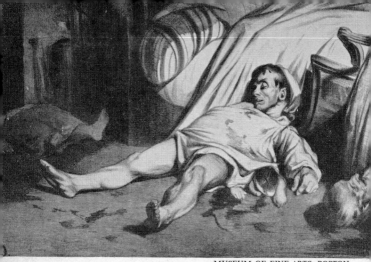

Daumier: Rue Transnonain, *1834*

Daumier: The Third-Class Carriage, *c. 1865*

PLATE VI

Courbet: The Painter's Studio, *1855*

Manet: Luncheon on the Grass, *1863*

PLATE VII

Pissarro: Maison Delafolie, *1885*

Renoir: Dance at Bougi-
val, *1883*

Monet: Woman with Umbrella

PLATE VIII

Degas: Ballet Rehearsal on Stage, *1874*

Seurat: Sunday Afternoon on the Island of
La Grande Jatte, *1886*

PLATE IX

El Greco: View of Toledo, *1600-1610*

Goya: The Third of May, *1814*

PLATE X

El Greco: Burial of Count Orgaz, *1586*

Goya: Maja Nude, *1795-1797*

PLATE XI

Cézanne:
La Montagne
Sainte-Victoire,
1885-1887

METROPOLITAN
MUSEUM OF ART

Cézanne:
Still Life—Apples and
Primroses, *1890-1894*

METROPOLITAN
MUSEUM OF ART

Cézanne:
Women Bathers,
1898-1905

PHILADELPHIA
MUSEUM OF ART

PLATE XII

Gauguin: We Greet Thee, Mary, *1891*

Van Gogh: The Starry Night, *1889*

PLATE XIII

Cassatt: The Bath, *1894*

ART INSTITUTE OF CHICAGO

PLATE XIV

Vuillard:
Mother and Sister
of the Artist, *c. 1893*

MUSEUM OF MODERN ART

Matisse: Odalisque

LUXEMBOURG MUSEUM

Rouault:
Miserere, Plate 46,
"The righteous, like
sandalwood, perfume
the axe that falls
on them,"
1926

MUSEUM OF
MODERN ART

PLATE XV

Braque:
House at
L'Estaque,
1908

COURTESY FRENCH
EMBASSY PRESS AND
INFORMATION

Picasso: Guernica, *1937*

Picasso:
 Girl Before a Mirror, *1932*

PLATE XVI

BELOW, LEFT
Picasso:
Les Demoiselles d'Avignon, *1907*

Picasso:
Man with a Hat, *1913*

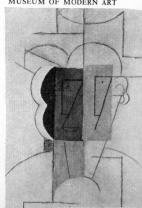

—often seem forced to stoop just to squeeze themselves into the picture. Still oftener, they appear to be starting out from the wallpaper or sinking into it. His mother—and he put her into many of his paintings—is the only figure that stands out clearly or sits solidly away from the wallpaper, the only personality to dominate her son's endlessly intricate patterns. As, indeed, she dominated his life.

It is quite apparent from some of Vuillard's earlier canvases that he was capable of strong and simplified forms which, if he had let himself progress in this direction, would have made him part of the rising stream of twentieth-century art. But he seems to have been overcome by a desire to crawl back into the cosy, cluttered womb of Victorian interiors. In parallel fashion, his art retrogressed during the last quarter-century of his life. Although he painted no great pictures at any time, some of the canvases he produced from the beginning of his career in 1888-89 until 1905 and, in lesser degree, until 1913, have an evocative charm and exercise a subtle fascination. Most of his paintings place before us intimately the petit-bourgeois home life of the end of the nineteenth century.

But the twentieth century arrived and soon marched on without Vuillard even though he lived through forty years of it. His period of greatest productivity—easel oils, decorative panels, lithographs, scenic designs—was from 1889 to 1908. From the start of his career his work was shown to critical and public approval in many exhibitions, at first chiefly with the Nabis during their ten years of active existence, and then in dealers' galleries, in the *Salon des Indépendants*, and the *Salon d'Automne*, of which he was one of the founders. A few years after the turn of the century, however, both critical and public interest in his work declined, and by the time of the first World War he had almost ceased to exhibit. In 1936 a large group of his early paintings was shown in a fiftieth anniversary exhibition of many of the artists with whom he had been associated. Two years later he was elected a member of the Academy and given a large retrospective exhibition. He died in June 1940, in his seventy-second year, shortly after leaving Paris ahead of the oncoming Nazi army.

Although Toulouse-Lautrec's paintings and lithographs are almost a day-by-day—rather, a night-by-night—record of his life, they do not reveal his inner self. Vuillard's offer a pictorial psychoanalysis of the subconscious impulses and tendencies that moved and ruled him. He never married and is not known to have had any love affairs unless his persistent passion for patterned wallpaper be accounted one.

One bright day in 1889, a young man serving his apprenticeship in an attorney's office in Paris took out from a secret hiding place—probably a file drawer—a secret desire and sold it for one hundred francs. That happy, unexpected sale changed the young man's life. Away with law books! If he could make a hundred francs that easily, why not yield completely to his secret desire and become a full-time artist?

The young man was Pierre Bonnard and what he sold that day was a sketch for a poster. It was, moreover, a poster he had created on his own as an advertisement for a certain brand of champagne—happy augury! So Pierre Bonnard's long and joyous career had its proper launching with champagne.

Bonnard, Lautrec, and Vuillard were the leaders in the poster and lithograph revival of the early nineties in Paris. The immediate surprise success of Bonnard's champagne poster—which delighted Parisians could see splashed on walls and hoardings all over the city—may be said to have sparked the revival. It was what drew Lautrec to the medium and to Bonnard. For years the two artists were close friends— Lautrec with his somewhat decadent obsession with night life and all that went with it, Bonnard with his more wholesome love for life in general. For both young men—and for the Nabis and others associated with them—the poster and lithograph offered an opportunity for the play of originality, wit and the spontaneity that belongs to youth. Except in the case of Lautrec, whose graphic work is closer in spirit and form to his paintings, poster and lithograph afforded much greater freedom of expression than the more serious medium of oil.

Bonnard carried this youthful spontaneity over into his oils—retained it, in fact, throughout his eighty years. He began exhibiting with nine paintings in the *Salon des Indépendants* in 1891 and, the same year, in the Nabis' first exhibition. His work in both was praised by leading critics. During the next few years, in addition to oils and graphic work, he collaborated in the design of sets and costumes, had twelve lithographs published by Vollard, and designed a stained-glass window—as did Vuillard—for Tiffany. In 1896, when he was only twenty-nine, he had his first one-man show. During the following half-century he was shown in countless exhibitions in Europe and the United States.

Bonnard's early paintings show the Japanese influence that reached him through the work of Gauguin. But the influence was thoroughly assimilated and can be traced only in Bonnard's individual handling of intersecting flat planes and unorthodox—according to the standards of Western art —arrangement. In all of his paintings Bonnard's color is a sensuous delight. His subjects have charm without special meaning and with no more emotion than pleasure in a sunny day, a lovely garden, an appealing face. His early paintings are fleeting impressions of a woman's head as she passes by, an intimate yet casual—rather than illustrative—domestic scene, a quickly caught glimpse of a street or river view. All of these were painted with the apparent ease and snapshot-speed of Impressionism and with obvious delight in color as its own excuse for being. Most of Bonnard's paintings depend as much as Monet's on the use of enchanting color alone, yet sometimes form is more solidly suggested.

Early in the twentieth century new and violent movements in art rose and fell and fought and clamored in Paris without affecting Bonnard's art except to strengthen it in its course and perhaps somewhat to deepen and enrich its color. But through it all, as throughout his life, he had no real struggle. His family life was harmonious, his pictures always sold, and painting was a pleasant recreation, as natural as song to a bird. He was in his eightieth year when he died, in January 1947. With his death the history of Impressionism—though not of its far-reaching effects—comes to a close.

10 THE FATHER OF MODERN ART

NATURE HAD ENDOWED WITH LITTLE TALENT and less facility the tempestuous, inhibited provincial from the south of France who was to become known as the "Father of Modern Art." Paul Cézanne is perhaps the solitary refutation of the old saw that an artist is born, not made. This statement will of course be challenged. It will be considered practically blasphemous. In the annals of modern art Cézanne is sacrosanct.

But if glory be demanded for the father of modern art, is it not more glorious that through decades of struggle this clumsy, artistically inarticulate man wrought out of desire and determination the magnificent paintings for which he is justly honored today? For forty years, with slight encouragement and almost no recognition, day after day, year upon endless year, he dug into the lonely crevices of his involuted soul to bring to the surface the richness of his deeply buried vein of genius. With most artists the struggle is with the external forces of poverty and non-recognition. Cézanne's real struggle was within himself, and it was titanic. The mountain labored—and brought forth a mountain which still stands solidly above the surrounding peaks of modern art. (Pl. XII)

Non-recognition was of course disappointing and embittering; it was a contributing factor to the artist's progressive withdrawal from society. But with the allowance and finally the inheritance from his father, Cézanne was free throughout his career to pursue art without worry about where his next meal was coming from or whether he would have a roof over his head. As it was not weighted with economic necessity, lack of recognition had only a negative effect on Cézanne; futhermore, his innermost conviction was that when he had become fully able to "realize his sensations" on canvas, he would receive his due. He became so inured to lack of appreciation that in the last few years of his life, when the younger generation of advance-guard artists discovered him and a few dared make pilgrimages to his studio, he was sus-

100

picious that they were either deriding or trying to flatter him with their adulation.

Paul Cézanne was born January 19, 1839, in the town of Aix-en-Provence in the south of France. His father was a hat-maker who by his industry and frugality became the town banker before Paul was grown.

As already related, Paul went to Paris to study art in 1861, gave it up to go back to Aix within the year, and the following year returned to Paris with no thought ever again of being anything but an artist. Until the Franco-Prussian war of 1870, he alternated between Paris and his father's home in Aix and his nearby country estate. Le Jas de Bouffan, with interludes at L'Estaque. After the war he maintained a studio in Paris—though he preferred Aix—and twice worked with Pissarro in Auvers and Pontoise.

Cézanne's only child, his son Paul, was born in Paris in January 1872. Six years later he moved the boy and Hortense Fiquet—whom he had not yet married—to Marseilles. He then tried to arrange for a larger allowance from his father. Unfortunately, however, Papa had opened a letter addressed to his son and discovered the liaison which Paul—always terrified of his parent—cravenly denied. Whereupon the frugal Cézanne *père* cut his son's allowance in half, from 200 to 100 francs a month, sardonically remarking that as a bachelor he did not of course need all of 200 francs to get along. Cézanne appealed to Zola to find him a job—any job—in Paris so that he could keep from starvation the woman and their son he had denied. Doubtless knowing how utterly inept in the workaday world his friend would be, Zola—in the first flush of prosperity from his novels—solved the problem by lending Cézanne a monthly sum paid direct to Hortense.

A year later, Papa Cézanne—perhaps as the result of an indiscretion of his own which Paul suspected—increased his son's allowance. But it was not until April 1886 that the artist finally married the woman who was not only the mother of his fourteen-year-old son but his most patient model. Six months later Cézanne's father died, leaving the artist wealthy for life. Two younger sisters shared with him their father's fortune. The older of these, Marie, had kept a sisterly eye on her two-years-older brother ever since their earliest schooldays. After the death of their father she took charge of her brother's affairs completely. He was, as he often said of himself, quite unable to cope with the everyday realities of life.

One would think that now, with plenty of money at his command, his domestic affairs completely undemanding, Cézanne could settle down to a more peaceful development of his art. But his hypersensitive, turbulent, prickly nature still rode his shoulders. From the earliest years of his career he had vacillated between extremes of behavior, intermittently trying to conceal the inward retreat of his fearful inferiority complex with outward aggressiveness. He had a passionate desire to be accepted by the Salon. Yet he ridiculed it, calling it contemptuously the "Salon de Bougereau" after its most currently favored artist whose voluptuous nudes received Academic honors and critical acclaim, selling for high prices in Europe and America.

Because he felt ill at ease and countrified with polished Parisians, he adopted an exaggerated Bohemianism accentuated at times with displays of boorishness. He not only admired the paintings—and probably the elegant urbanity—of Manet, but urged Zola on to ardent defense of the painter's *Olympia*. Yet he was so shy and unsure of himself in Manet's presence that on one occasion, meeting him with a number of other artists, he shook hands with all but removed his hat with mock humility before his idol, saying: "I'm not offering you my hand, Mr. Manet. I haven't washed for eight days." At another time, when Manet—who, quite understandably did not like him and thought his painting "atrocious"—asked him what he was working on for the Salon, Cézanne replied with a rough obscenity. Despite all this, Cézanne labored for years to produce intermittently a series of paintings which he called *Olympia* or *The Modern Olympia*, which were plainly variations—some of them awful in their grandiloquent absurdity—of Manet's masterpiece.

Cézanne, whose great and lifelong idol was Delacroix, was an admirer of the palette-knife technique used by Courbet. But where Courbet handled the knife with a certain restraint, Cézanne early in his career simply loaded his with pigment. Occasionally, it was reported by eye-witnesses, he would in a moment of frenzy pick up great gobs of paint and with his hand plaster them on canvas. One writer, after a visit to Cézanne's studio, said he saw the artist fill a spoon with thick green color and apply it with a daubing, twisting motion to the canvas. In his early pictures Cézanne used a great deal of black, but whatever he used he laid it on in thick impasto. In keeping with his dark, heavy palette, his subjects—except for his portraits—had a wild and gloomy romanticism. These "black idylls" were all products of his imagination as of course he never saw such melodramatic scenes as those he painted in fine frenzy under the titles of *The Rape, The Murder,* his various *Olympia canvases,* and *The Picnic.* In spite of its crudity, the last-named has a brooding power and is melodramatic only in atmospheric effect.

When he began working from landscape with Pissarro,

Cézanne's palette lightened and brightened though he still used such a heavy impasto that when he showed in the Impressionist exhibition in 1874 one of the critics called him the "pistol painter," declaring that he must have shot his color at the canvas with a pigment-loaded pistol.

But when he showed for the second—and last—time with the Impressionists, in 1877, Cézanne's genius had begun to emerge, though no one yet recognized it, least of all himself. As he worked on into the 1880's he developed his remarkable *weightless* technique of laying color upon color so lightly that the entire canvas is smooth to the touch. In his final period he returned to a somewhat heavier method but never to the slashing palette knife of his early canvases.

One of Cézanne's two most famous statements gave artists of the next generation the cue to bring on stage the greatest and most pervasive art movement of the twentieth century—Cubism—the clue to which, guided by his statement, they thought they found in his works: "Everything in nature is shaped after the cylinder, the sphere, the cone." And the amplification of that statement in his advice to *"See* in nature the cylinder, the sphere, the cone, putting everything in proper perspective so that each side of an object or plane is directed toward a central point." In the other famous statement Cézanne defined both his aim and his achievement: "I have wanted to make out of Impressionism something solid and enduring as the paintings of the museum."

Hewing away year after year at his art like a sculptor pounding and chiseling rock, Cézanne painfully wrought out of the rich chaos of his genius canvases that approach the conceptions he could never completely bring forth. He said: "I can't seem to express the intensity which beats in upon my senses." In despairing rage he would often slash a canvas to pieces, toss one out of the window, leave another abandoned in the field when he took easel and paints home after a day of struggle.

But he did not always give up in despair. When painting a portrait he had no mercy on the sitter. Vollard, the young picture dealer who in 1895 began to buy up all of Cézanne's available works, had 115 sittings for his portrait. Even then it was not finished, Cézanne merely remarking that "the front of the shirt is not bad."

He did not permit the sitter to utter a word and he allowed few rests. If there was the slightest involuntary movement, he would admonish severely: "You must sit like an apple. Does an apple move?" Even apples, however, were not entirely satisfactory as models for Cézanne's still lifes; they decayed after a few weeks. Oranges were almost as bad. Flowers, of course, were impossible, so Cézanne used paper flowers. But even paper flowers faded, so he was reduced to using engravings of flowers as occasional models. He found skulls very satisfactory, however. They did not move, they did not fade, and their decay was a thing of the past.

In his early studies at the *Académie Suisse,* Cézanne worked at times from nude models both male and female. In 1865 he did a magnificent figure painting of a Negro, *Scipio,* but it is unique in quality among all his other figure paintings of that or any of his periods. From the beginning, his rugged, undetailed portraits, in heavy, slashing impasto, showed the power of which he was capable. In 1870 he produced one of his finest still lifes, *The Black Clock,* with its broadly painted, dramatic contrasts. Throughout his subsequent career he continued to experiment with still life, particularly of fruit—apples and oranges—placed on a table; these are among his most characteristic works.

But it is in the field of landscape that Cézanne is supreme. His great teachers were the masterpieces in the Louvre, which for years he studied intently. He said, of France's seventeenth-century master landscapist, that he wanted "to make Poussin over according to Nature," and that is exactly what he did. Poussin was the most architectural of painters; his landscapes were always "arranged" with meticulous regard for perspective and placement. Cézanne's landscapes by-passed architectural rules to strike through to fundamental architectonic form. The difference between his painting and that of Poussin's is the difference between a grove of great, arching trees and the man-made imitation of them in the Gothic cathedral. The one is organic; the other constructed.

Cézanne's mighty struggle to wrest organic harmony out of his chaotic genius is reflected in the great positiveness and power of his master paintings—even in his portraits, his still lifes and in some of his landscapes with figures. In the Philadelphia Museum's *Women Bathers* the crudely drawn nudes are not women so much as elements of the landscape; they compose into architectonic forms as much as the trees that arch above them. (Pl. XII)

But Cézanne's greatest landscapes are those of his favorite model—the Monte Sainte Victoire which dominated the landscape around Aix. Cézanne painted this mountain again and again; in fact, to know any of his canvases of Monte Sainte Victoire is to know Cézanne. In the magnificent volumes and planes of these paintings he most fully achieved his aim of making art "solid and enduring."

The technique of this achievement is what makes Cézanne the father of modern art. He built his architectonic forms not with lines or strokes but purely with color—not by *juxtaposition* of colors but in depth, in tone, in varying intensities of color. He said: "I try to render perspective only by means of color." He broke up his forms into planes not by modeling but by infinitely subtle modulations. He completed the revolution begun by Delacroix whose battle cry was: "Color is line!" Through his paintings, Cézanne declared: Color is form! He said: "As the harmony reaches its fullness, the design reaches its completion."

And while this great achievement in art was taking place, the world of art totally ignored it and the artist. He withdrew more and more to Aix and was so little in touch even with his old friends that many of them thought him dead. He had little to do with the townsfolk of Aix, who kept at a respectful distance—respectful because he was the rich man of the town, certainly not because he was an artist.

They disapproved of Cézanne anyway, considering him a madman. What they thought of his paintings was even worse. Cézanne could not bear to have anyone watch him paint. He took care to set up his easel in a remote field or on a hillside, but if he saw anyone at a distance who appeared to be looking at him, he would pack up his things and return to his studio for the day. But he was pathetically responsive to even a casually polite remark about his work and would give a canvas to anyone he thought had expressed the slightest appreciation of it.

When word got about Aix that another madman was in town—a Monsieur Vollard from Paris who was crazy enough to pay 150 francs for a painting by Cézanne—the madman was shown canvases hidden in outhouses, attics, cellars, and on dark stair landings used as catchalls for broken or unwanted household utensils. Vollard bought all the Cézanne canvases he got trace of in the village—all except those owned by the great woman of the town, a Comtesse R. When he asked to see hers she told him scornfully that they were not art. He asked to buy them, sight unseen. "I'm no shopkeeper!" she snapped, and added that she kept the paintings in her granary. "But the rats—," suggested Vollard. "Let my rats eat my Cézannes!" she flared. And perhaps the rats did, for Vollard never got the paintings.

Through it all and apart from it all, Cézanne painted. In Paris *Père* Tanguy, the artists' supply dealer with whom Cézanne in times past had exchanged paintings for paint, would show young artists his treasures with the shy but beaming pride of a fond mother displaying her offspring.

Ambroise Vollard became acquainted with Cézanne's paintings through the auction of *Père* Tanguy's collection after the death of that gentle little godfather of modern art. Being apprised of their worth by Pissarro, the shrewdly intelligent young art dealer decided to buy up as many as possible and then to launch Cézanne in a one-man exhibition. It took Vollard months to locate the artist, but in the fall of 1895 he opened a large exhibition of his works. Except for the single painting which had entered the Salon of 1882 by the back door, it had been almost twenty years since any work by Cézanne had been seen in Paris. The new crop of critics—and some of the old ones still on the scene—were as savagely denunciatory as ever and the public decided to be outraged as usual. But Cézanne's old comrades were joyfully amazed. Pissarro wrote his son: "My enthusiasm was nothing compared to Renoir's. Degas himself was seduced by the charm of this refined savage—Monet, all of us."

On October 17, 1906, Cézanne was caught in a downpour as he was painting in a field. For two hours he continued to paint, then he started for home. But exhaustion overcame him—for some years he had been suffering from diabetes—and he fell, to be picked up and taken home by the driver of a passing laundry cart.

Although still weak from a feverish night, the next day he insisted on going into the garden to continue work on the study of a peasant. He fainted at his easel and was put to bed. He died on October 22, almost literally fulfilling the desire he had expressed not long before: "I wish to die painting."

He was within three months of his sixty-eighth birthday. Seven years earlier, when he was sixty, he had felt a gleam of hope that he was making some progress in his art. He wrote a friend: "I believe that at last I have arrived at realization. I work ceaselessly. I see the Promised Land. Shall I be like the great Hebrew leader, or shall I be allowed to enter it?"

Paul Cézanne never entered his Promised Land. Unlike Picasso with his oft-quoted statement—"I do not seek, I find!" —Cézanne forever sought. Except in a very few of his canvases he never found what he sought. It was too big. But the bigness of the thing sought comes through his paintings to foreshadow perhaps a greater art. Cézanne's art came into flower with the beginning of our century. Possibly, before our century ends, its full fruit will be apparent in the work of some other artist or artists, for all modern painters since Cézanne have consciously or unconsciously received an impulse from him.

11 TWO TORMENTED ONES

VINCENT VAN GOGH WAS A COMPLETELY VUL-
nerable man. In a world inhabited largely by crustaceans, he
had never grown around himself that protective shell most
people acquire through caution or buffetings by the time they
are adult. He was deeply intelligent but was ruled entirely by
emotion—chiefly the emotion of an outgoing love. He loved
humanity, especially the unfortunate and downtrodden, and
in a simple, direct way wanted humbly to be of service to it.
He was passionately sensitive—toward others, not toward
himself. His outgoing nature finally found release in a new
form of art: Expressionism. (Pl. XIII)

Paul Gauguin was brilliant, sophisticated, highly complex,
arrogant. He knew his way about Paris and the world. A
successful stockbroker, making considerable money with little
effort, he suddenly fell in love with painting, first as a collector, then as a Sunday painter. Finally, with a confidence
born of quick success in an entirely different field, he asked
himself: If others can devote their lives to painting, why not
I—and make money at it? He gave up his lucrative job and
turned completely to painting; he made no money. He continued to paint; he lost all that he had—money, family,
standing in his world. He went on painting, and renounced
civilization. Out of his complex nature and widely varied
experiences he developed a form of art he called Synthetism.
(Pl. XIII)

The lives of these two artists came together briefly and
tragically. They separated, each to go on to his private
Gethsemane and death, one under brilliant tropical skies, the
other in a wheatfield warmed by the sun of southern France.

Vincent van Gogh was born, in 1853, in the little town of
Zundert, The Netherlands, eldest of six children in the family
of a Dutch pastor. Sent to a boarding school when he was
twelve, he came home at sixteen the same sensitive, homely,
emotional redhead, taller, heavier, hairier, and no better
equipped to meet and make his way in the world. But an
uncle who was manager of The Hague branch of the Goupil

art gallery of Paris took him on as handy man and junior salesman. There Vincent had his first experience with art. Awash with enthusiasm, he thought he saw in minor works by Rembrandt, in Dutch *genre* paintings, in pictures by the Barbizon group, Corot and especially Millet, a universal chord of love for humanity. He put his soul into selling such paintings and did so well that he was transferred to the London branch of the firm.

Here for the first—and last—time in his life, Vincent van Gogh was a success. He dressed well, he was a splendid salesman—and he fell in love with Ursula, daughter of his landlady. After months of secret passion, idolizing and idealizing her, he poured out his love, asking her to marry him. She laughed in his face and abruptly informed him she was engaged to another. To shut off his importunities, she slammed the door on him.

Shocked into despair, van Gogh turned to a half-baked religious fanaticism, spouting noble sentiments in the gallery instead of selling pictures, and quarreling with anyone, including the customers, who disagreed with him. He had been such an excellent salesman, however, that the firm transferred him to Paris, hoping the diversion might restore his balance. But he sank even more deeply into despondency. Mixing religion with philosophical theories of his own, he presented the *mélange* in bad French to Goupil's rich and fashionable clients. Before the firm could dismiss him, he handed in his resignation, determined to make religious service his life.

He obtained a poorly paid teaching job in London, and served as an unpaid social worker in the slums. Then back to Holland where his disapproving family finally agreed to help him through a theological seminary in Amsterdam. It was a seven-year course in Greek and Hebrew, ecclesiastical dogma, and dry scholasticism. After six months of intensive, night-and-day study—against which his native intelligence and practical humanitarianism instinctively revolted—he could take no more. He was near a nervous breakdown and no nearer Christ. "What has all this to do with the Gospels?" he asked.

He decided to be a lay-preacher in the terrible coal mining district of the Borinage, near Mons, Belgium. Sent there by the Society for Evangelism of Brussels, he found conditions much worse than he had anticipated. But here at last was work into which he could throw heart and soul. These people needed acts, not words. He nursed the sick, taught the neglected children to read and write, comforted the bereaved and the old, gave the destitute his clothes, his blankets, his food. He slept on a pallet of straw and shared the miserable food of the miners. In return, he received their love—and, within a year, dismissal by the authorities in Brussels, who considered such literal Christianity shocking.

Now, at the age of twenty-seven, he was again a failure. His parents were bitterly humiliated, their friends despised him. Even his devoted brother Theo, four years his junior and now in Paris working at the Goupil gallery, was almost in despair. But no one despaired more than Vincent. He wrote Theo:

> *Now for more than five years, I don't know exactly how long, I have been more or less without employment, wandering here and there; yet my only anxiety is: How can I be of use in the world, cannot I serve some purpose and be of any good? . . . There is something inside me, what can it be?*

Within a few weeks the answer came. He again wrote Theo:

> *In spite of everything I shall rise again. I will take up my pencil, which I have forsaken in my great discouragement, and I will go on with my drawing, and now everything seems transformed for me.*

Then began an amazing demonstration of brotherly faith and love that gave the world a great artist. For the next decade—all that was to be left of Vincent's life—Theo as regularly as possible sent his brother everything he could spare from his slender earnings. With his zealot intensity at last channeled in the right direction, Vincent began to pour out drawings, Millet-like in their simplicity and strength, of Dutch and Belgian peasants and of the life of the poor Borinage miners so deeply etched in his memory. All that Theo could send was not much, and Vincent tramped the countryside, sometimes begging his bread, sleeping in haystacks, talking to toilers in the field. He always identified himself with the poor and lowly, as his drawings of this period show.

He achieved the great picture—and it is a very great one— of his Dutch period in 1885: *The Potato Eaters*, a dark gloomy canvas of tremendous inner power and compassionate humanity. Nothing can better describe it than Vincent's own words in a letter to Theo:

> *I am working again at the picture of those peasants around the dish of potatoes in the evening. During these days in which I have been working on it, it has been a regular battle. I have tried to make clear how these people eating their potatoes under the lamplight have dug earth*

*with those very hands they put in the dish. I have wanted
to give the impression of quite a different way of living
than that of us civilized people. Therefore I am not
at all anxious for everyone to like or admire it right
away. It would be wrong, I think, to give a peasant
picture conventional smoothness. If a peasant picture
smells of bacon smoke, potato steam, all right; that is
not unhealthy. If a stable smells of dung, all right; that
belongs to the stable. If the field has an odor of ripe
corn or potatoes or guano or manure, that is healthy,
especially for people from the city. To be perfumed is
not what a peasant picture needs.*

The following year Vincent went to Paris to live with his
brother in a studio apartment in Montmartre, at that time a
somewhat sparsely settled section at the edge of the city. In
addition to being a wonderful brother, Theo was in advance
of most of the art dealers of the period; he had an acute and
sound perception of artistic values. He was now manager of
a small Montmartre branch of the Paris art firm of Boussod
& Valadon which dealt chiefly in works by Salon artists and
well-known Academicians. Somewhat skeptically, they were
letting Theo try his hand at building up a clientele for works
by the Impressionists, chiefly Monet, Pissarro, and Degas.

After his years of lonely, impoverished striving, bereft of
almost all creature comforts and totally lacking in the deep
satisfactions of congenial human companionship, Vincent was
overjoyed and tremendously stimulated by his new life in
Paris. It was like coming up out of a dank, cold cellar into the
light and warmth of day. Soon the murky greens and browns
that had reflected the drabness and despair of his life in Holland yielded to the color and spontaneity of the Impressionists
he met through Theo. For a few months he attended the
classes of Cormon, a popular Academic teacher in Paris.
Then he turned to Paris itself, with all its art treasures and
artists, as his only school. In a veritable orgy of sampling and
assimilating, he absorbed new art theories, techniques, and
styles. The dean of Impressionism, the bald and benevolent
Pissarro, explained its principles to Vincent and introduced
him to neo-Impressionism, or Pointillism. Vincent tried out
both methods, adopting one after the other. He had discussions
with Toulouse-Lautrec, whom he had met at Cormon's studio. He studied Seurat's intricately worked out masterpiece,
Sunday Afternoon on La Grande Jatte. He met and mingled
with most of the advanced—and as yet unrecognized—painters
of the day, including Gauguin. And he did not neglect the
Louvre, where he was most impressed by Delacroix.

Not least important, he was taken to the little shop of *Père* Tanguy and these two gentle souls struck up a great and lasting friendship, with the result that once again Tanguy exchanged paints and canvases for unsaleable paintings. With his amazing artistic instinct, this little man placed van Gogh beside his other favorite, Cézanne, in the greatness of their art. Out of their friendship grew one of van Gogh's most touching and delightful paintings, his endearing *Portrait of Père Tanguy*.

In the background of the Tanguy portrait is evidence of van Gogh's interest at this time in Japanese prints. He had begun the study of them in Antwerp. In Paris he extended this study and began to absorb into his work a deeper understanding of the technique. Before the year was out, other influences evident in his painting were the experiments and developments being made by Cézanne, Seurat, and Gauguin.

Within less than two years van Gogh had completely transformed his art. Now he was ready for the last two years of that art and his life. For some months, with his sensitive perception of others, he had been feeling that his failure to succeed as an artist was a drag on his brother, who was having hard enough going to make profitable sales of the Impressionist works he had taken into his gallery. And he was beginning to long for a simpler, more rustic life than that of Paris. Toulouse-Lautrec, city-lover though he was, described in glowing terms the sun-drenched landscape of the south of France. And Cézanne lived there. These obvious attractions would serve to conceal his real reason for relieving Theo of his presence.

On a February day in 1888, Theo came home to find the studio apartment spick-and-span, sweet with flowers and colorful with the canvases Vincent had neatly tacked on the walls. There was a note from Vincent, too, which told of his longing for a fresher wind, a brighter sun, and "the warm, sweet smell of the ploughed field."

In the little town of Arles, in Provence, Vincent van Gogh found himself completely. For the remaining two years of his short life he painted with such violent energy and ebullient joy that his pictures radiate a vitality of color, rhythm, and form. Although he used the varicolored brush strokes he had originally learned from the Impressionists, his were larger, freer, stronger; they served a different purpose and produced a far different effect. He wrote his brother of this difference in method and purpose:

Instead of trying to reproduce exactly what is before my

eyes, I use color more arbitrarily so as to express myself more forcefully.

Not with the mathematical color calculations of Seurat, but carried forward on waves of an almost physical passion, he achieved what he called "the marrying of form and color." With powerful brush he swept his canvas free of the multiple niggling juxtapositions of Impressionism and renewed in vibrating color the large simplifications of form that make him heir to Daumier. In an ecstasy of self-liberation—what liberty is so great as the freedom to be completely one's self? —he painted everything and everyone that came within his range of vision.

Coming from the cold and cloudy north, he fell in love with the sun and with the color of the sun. Yellow—for him "the color of love"—became his passion, and the sunflower its symbol. The one critic, Albert Aurier, who perceived something of his greatness—and this only a few months before Vincent's death—wrote of him: "In his insolent desire to look at the sun face to face, in the passion of his drawing and his color, there is revealed a powerful one . . . an illumined soul. . . ."

Vincent continued his voluminous letters to Theo—van Gogh's letters constitute one of the great documents of art— and also corresponded with Gauguin, at that time in Brittany and poorer even than van Gogh, for he had no devoted brother to send him a regular stipend. Vincent conceived the idea of having Gauguin join him and share Theo's generosity. Theo agreed—and then found he must even supply Gauguin's fare to Arles.

Preparing to welcome his fellow-artist, Vincent put in order a little house he had rented in Arles for fifteen francs a month. A frenzy of domesticity took hold of him. He cleaned and painted the entire interior and had the outside painted yellow—"because I want it for everyone to be the House of Light." While he worked on his house with such feverish joy, Vincent's mind was busy with his long-nurtured dream of a brotherhood or association of artists. This was to be the first step—a house for art, "The Atelier of the South."

Gauguin arrived in October, and immediately took over. Wherever he was, he asserted mastery and not only boasted of his superiority but often proved it. He argued with van Gogh about the merits of painters—particularly Delacroix and Daumier—that Vincent most admired. He told Vincent what to do and how to do it, how and what to paint. Although Vincent stoutly held out for his artist-idols, he was willing enough to discuss painting techniques and adopt those he considered worth while. Gauguin taught him how to grind his own colors, how to make his own frames. And Vincent happily ate—and happily applauded—Gauguin's superb cooking.

But the constant discord of arguments, the excitement—pleasurable or otherwise—that Gauguin always generated around himself, began to wear van Gogh's nerves thin. And the absinthe drinking they indulged in did not help. Shortly before Christmas the explosion came. That evening, in the café, van Gogh began to talk eloquently of his idea for a brotherhood of artists. Gauguin ridiculed it. Van Gogh sent a wine glass whizzing at his friend's head. Gauguin dodged it. Van Gogh collapsed, and Gauguin carried him home and put him to bed.

The next morning Vincent, frantic with remorse, begged Gauguin's forgiveness. But at midnight madness descended upon him. As Gauguin left the house for a stroll, Vincent went after him with a razor. Gauguin commandingly ordered him back to the house, and put up at a hotel himself. Sometime during the night Vincent cut off his own ear, wrapped it and delivered it to the town brothel addressed to a prostitute to whom he had once jokingly promised it.

In the morning he was discovered seriously weakened by loss of blood. After a few days under a doctor's care he began to regain his strength. Patient Theo had come down at once, summoned by Gauguin, and the two left together when they saw Vincent was well on the way to recovery. For a time he made a great effort to avoid excitement even in his painting—which at any time was apt to send him into a fury of work. But although he was for the moment able to keep a tenuous hold on his own emotions, he was now an object of morbid interest to his neighbors and the town. Children mocked him on the street, calling: "Give us your other ear, madman!" and the townspeople watched him with unconcealed curiosity, often gathering in groups—Vincent wrote his brother he once counted fifty—to look up at the windows of the poor little house where the exalted dream of a brotherhood of artists had crashed.

Unnerved by such cruel spotlighting, Vincent's control snapped. He broke down completely and his brother sent him for a year to the asylum at Saint Remy, near Arles. After a few weeks there he was allowed to paint as much as he liked. Instead of being depressed by the confinement, he came to welcome it as a peaceful retreat from the mad and maddening world. Despite occasional dismaying occurrences both on his part and that of others confined there, he began to take an interest in his fellow-inmates. He painted some of his finest canvases in the asylum. (Pl. XIII)

He was a year at Saint Remy, his paintings and drawings —their twisting, writhing movements, the excitement of their blazing colors—indicative of the violence of his recurring, probably epileptic, attacks. He regained complete sanity between the seizures which, however violent, were of short duration and were actually of little danger to anyone but himself. It was not *during* an attack, but in the aggravated nervous tension building up to an attack that he threatened Gauguin and cut off his own ear.

Toward the end of van Gogh's year at Saint Remy, two joyful events occurred. Theo sold a painting by Vincent—for four hundred francs! And a son was born to the devoted brother, who had married soon after Vincent had left the studio apartment at Montmartre to live in Arles. The son, Theo wrote his brother, was to be named Vincent.

Vincent rejoiced for the brother who had done so much for him. But he felt—though the surer he became, the less he mentioned it—that there was not much time left for him. Theo suggested that he spend the earnings from his painting by going to a private sanatorium at Auvers. It was a pleasant retreat near Paris and it was kept by the Dr. Gachet, something of an artist himself, who had been one of the first to buy a painting by Cézanne.

In May 1890 Vincent made the change, stopping in Paris to see his new godson and a few old friends. Three days later Theo took him on to Auvers. There Vincent settled down to a quiet life under the kindly eye and with the frequent companionship of the understanding Dr. Gachet. Although Vincent still painted with fervor, he seemed otherwise tired and dispirited. Late in July he looked at the calendar. His attacks were now coming in regular two- or three-month cycles. Alone, he made a decision. One evening he went out to the nearby field, sat down under a tree, and shot himself in the abdomen. He had left a last note for his brother:

I am risking my life for my work and for it my sanity has half-foundered.

But he did not die immediately. As usual, he had fumbled the job. Theo came in great haste and Vincent told him: "I have failed again." Two days later, on July 29, 1890, he died, his brother beside him. Strangely, the separation was not for long. Six months later Theo followed him, and the two brothers lie side by side in the little cemetery at Auvers, their graves bordered by the sunflowers Vincent so loved to paint.

In the crowded ten years of van Gogh's career as an artist he painted more than 700 pictures and produced over 1,000 drawings. In addition to the landscape Theo sold for 400 francs ($80), van Gogh had one portrait commissioned for 20 francs ($4), and sold about twenty drawings at an average price of $1.25 per drawing. These comprised his entire sales during his lifetime, from which he realized a total amount of little more than one hundred dollars. One of his paintings of sunflowers he modestly estimated should bring 500 francs ($100), but there was no sale of it during his lifetime. Twenty years ago, one of these sunflower paintings sold for $50,000 and would unquestionably bring twice that amount today. In fact, just a century after his birth in 1853, an offer of $175,-000 was made for another of his flower paintings, but the owner refused to sell.

Short though it was—and utterly ignored during his lifetime and for almost a decade after his death—van Gogh's ten-year period in art has been one of the major influences in modern paintings of the twentieth century. And still is. Even the most avant-garde of today's artists—and today one is not avant-garde unless an abstractionist—insist on being called abstract-*expressionists* as though unwilling to have their uncommunicative paintings judged as devoid of emotion as they are of meaning. Even many of today's artists who think they abjure emotion in their paintings make use—consciously or not—of van Gogh techniques. For example, the present craze for "texture" in painting—though borrowing also from Picasso's and Braque's experimental use of string, sand, screening, and rags literally painted onto the canvas—stems back to the richly varied, heavily pigmented brush stroke of van Gogh. With this difference: to the "texture"-minded artist of today the mere appearance of texture is sufficient; to van Gogh, the brush strokes that created the effect of texture—no matter how masterful—were nothing in themselves but a means to an artistic end in the completed painting. He developed as *tools* what some contemporary artists congratulate themselves are achievements.

Van Gogh made painting the vehicle of emotion, developing techniques so forceful and passionately expressive that the emotion *and its meaning*—be it the character and life experience of a sitter to one of his portraits, the happiness of small red bugs disporting themselves in a forest of grass blades, the empty despair of an almost deserted café, the quivering movement of a cypress caught into the rhythm of earth and sky, or the wheeling irradiance of stars and moon unrolling infinity above a sleeping village—instantly communicates itself to the spectator. In the paintings of this artist who died when he was only thirty-seven, there is unquenchable life.

Often called the "civilized savage" Gauguin was not so much a civilized man who went native as a natural man for whom civilization was a cocoon in which unthinkingly he grew until the awareness of art entered his consciousness, expanding it until it broke through his comfortable bourgeois enclosure and freed him to paint, to starve, and to suffer.

Paul Gauguin was born in Orleans, June 7, 1848, the year of the second French Revolution. His mother's ancestry was Peruvian, intermingled with other exotic strains. His father was a French journalist with strong Republican sympathies. In 1851, when Louis Napoleon eased himself into power through a bloodless *coup d'état*, the Gauguins prudently set sail for Peru. Gauguin *père* died on shipboard. Paul and his mother then lived for four years with well-to-do relatives in Peru.

In 1855 they returned to Orleans, where Paul received his schooling. At the age of seventeen he entered the French merchant marine as a cadet, making several voyages between Le Havre and Rio de Janeiro. After three years of naval training he served on a cruiser. When he was nearly twenty-three, at the time of the French defeat by the Prussians in 1871, he quit the sea to go into a stockbroker's office in Paris. There he became very friendly with a fellow office worker, Émile Schuffenecker, and two years later married a beautiful Danish girl from a stolidly respectable, moderately prosperous Copenhagen family.

Gauguin was now firmly set on the road to a substantially successful bourgeois existence. He prospered in business, his attractive wife enjoyed the social activities increasing prosperity brought into their lives, and they started a family. Gauguin discovered in himself a talent for decorating his house in somewhat bizarre fashion and developed an interest in craft work, especially in woodcarving. He casually amused himself by drawing.

With his friend Schuffenecker, who was an amateur painter, he began attending art exhibitions and, modestly at first, started a collection of pictures—chiefly by those revolutionaries in art, the Impressionists everyone was talking about and no one was buying. It was not long before he became a Sunday painter, in emulation of friend "Schuff." In 1876 he sent up a trial balloon in the form of a conservative landscape which he submitted to the Salon. It was accepted.

Gauguin became less casual about painting. He met Pissarro. Encouraged and instructed by that kindly soul and superb teacher, little by little he took steps in the direction of Impressionism. Three years later he spent his summer holidays with Pissarro in Pontoise. On his return to Paris, he rented a studio and the following year, 1880, had seven paintings and a sculpture in the fifth Impressionist exhibition.

Now painting absorbed all his waking hours not devoted to business, in which he continued to prosper. He exhibited in the sixth Impressionist show and was praised by the important critic Huysmans. But in the seventh, in 1882, his work was dismissed by him as showing no progress.

That was a challenge Gauguin could not resist. Determined to show the world and the critics what he could do if he painted all day, he quit his job in the spring of 1883 despite the alarmed remonstrances of his wife and the protests of his business friends. His artist friends were thunderstruck; they knew the pitfalls, the roadblocks, and the lions in the path of art. They tried to warn him. But he had been quickly successful in business; why should anyone imagine he would fail as a painter? The artists shook their heads rather wistfully; gaining a fellow-worker who would probably soon be as poor as themselves, they were losing a valued patron who the previous year had made 40,000 francs and spent almost half of it buying *their* paintings! But the foolish fellow was determined on his course.

He had some savings. To make them go as far as possible, and also to be near Pissarro, he reduced living expenses by moving his family, which now included five children, to Rouen. Within a year his savings were gone. He yielded to his wife's entreaties to move to Copenhagen where she felt he could find work through family connections and might be induced by family pressure to give up unpaid painting for a paying job. For a time Gauguin tried it her way. He became a commercial representative, but the undertaking failed. At the same time a Copenhagen exhibition of his own works received such a shocked and hostile reception that it was ordered closed by the Danish Academy five days after it opened.

In June 1885, after quarreling bitterly with his wife's family, he left for Paris, taking his six-year-old son with him. Desperately poor, unable to sell a painting or find any work suited to his considerable and varied abilities, he took any sort of odd job he could get, including that of bill-poster. He and his poor little son suffered incredible hardships, often going without food, shivering nights without warm bedding, wearing their shoes through, their stockings simply a collection of holes. Finally the child's mother came to Paris and took the little boy back to Copenhagen.

Then began Gauguin's years of wandering. For a time he abandoned his futile efforts even partially to support his family or any member of it. He became completely absorbed in painting. In the spring of 1886 he had nineteen paintings in the eighth and last Impressionist exhibition. The summer of that year he spent in the village of Pont-Aven in Brittany, living at an inn run especially for impecunious artists where food and lodging were cheap and where he was able even to get credit. Setting to work with a grim determination that excluded most of the other artists, he began experimenting with cruder forms and stronger colors than those of the Impressionists. A few of the younger artists were attracted by this bold approach to art. They gathered around him, listened to his burgeoning theories and watched his first attempts to embody them in painting. In the fall Gauguin returned to Paris.

For several years, now, life had been gray with failure and poverty. The blood in Gauguin's veins and his youthful experiences of travel to distant lands demanded a change to sunshine and bright color. With a young painter he set out for the tropics by way of Panama, where the Canal was being dug. Rumor said there was much money to be made there quickly. The only job that offered, however, was digging the Big Ditch. But it paid well—for ditch digging—so for a few weeks the two artists wielded shovel and pickaxe instead of paintbrush. Then they took ship for Martinique, in the West Indies, a nearer paradise than the islands of the Pacific which had been their goal.

Early in 1888 the two were back in Paris, Gauguin weakened by dysentery, his friend almost a wreck from malaria. Gauguin had brought back with him two dozen paintings which showed Impressionism yielding to the bolder, richer colors of the tropics.

In the spring Theo van Gogh gave a small exhibition of Gauguin's Martinique and earlier Brittany pictures. A few were sold at low prices, and brought in the small amount needed for another summer at Pont-Aven.

It was there in the summer of 1888 that Gauguin turned definitely from Impressionism to work in broad, flat planes, simple lines, and pure, brilliant, sometimes clashing color. He became convinced that Cézanne was on the right course in abandoning Impressionism for painting that had more substance and structure. In fact, he was so outspoken in his admiration that he alarmed the timid, ever-suspicious older artist, who feared that Gauguin was preparing to steal his ideas and technique.

But Gauguin was working out his own ideas and individual technique in so definite and original a fashion that he became the leader of most of the young painters in Pont-Aven. Basically, the new style was a *synthesis* of nature (or the actual or real) with the idea in the artist's mind, the natural forms or realistic shapes being simplified or even at times distorted and the natural colors exaggerated or arbitrarily changed to convey, emphasize, or even to *symbolize* the idea in the artist's mind—hence the labels "Synthetism" and "Symbolism" though Gauguin himself soon scoffed at both labels.

It should not be supposed that Symbolism was meant to designate the use in painting of such tritely obvious and commonplace symbols as, say, a lily for purity, a devil's mask for evil, a baby's face for innocence, etc. It was much more subtle and subjective, an emanation or evocation from the painting itself which might or might not—it didn't matter—convey to the viewer the idea in the painter's mind. What did matter was the power of the painting to evoke. In the paintings of Gauguin it is *mood* or *atmosphere* that communicates itself to the viewer—an evocation of purity and peaceful beauty in a primitive paradise, a sense of shining Sunday calm and reverence as the Breton women kneel before the crudely drawn, violently colored Figure on the Cross. The very crudity and violence by some strange alchemy transcend actuality (perhaps because they contradict its familiar form) and lift us to freer, purer realization.

In the fall and early winter of 1888 occurred Gauguin's visit to van Gogh—unfortunate except that each gained something artistically from the other. Back in Paris—agog with the World's Fair of 1889 of which the newly built Eiffel Tower was the chief attraction—Gauguin and his Pont-Aven followers hung an exhibition of their own works in the restaurant of the Café Volpin. It created no stir in the established art circles of Paris, but it had considerable impact on the younger artists of that city. Gauguin of course was the leading spirit and the chief exhibitor, and the show served to introduce his works to the youthful rebels who were about to launch the Nabis.

After hanging the Café Volpin exhibition, Gauguin returned to Pont-Aven which was beginning to be thronged with artists and would-be artists largely through the controversy, excitement, and genuine interest—unfortunately, none of it financial—which Gauguin's theories of art and his paintings generated. In September he moved on to Le Pouldou, a small village farther along the coast which had not yet felt the drawing power of his personality. There he painted several important pictures including *The Yellow Christ*, an early example of his simplification and arbitrary placement of form and color to convey the idea—in this case, "rustic and superstitious simplicity." In place of modeling, he emphasized outline or silhouette, and one sees the beginning of his abandonment of perspective for flat, two-dimensional design. This was to become one of the chief characteristics of his painting. At first it seemed faintly related to the Egyptian (because of his early emphasis on the silhouette) but later it tended more toward the Oriental, finally developing a subtle relationship with the static serenity found in the finest Chinese painting.

Now Cézanne no longer believed that Gauguin was out to "steal his stuff," as indeed he was not. Although he admired and emulated Cézanne's abandonment of Impressionism, he never imitated the form it took. The technique and work of the two artists are diametrically opposite. After Gauguin's death Cézanne remarked: "He never understood me. I have never desired and I shall never accept the absence of modulation or of gradation: it's nonsense. Gauguin was not a painter, he only made Chinese images."

It is equally true that Cézanne never understood Gauguin's art and could not, of course, foresee that it was to have almost as far-reaching effect as his own on the art of the twentieth century. Yet Gauguin, as quoted by Maurice Denis, expresses in a few words not only the revolt from both Impressionism and Realism but the new attitude that was so soon after his death to become a dominant influence in modern painting. Denis writes: "Gauguin freed us from all the restraints which the idea of copying nature had imposed upon us. For example, if it is permissible to use vermilion in painting a tree which seems reddish . . . why not stress even to the point of deformation the curve of a beautiful shoulder or conventionalize the symmetry of a bough unmoved by air?"

In a letter to a friend, Gauguin challenged (and how that challenge has since been repeated by modern art and modern architecture!) the ideal of symmetry which is the *summum bonum* of Greek art and architecture. In 1897 Gauguin wrote to a friend: "The great error is the Greek, however beautiful it may be. . . . Keep the Persians, the Cambodians, and a bit of the Egyptians always in mind." And "It is the eye of ignorance that assigns a fixed and unchangeable color to every object. . . . The eye seeks to refresh itself through your work; give it food for enjoyment, not dejection."

Gauguin had enjoyed pontificating before a steadily growing group of young artists, but now he decided that he wanted to escape from all the bonds of civilization and its constant "struggle for money," as he phrased it. A struggle, it may be added, in which he had engaged unsuccessfully ever since he had turned full-time artist. At first it had been difficult for him to paint pictures without the immediate expectation of selling them. This logical attitude was so novel that it amazed artists grown poor in the service of art.

Now Gauguin was on the move. He had selected Tahiti as

his retreat from the world, and friends helped speed him on his way. An auction was held at the Druot galleries, and thirty paintings brought almost $2,000. In April 1891 Gauguin set forth.

In Papeete, port of Tahiti, Gauguin shed the restraints of civilization too abruptly. Capital of the French protectorate, Papeete had a population of about 3,500, half of which was French or French half-castes and miscellaneous whites, who were trying with more or less success to "civilize" the natives unfortunate enough to share the town with them. And here was a white man, even a Frenchman from the most civilized city in the world, threatening by his amoral actions to upset the rickety apple cart of their white propriety and superiority! On his part, Gauguin was disgusted with the encroachment of officialdom—a mere veneer when it wasn't a travesty of European civilization—of what he had fondly believed would be an island paradise. Officialdom—the colonial government, the clergy, the leading citizens, etc.—was even more disgusted with his determination to revert to primitive manners and morals (or lack of them) within sight and hearing of their own little Europeanized community.

The immediate problem was solved by Gauguin's move to a native village twenty-five miles along the coast. There he quickly acquired a hut with an exquisite view of mountains and ocean, and a young Tahitian who became his *vahiné* or native wife. Now he felt civilization slip from him while he dwelt for a time in the paradise he had dreamed of. Food was abundant and cost little more than a few cents to a fisherman if one were too lazy to do his own fishing; and even a lazy man could pluck breadfruit from trees he had not planted, pick ripe mangos and other luscious fruits from vines and bushes he did not need to tend. The sun was golden, the colors and forms—including the human—glorious, the natives gentle and yielding. Within the year Gauguin produced more than sixty pictures and many drawings and carvings. (Pl. XIII)

But he became ill, lost weight seriously, and had to go to the hospital at Papeete. After some weeks he was able to return to his hut but was far from well. And he was again without money—the long voyage, his first carousing month in Papeete, and finally the hospital there, had taken it all. Even in paradise, it seemed, at least a little money was essential. His Tahitian pictures, which he had sent back in groups to dealers and friends in Paris to be disposed of, had aroused great comment but had not sold.

Ill and penniless, Gauguin now yearned to return to the comforts of the civilization he had so grandly discarded less than two years before. After pressure and persuasion from friends, the French Government repatriated him, and he arrived in Marseilles without a sou. By chance it was a significant anniversary for him. Exactly a decade earlier he had walked out of his brokerage job. Ten years devoted to art and not a sou to show for it.

A friend in Marseilles lent him a little money and he went on to Paris. There good fortune—which for so long had persistently gazed in the opposite direction—smiled briefly on him, presenting a $2,000 legacy from an uncle who had been kind enough to die at the right moment. Immediately Gauguin's aches and pains vanished—unexpected money is sometimes a miracle healer—and he blossomed out in all directions. He took a large studio in Montparnasse, furnishing it with an odd and colorful jumble of French furniture, Tahitian mementoes, Chinese hangings. He acquired a pet monkey and an Indonesian model named Annah who soon became his mistress. Sartorially he fitted himself out with a pearl-buttoned blue frockcoat, yellow trousers, and a blue weskit embroidered in yellow and green. He topped it with a large felt hat banded with a bright blue ribbon. As a finishing touch he wore a pair of hand-carved—by himself—Breton shoes, and carried a heavy wooden cane on which he had carved curious figures climaxed by a nude man and woman in embrace.

He used his studio—on a wall of which he had inscribed: "Here one makes love"—not for painting but for parties, as many a lesser artist has done before and since. Writers and artists and noted people from many levels of Paris life thronged the parties. For a brief time Gauguin, that despiser of civilization, lived this life to the full, enjoying the notoriety and excitement, holding court in his studio or swaggering along the boulevards, his pet monkey perched on his shoulder, the exotic and enigmatic Annah at his side.

In November Durand-Ruel gave an exhibition of Gauguin's Tahitian paintings. None but a few artists and even fewer critics considered the paintings art, but the public came to see the odd pictures of a strange and luxuriant land, copper-colored, half-nude women, and outlandish colors—there was even a red dog and a pink horse to add to the fun. His old Impressionist friends came, too, and were shocked and troubled. What kind of painting was this, asked Monet, Renoir, and Pissarro, forgetting that they too had once been targets of such questions. Only Degas approved; his failing eyes saw further into the future and deeper into the paintings. He alone of the Impressionists bought Gauguin paintings.

Gauguin went to Copenhagen briefly to see his family. Returning, he closed his Paris studio—by this time he had spent most of his inheritance—and went for the summer of 1894 to Pont-Aven, taking Annah and the monkey along. But his sartorial and other exhibitionisms annoyed his artist friends and caused the Breton peasants to draw stiffly away from him. He quarreled, painted little, and was by fits and starts morose or alcoholically gay. One evening, strolling with Annah and the monkey, he took offense at some jocular insults cast his way by a group of sailors. A brawl resulted and Gauguin with his heavy cane called into emergency service his early training as a fencer. Then his fists went into action with remembered boxing skill. He was gaining over his half-dozen adversaries when a departing opponent from behind aimed a vicious kick with his wooden clog and broke Gauguin's ankle.

During the melee Annah disappeared and did not stop going until she reached Paris, looted Gauguin's closed studio, and had made off with every movable object of value. Gauguin's partial recovery—his ankle never healed completely and he walked with a painful limp the rest of his life—left him dispirited and not at all well. He returned to Paris and soon decided it was time to make his final farewell to civilization. At an auction which brought him little more than $2,000 he disposed not only of his paintings but of everything he owned.

The summer of 1895 saw him back in Tahiti, again squandering money freely. Unwisely he built a two-room hut on rented land, which he later had to move when the land was sold. He acquired another *vahiné,* who shared with him his descent into poverty. Often they had only water and rice to eat. Money was slow coming from Paris for the paintings he sent to be sold. Even his ability and desire to paint were weakening. Too often there was no money for paint and canvas. When he had money he frequently found it necessary to spend it at the hospital for treatment of his complication of diseases.

His days of arrogance and self-confidence were gone. He begged his friends in Paris to organize a group that would provide the $40 a month he needed for living expenses and art materials, taking in exchange paintings. He suggested that each individual in the group contribute $32 annually, for which he would give each a painting. He humbly pointed out that his pictures should reasonably be worth $32 and that perhaps those who put up that sum would in the future find them not a bad investment. (Within a year of his death—only a few years away—those paintings he offered for $32 would easily have sold for many times that amount; today the same paintings would bring from 2,000 to 4,000 times $32.)

But there were no takers, so Gauguin desperately wrote friends and agents to sell his canvases for whatever they could get. Occasionally a painting was sold and he received some money from Paris. And then for long stretches there would be no money at all. At last he could stand it no longer. He painted what he thought would be his last picture—a large painting on sacking, as he could purchase no canvas. This major composition, now owned by the Museum of Fine Arts in Boston, he called: *Where Do We Come From? What Are We? Where Are We Going?* He left it in his hut as his fare-well to the world.

Painfully he climbed the mountain back of his hut, swal-lowed arsenic, and lay down to die. But he had apparently taken an overdose. Retching in agony, he stumbled down the mountain, fell into his hut, and slowly recovered to take up again the wretched business of his life. For a year he gave up painting and, when not too ill, worked as a Government clerk in Papeete. Eventually some money arrived from France. Gauguin took heart again, gave up his miserable job, and returned to painting. Within the year he began quarreling with Government officials and decided to get farther away from even the outposts of civilization. He sold his hut and in November 1901 took himself and his belongings to Atuana on the island of Hiva Oa in the Marquesas. This time no *vahiné* accompanied him.

The money that had come earlier from Paris had been sent by Vollard, the art dealer, who in 1900 agreed to send Gauguin a monthly stipend of $60 in exchange for paintings rated on a sliding scale of $40, then $50, and finally $60. After a year or two Vollard's remittances became irregular and Gauguin, again beset with money troubles and plagued with recurring illnesses, began quarreling with the Colonial ad-ministrators over injustices he felt were being done the na-tives. Early in 1903 he was sentenced to a fine and a jail term. Preparing to return to Tahiti to appeal the sentence, he be-came too ill to go. On May 8, 1903, he died, alone and un-cared for.

Like vultures, the officials took charge, destroying some of his belongings, including the carved walking stick, and auc-tioning off as laughable souvenirs his wonderful paintings. Someone paid the equivalent of $1.50 for the last picture he ever painted, a remembered scene of Brittany. Meanwhile, in Paris, the shrewd Vollard was quietly cornering the market on Gauguins, from which he subsequently realized a fortune.

There were others in Paris who were beginning to realize the value of Gauguin's paintings, not in financial terms but in their importance to the forward movement of art. These were artists younger than the ones who had listened to his theories and watched him paint at Pont-Aven a dozen years earlier. Through this new generation Gauguin's influence was to enter the mainstream of modern art almost immediately, as would become apparent in the 1905 exhibition of the *Salon d'Automne*. Visitors to that exhibition were startled, indignant, scornful, and utterly bewildered by the paintings of a group of obscure young artists with unfamiliar names— Matisse, Rouault, Braque, Derain, Dufy—whose works were considered so radical, even violent, that they were herded into a single room which a critic promptly dubbed *Cage aux Fauves* or Cage of the Wild Beasts. And so the Fauves came into being.

The rest of the world—those who love and enjoy art without being able to put it on canvas—received an even greater inheritance from Gauguin. He counseled artists: "The eye seeks to refresh itself through your work; give it food for enjoyment." This Gauguin gave in overwhelming measure. The island paradise he sought, and only in brief interludes could enjoy, he lavishly bestowed on the world through paintings of abundant peace and glowing beauty.

12 THE TWENTIETH CENTURY

EXPLODES IN COLOR

EACH SUCCEEDING GENERATION PROBABLY feels that it is living in "times that try men's souls" or at least that the century enclosing its particular generation is one of great change and upheaval. And that has been true, century after century. But as the twentieth century advances past the halfway mark, it becomes abundantly clear that in no previous century has the knowing and knowable world expanded so far so fast—and simultaneouly contracted so rapidly in the time and space required for communication and accessibility. Before mid-century the opposing pulls of expansion-contraction reached ultimate expression in the splitting of the atom.

Art in the twentieth century not only kept pace with the headlong acceleration of world change but often out-paced it, not only reflected world conditions but sometimes foreshadowed them. Artwise, the century opened with the explosion of color called Fauvism; a few years later came the disintegration of form known as Cubism. The four artists of the nineteenth century usually referred to as *the* Post-Impressionists*—Seurat, Cézanne, van Gogh, Gauguin—prepared the way, the first two laying the foundation for Cubism, the latter two having the most immediate effect on the earlier Fauve movement.

Three young artists—Matisse, Vlaminck, Derain—walked into the van Gogh memorial exhibition held at the Bernheim-Jeune Gallery in Paris in 1901, and walked out tremendously impressed. Vlaminck later said: "That day I felt I loved van Gogh more than my own father." It was van Gogh's riotous use of color that most affected the young artists; its emotional expressionism they largely overlooked or ignored.

Two years later these three joined several other artists to found the *Salon d'Automne*. Its first exhibit opened in October 1903 in the basement of the Petit Palais on the Champs-Elysées, its most notable feature a memorial show of Gauguin's paintings. The following year the *Salon d'Au-*

tomne was refused even the basement of the Petit Palais. The Director of the *Beaux-Arts,* strangely enough, came to their rescue. He obtained exhibition space for them in the Grand Palais de Champs-Elysées. For its second Salon the Committee organized a large retrospective show of the works of Cézanne.

This aroused enough comment to alert the conservative press and the Academicians to the encroaching dangers of modern art. Together they vigorously opposed any more *Salon d'Automne* showings in either Palais. But a strong champion arose and forced the Grand Palais to relent, and so it became the scene of the famous *Salon d'Automne* of 1905 in which the paintings of the younger, more radical artists—among them: Matisse, Derain, Vlaminck, Rouault, Friesz, Marquet, Van Dongen, Dufy—were given a special room, derisively christened by a critic "the cage of the wild beasts (*fauves*)." Fauvism, as a movement and as a group, lasted only about five years, but it had a tremendously liberating effect on art as it moved out of the nineteenth into the twentieth century. It was the final step but one—and that was to come soon in Cubism—that set the creative imagination free from any obligation to imitate nature.

Foremost of the Fauves was Henri Matisse. Until he was nearly twenty he had not the slightest desire to become a painter and would have rejected as fantastically impossible the very idea that he was destined to spend the next sixty-five years of his long life in the pursuit and happy capture of art and through it, finally, a sizeable fortune. (Pl. XIV)

Henri Matisse was born in the north of France (Picardy) in Le Cateau, December 31, 1869. His father selected the magistry as a career for his son and young Matisse, after the required early schooling, took up the study of law. He was not particularly attracted to it, neither did he rebel against it. He accepted it as a matter of course; a man must earn a living and this seemed as good a way as any. Then destiny took a hand. Matisse was stricken with appendicitis. To lighten the boredom of a slow convalescence, a friend suggested that he try his hand at painting. Mme. Matisse, who had a pretty talent for painting flowers on chinaware, bought her son a paintbox, the Goupil book "How to Paint," and a few color reproductions to copy. Suddenly, with a paintbrush in his hand, Matisse to his own amazement was "transported to a paradise where I felt gloriously free, at ease, and on my own."

That finished his law career almost before it was begun. When he was twenty-two Matisse took up the formal study of art in the studio of the leading Academician, Bouguereau.

Not finding it to his liking, he moved on to the studio of the artistically liberal Gustave Moreau, a splendid teacher who used no formula but encouraged his pupils to develop their individual talents. In this studio Matisse met some of his future fellow-Fauves, including Dufy and Rouault. Part of the training was of course the study and copying of the Old Masters in the Louvre, at which Matisse became so expert that he sold every copy he made.

In 1894 and 1895 he exhibited paintings of his own in which the Chardin influence was evident and which, possibly for that reason, received favorable reviews. Two or three years later he adopted for a time an Impressionist technique. Then he rapidly went through a series of experiments with Pointillism, heavy impasto, and the two-dimensional arrangement of space. Paradoxically, the man who was to be called the leader of the "Wild Beasts" was cautious rather than impulsive. He was no radical, wild-eyed artist. He experimented thoughtfully, he considered, he decided. Unlike van Gogh, he felt no burning need to express himself, no longing to give a message to mankind. He did not want either to denounce or renounce the world, as had Gauguin—intermittently.

It was van Gogh's break with tradition in the use of color, his daring freedom in it, his wild exaggeration of it, that had taken Matisse and his colleagues by storm. It was Gauguin's decorative use of flat color, his two-dimensional patterns, his willingness to distort natural form for esthetic emphasis or to fill out or make more exciting the design of a painting, that completed the freeing of these young men from natural shapes and colors. In full swing after their baptism as Wild Beasts, the group as a whole and individually rejected the soft vagueness of Impressionism, the realistic forms of naturalism, the cozy Victorianism and sentimental nuances of the group that immediately preceded them, the Nabis.

The Fauves imperiously ignored or rearranged perspective, handled form roughly, and let intensity of color—sometimes in arbitrary splotchings of paint—take the place of volume. In one of his first Fauve portraits, instead of shading, Matisse used a strip of green to model nose and upper lip, a splash of green across the forehead, a streak of red to indicate the shadow cast by the curve of the neck. In another very famous painting (*Portrait with the Green Stripe* owned by the Royal Museum of Fine Arts, Copenhagen) the woman's hair and eyebrows are a dark blue, a stripe of acid green from hairline to lower lip forms the nose and upper lip, the right side of the face is yellow, the left side yellowish-pink. The background of the portrait is laid on in three irregular flat areas of green, orange, lavender. In spite of this slashing contradiction of

reality, the painting *is* a portrait. And it is more. It is a remarkable example of Matisse's genius in combining the most
shrieking color contrasts in a somehow satisfying and at the
same time exciting whole, as an expert musician blends dis-
sonant chords into a magnificent, crashing climax.

This working of unexpected and stridently clashing colors
into a unified composition is often referred to as "color orchestration" and was the early identifying characteristic of
Fauvism. As the years wore on, some of this violence in paint
wore off. Color, often just as intense and always magnificently
handled, was related more naturally to the subject by the
painters who emerged from Fauvism into brilliant individual
careers. Matisse was a born colorist, probably the greatest in
all modern art.

For the few years of his experimental period between his
abandonment of Impressionism—just becoming popularly
saleable—and the somewhat equivocal fame he suddenly won
as the leader of the Fauves, Matisse had a severe financial
struggle. His wife helped out with a small millinery shop and
for a time the grandparents took the children. By 1908, however, he was selling moderately and was sought out by students, most of whom wanted to become Fauves overnight.
Matisse frowned on this and insisted that his students subject
themselves to the discipline of nature before they tried to
distort it. They were trying to begin at the wrong end, he told
them. "Before you start tightrope walking," he said, "you must
learn to walk firmly on the ground."

Although the 1901 van Gogh exhibition was the initial impulse that led to Fauvism, and the 1903 Gauguin added its
impact, it was Cézanne's organization of space and architectonic relationships that had the deepest and most continuing
influence, particularly on Matisse. Other contributing factors
to the formation of his art developed from Persian ceramics
and Byzantine mosaics and from his study of Oriental art. In
1903 he went to Munich to see the big exhibition of Moham-
medan art. In 1918 he visited Morocco and, like Delacroix
before him, found much in its exotic colors, patterns, and
customs that he carried over into his own art. These influences, particularly the Persian, are suggested in his Odalisque
series. (Pl. XIV)

In comparable degree with his genius as a colorist, Matisse
was master of the arabesque. This is most immediately apparent in his beautiful drawings, where line flows into line
or with airy sureness weaves in and around or darts off in
fresh tangents. His distortions of form are like frozen music,
ready on the instant to melt into new and seductive rhythms.
Every object—a flower, a tree, fruit, a vase, a woman's body

—was for him a point of departure into an evolving pattern.

In 1908 Alfred Stieglitz—at the instigation of the famous American photographer, Edward Steichen—gave Matisse an exhibition in his New York gallery "291," the artist's first one-man show in the Western Hemisphere. Within the next five years his reputation grew internationally through one-man exhibitions in London and Berlin. During this period he visited Moscow, where he painted two mural panels for the palace of a wealthy tea merchant. This stimulated a desire in Russia for his paintings, with the result that the Museum of Western Art in Moscow owns one of the world's finest Matisse collections. His reputation was world wide when in 1925 France made him Chevalier of the Legion of Honor.

In the last decade of his lengthy and fruitful career, his work became completely two-dimensional, the forms large and greatly simplified, sometimes entirely abstract. In 1943 he moved to Vence, in Southern France where, somewhat of an invalid, he devoted much of his time to book illustrations and to cutting forms out of colored paper which he arranged in mural-size designs. Between 1948 and 1951, despite physical disabilities, he designed the building for the Chapel of the Rosary in Vence and decorated it—stained glass windows, mural, and even the vestments worn by the celebrant of the Mass.

As he advanced toward his mid-eighties, he would sometimes from his bed wield a piece of charcoal attached to a long, slender pole, drawing designs and outlining figures on his high white-plaster wall. On his good days he sat on a comfortable small chair before the wall and directed an attendant to stick his colored cutouts on the plaster in patterns he indicated.

Finally, full of honors and still delighting in the creation of "an art of balance, of purity and serenity" which he had declared many years earlier should rest and relax one "something like a good armchair," Matisse died in Nice while working out a design of a stained glass window for the Chapel of the Rosary. It was November 3, 1954, not quite two months short of his eighty-fifth birthday.

André Derain was born in 1880 at Chatou, France, the son of a pastry shopkeeper who was ambitious for him to be an engineer. But the boy's painting at the early age of fifteen showed clearly his course in life. In 1898 he was sent to the *Académie Carrière* in Paris where he met Matisse. The following year Derain and Maurice de Vlaminck—the two had met in a minor railway accident and had found much in common besides the accident—painted together on the Island of Chatou. They had rigged up a studio there in a dilapidated old house which they rented for ten francs a month and which, Vlaminck wrote, ". . . always seemed on the verge of lurching over into the Seine!"

In a curious way, Derain seemed to seek a balance between his two friends: Matisse, who always strove to "organize his brain" and paint as it directed, and Vlaminck, who tossed caution and calculation to the wind, painting only as instinct and emotion led him.

Derain's artistic ambivalence was evident throughout his career. Rather than a weakness, it indicated a richness of talent. But the pulling in opposite directions—before he finally resolved it by giving in to it and becoming one of the most varied of modern artists—gave the young painter periods of self-doubt at the start of his career despite the fact that he quickly attained command over any technique.

Early in his career, too, he received a reassurance for which some greater artists had waited a lifetime in vain—notably van Gogh and Gauguin. In 1905 Vollard, the canny Paris art dealer, bought all the paintings in the twenty-five-year-old artist's studio.

In his Fauve days, Derain's color was startling in its exuberance even for a Wild Beast. Yet, although with his fellow-Fauves he disregarded the normal hues of objects and scenery, he avoided the clash of bold color juxtaposed against bold color by intermingling more subdued tones.

With Matisse and Vlaminck, his first impulse toward Fauvism came from van Gogh but he did not come under the influence of Gauguin so much as did Matisse. He felt the need for the more architectonic order evolved by Cézanne. In 1907 his forms became more simplified, his volumes a part of the underlying composition. The following year he abandoned the pure strong colors of Fauvism to work, via Cézanne, toward the system of blocked volumes that was to be one of two starting points of Cubism. At this time also he was somewhat influenced by the new passion of the Paris art world—African Negro sculpture—which was to have such impact on twentieth-century art. This influence, plus his study of primitive sculpture, is evident in the stone carvings he produced at this period and in the masks he sculptured from copper shell cases during his service in World War I.

For several years his work showed a certain kinship with Cubism though it cannot be classed with that school. His landscapes have much the strength of Cézanne's but are far more simplified. His figure paintings and portraits are distinguished by the same qualities. After World War I the Cubist and African Negro influences diminished and his work took on a classic serenity that certainly has been one of the contributing factors to its popularity. (It is modern art that is "easy to live with.") At the same time it shows in some degree the romantic inheritance from Delacroix, Courbet, and Manet, even though it retains a slight Cubist "stiffness" in figure painting and portraiture and a Cézanne-like order in landscape.

In 1928 Derain won first prize in the Carnegie International held in Pittsburgh. In his fifties and sixties he continued vigorously working in southern France. In 1945 he did a series of superb color woodcuts for a special edition of Rabelais' "Pantagruel." Later that year he designed stage sets for a London production. In the summer of 1954, while crossing the street, he was struck down by an automobile. A few weeks later he died. His work is owned by a great many museums and private collectors.

Maurice de Vlaminck, born April 4, 1876, in the crowded center of Paris, loves the country and has lived most of his life in it. He is the son of a Belgian father and a mother from Lorraine, both of them musicians. He is a big, blond—now gray-haired—rugged man who all his life has hated regimentation and conformity.

He taught himself to paint, but not at the Louvre. Even though, early in his career, he occasionally visited that palace of art and "spent long moments in front of the paintings that corresponded with my temperament" he felt that "in painting, every generation must start out anew . . . without exhuming Corot, without perfecting Courbet, without speaking of Poussin as a close relative. . . . The individual must create everything; to look at the Masters does not mean to copy their works." He explained more fully: "I went to the museums as I went to brothels, but I never 'went upstairs.' " Soon he renounced museums altogether—though he does not seem to mind that a great many own pictures by him.

Though for a short time he turned to Cézanne, van Gogh was the only artist of whose influence Vlaminck was consciously aware. But at the 1901 exhibition when he felt so strongly the impact of the Dutch artist's works, van Gogh was far from being recognized a master either inside or outside museums.

It should be stressed again, however, that not one of the three young artists who were so soon to become the nucleus of the Fauve movement was influenced by the *emotional* power of van Gogh's canvases. They were overwhelmed solely by its forceful *painterly* results. Vlaminck was the most greatly affected. To this day, his work—which has changed in character very little during the intervening half-century, still bears a slight surface relationship through its forthright freedom of form and color.

When he was seventeen, Vlaminck, whose parents struggled to support their five children by giving music lessons, was the unexpected recipient of a brand-new and long wished-for bicycle. He put it to immediate use touring the countryside. He was so happy in this widening view of the beautiful world of "water, sky, clouds, and trees" that the urge to paint came upon him and out of the exuberance of life he began painting just for himself.

But he had to earn his living and no way seemed open to him except teaching music. He could not remember a time when he did not play the violin, and with so much music and music-teaching going on at all times in the household, he shuddered at the thought of adding to the cacaphony. And then a magnificent idea came to him. In his exploration of the countryside he had become an expert bicyclist—and bicycle racing was the rage in France, with prize money in considerable amounts. Soon he was earning a good living and vanity-tickling fame as a winning bicycle racer. He was not to enjoy this carefree, exciting existence for long, however. After recovering from an attack of typhoid fever he was called up for military service.

He had married at eighteen and now had two small daughters. To support his family, when he was returned to civilian life, he played in gypsy orchestras in Paris night clubs. To relax during the daytime he again took up painting, which he had neglected during his military service. In 1899 he met Derain and a close and inspiring friendship was formed. Derain knew much more about art, but Vlaminck's passion for painting, his instinctive, almost explosive use of strong pure colors infected Derain with like enthusiasm. When Derain brought Matisse to Chatou to see their work, the older artist realized that here was something new, something that lay in the direction toward which he had been groping—and the foundation of the Fauve movement was laid.

When, after the 1905 christening of the Fauves, Vollard bought all of Derain's paintings, the artist suggested that he take a look at Vlaminck's also. Vollard did—and bought them all for a total of 1500 francs! Stunned with happiness, Vlaminck later remarked uneasily that he was afraid he might "have done the poor man in." The 1500 francs—equivalent at that time to about $300—enabled Vlaminck to move his little family from a depressing, dirty suburb of Paris into the real country. There he was able to devote all his time to painting, as it was not long before Vollard began to interest buyers in his work.

In 1908 Vlaminck abandoned pure color, turning for a time to the study of form in Cézanne's works. When the rising Cubists claimed the Master of Aix as their progenitor and patron saint, Vlaminck violently rejected their assumptions but when they explained their theories—how they loved to explain and air them!—pointing out the genesis of Cubist forms in Cézanne's work, Vlaminck's intelligence recognized the validity of their claims. But with his abhorrence of formula he could not accept them for himself. He fought to free himself from all outside influence and to find only in himself and in nature the inspiration for his painting.

He loves to paint lowering skies, rows of leafless trees, tiny huts on the windswept countryside, boats moving over dark and turbulent waters. He seldom paints an actual storm. It is the threat of storm that seems to appeal to him and even in his blue skies and calm waters there is always a sense of movement that presages change. When he paints flowers it is as though they have just been plucked and dropped in a mass on a table, or a few carelessly stuck into a vase. Even a loaf of half-cut bread, with knife and water jug near by, has a casual, impermanent air, as though someone has been interrupted in cutting the bread. His snow-clogged streets, though there may be a few pedestrians, seem vast and lonely. Something of what one feels through his paintings is expressed in a written statement by him: "I live in the country. What grandeur solitude expresses! What sincerity it compels! Thanks to it one understands—or, rather, one feels—true values, life's essentials, and internal peace more deeply."

A painter first of all, and a musician from early childhood, Vlaminck is also a writer of both prose and poetry, with ten published books. He wrote his first novel in 1901, which Derain illustrated with more than thirty sketches. Living in the country north of Paris, Vlaminck farms his land and claims that he prefers to be known as a farmer rather than an artist. He has won several prizes at international exhibitions such as the Carnegie, and has produced ceramics, woodcuts, lithographs, etchings, and watercolors as well as his major works in oil. His work hangs in leading museums and is represented in the private collections of many countries.

It is a curious circumstance that this ruggedly independent painter, who despises schools and groups of art, should have been one of the three most responsible for the Fauve movement. It is even stranger that through the chance purchase in 1900 of an odd little statuette from a café owner, he should unwittingly have set in motion the chain of events that resulted in Cubism. The little figure he bought for a few francs was a piece of African Negro sculpture—the first ever acquired by a French artist. He took it to Derain at the Chatou studio, both of them regarding it more or less as a small piece of curioso. Matisse saw it there and was immediately struck by its artistic qualities. He began to make a serious collection of African Negro sculpture, which he later introduced to Picasso, Braque, and other artists. Within a few years it was the rage in Paris art circles and became the secondary influence that brought about Cubism.

Delightful Dufy! His was not a major talent, but the gay charm of his paintings, instantly beguiling, has probably done more than weightier works to win the indifferent and even the hostile to modern art. His quick-moving line reaches further than a century back to the drawings of Watteau (although more akin to his nearer artistic ancestor, Constantine Guy of the Napoleon III era) and across three thousand miles of ocean to his American contemporary, John Marin, a greater and more serious artist but one whose darting line bears distant kinship.

Until the latter third of his career, Dufy's color had the rich beauty—without, of course, the conventional placement and handling—of Fragonard. From 1935 on, it became lighter in tone, with a more delicate interplay; also in this later period he sometimes used brownish reds with great effect over an entire canvas.

Raoul Dufy was born at Le Havre, June 3, 1877. At the age of fifteen he began attending evening classes there at the *École des Beaux-Arts*. Winning a scholarship in 1900, he went to Paris where he studied under Gustave Moreau, the teacher who encouraged several future Fauves (as well as all the art students who worked under him) to give reign to their individual talents.

Dufy's original tendency was toward Impressionism. He met Matisse in 1901 but was not greatly influenced by the older artist until he saw the earliest version of his *Luxe, Calme et Volupté*. This painting had the power of a revelation for Dufy—not that it showed him *what* to do or *how* to do; rather, it suddenly opened his eyes to what *he* could do. Impressionism's hold dropped from him and he threw in his lot with the Fauves, happy to exchange even Impressionist non-traditional imitation of nature for the free play of imagination in form and color.

Such artistic freedom was temperamentally suited to the ebullient Dufy, whose *joie de vivre* and buoyant wit sought outlet in line and color as well as in words. He plunged joyfully into pure and riotous color. Although at first his forms were heavier, his lines deliberately thicker than we now think characteristic of his work, his paintings even then had a sparkle and vivacity not common with the Fauves. Two or three years later, for a short time, the Cubist influence showed in restraint of color and more sober design. But he soon emerged from this period of development with a brighter palette and more decorative design, painting the fashionable beaches and holiday world of the Mediterranean coasts of southern France, Italy, and Morocco, their Arabian Nights casinos, their palaces of past grandeur, the fishing boats and fleets, the race tracks with jockeys, top-hatted sportsmen and parasoled ladies, and lush and lovely gardens ornamented rather than hidden by iron gates. Dufy's allegro touch and virtuoso handling of color were also perfectly in key with the "renderings" of musical compositions he delighted to put on canvas, as in *Blue Mozart* and *Red Concert*.

From 1911 to 1930 Dufy engaged in various artistic endeavors, doing woodcuts, book illustrations, textile designs, ceramics, tapestries. In 1937 he painted a 200-foot mural, thirty-five feet high, for the Paris World's Fair. Along with all this he turned out a continuous stream of oils, watercolors, and drawings which were eagerly bought in Europe and in America. Color reproductions of his works are tremendously popular. His paintings are exceptionally well suited to flawless reproduction—and, it must be said, to the facile brushes of imitators, who have found the selling of Dufy-esque works both easy and profitable.

In 1951 Dufy went to Boston for treatment of arthritis so crippling that he could grasp his brush only with the greatest pain, when at all. He received relief, and improved to the point where he could again command his hands in the joyous service of art. On November 23, 1953, he died in Provence of a heart attack. The felicitous line and enchanting colors of his paintings will live for many years.

No contrast could be greater than that between the paintings of Dufy and those of Rouault—the most lighthearted and the heaviest laden produced by that group of artists first known as the Fauves. As Dufy's inviting canvases say to the spectator, "Be gay with me!"—so Rouault's solemnly intone, "Abandon hope, all ye that look at me. Flagellate yourselves for the sins and sorrows of the world."

As each followed the line of his own artistic individuality, the progressive paths of their painting became more and more divergent, as indeed Rouault's art from the beginning of his association with the Fauve group in 1903 diverged from the art of all his contemporaries. Then, and now, Rouault stands alone and lonely in art. One must go back to Daumier, who died when Rouault was five years old, for even a slight kinship close in time; back of Daumier to Rembrandt, two centuries before; then, beyond all and above all, to the anonymous cathedral craftsmen-artists of the Middle Ages, five centuries in time away from Rouault but closer to him than all others in spirit and in art.

Georges Rouault was born May 27, 1871, in the basement of a house in the Belleville section of Paris when the city was under merciless bombardment, night and day, by the Versaillists. As he emerged from the darkness of the womb into the murk of the cellar, the house above him received the direct salute of an exploding shell. But his boyhood was reasonably peaceful and quiet, shepherded by a devoted grandfather who loved the works of Manet, Courbet, and Daumier. The old man often showed the little boy engravings and prints of their work, and sometimes took him to the Louvre to see paintings by earlier artists, for not as yet had the grandfather's three favorites achieved the place they now hold on those august walls.

In his early 'teens, Georges was apprenticed to a stained-glass artisan and helped with the restoration of medieval church windows. Evenings he attended classes at the *École des Arts Décoratifs*. When he was twenty he left his apprenticeship for full-time study at the *École des Beaux-Arts,* soon coming under the instruction of Gustave Moreau, the Academician who had such a remarkably liberal teaching attitude. It was in his studio that Rouault met Matisse.

Rouault's deeply religious nature undoubtedly received subconscious visual enrichment during the formative years of his adolescence when he worked on stained glass windows. This became apparent later in the thick black lines, like leading, he used to outline contours and mark off areas of light. It was also evident in his use of rich dark colors relieved by colors as rich but through which light seemed to glow. An early outward sign of his religious preoccupation was indicated in the series of subjects which won him first prize at the *École des Beaux-Arts* in 1892. During the next three years he was awarded two or three other prizes, but not the coveted *Prix de Rome,* for which he twice competed. On the advice of Moreau, to whom he had become deeply attached, he left the École in 1895.

In 1898 Moreau died. Shocked and grief-stricken, Rouault accepted the position of Curator of the Moreau Museum although the salary of 2400 francs a year was not enough to support him and his dependants. It was a difficult period for him, filled with financial, emotional, and spiritual crises. He became ill. During his convalescence he was suddenly filled with revulsion for his own brand of Academism—dark-brown canvases with smoky shadows vaguely derivative from Rembrandt. He moved away from such painting and during the next two or three years began working out new techniques as he developed new conceptions of art. With Matisse and others, he was one of the founders of the *Salon d'Automne* and became interested in the beginnings of the Fauve movement.

In 1903 he showed in the first *Salon d'Automne*. The following year he exhibited eight paintings and thirty-two watercolors in his newly formed style. In the famous 1905 Salon he showed three important works. They were not hung in the room later labeled *Cage aux Fauves* but his break with tradition in color and form were so equally shocking that he was generally classed, by critics and public, with the "Wild Beasts" with whom, of course, he was known to be personally associated. Actually, he was never one of the Fauves in an artistic sense though often, even now, he is more or less classified with them.

In 1904 Rouault became acquainted with two fervent Catholic writers, Huysmans and Léon Bloy. Huysmans was trying to form an association of Catholic artists to bring religion back into painting and painting into religion. Bloy felt that a return to primitive Christianity was the only salvation for a world sunk in sin and misery. He became an intimate friend and exerted a profound influence on Rouault who, seizing on sin rather than on salvation, responded with a stream of darkly luminous paintings of prostitutes in the last stages of degradation, in gross and ugly physical deterioration.

During this period Rouault also painted clowns as they really were, away from the blare and color of the circus ring—sad, dejected faces, wearily slumped bodies. The third subject that absorbed him at that time was the police-court judge. In addition to these three predominant subjects, he painted a few somber landscapes, scenes from the daily life of workers and peasants, and an occasional individual study such as *Portrait de Monsieur X*—all of these with heavy shadows outlining contour.

In 1907 both his color and line changed somewhat and he began his great series of clowns and circus people. The faces are as sad as before, but Rouault's colors—though still thickly laid on—are lighter and the forms firmly defined with the heavy black line that is so like the leading of stained glass windows. In his clown and acrobat pictures this line often seems to separate body and limbs into the jointed parts of a marionette. This technique intensifies the suggestion implicit in the paintings that those who entertain the world are detached from it and see it with the disillusioned eyes of their own sorrow and their pity for the world of reality.

A little later Rouault again took up the theme of the judges, remembering the faces of the police magistrates he had earlier observed but depicting with much greater power their heavy stupidity, their dull bestiality. When we see a Rouault picture of a judge we shudderingly ask ourselves who (and by what sanction) dare put such animal venality on high to pass sentence on the unfortunate children of men?

In 1908 Rouault was married. A year or so later he had his first one-man show. During the next few years he painted a variety of subjects—family life, peasants, workers, a few portraits—all of them in heavy brush stroke, thick contour lines, and luminous color, still richly glowing even in the lighter tones. He then began a return to specifically religious subjects.

In 1916 Vollard became his exclusive agent and persuaded him to turn chiefly to illustration. He even fitted up a studio in his own home—ostensibly as a convenience for the painter but perhaps more so he could keep an eye on Rouault's production. Vollard was obsessed with the ambition to produce the most beautiful books in the world, illustrated with great and original art especially created for them. Except for unsurpassable illuminated manuscripts of the Middle Ages, he succeeded in his ambition. No book-making of modern times compares with that of Vollard. He had the farsighted perception that enabled him to select the most advanced and perfect artist for each of his publishing projects. In Rouault he had an amazing artistic amalgamation of the intensely medieval with the completely modern. Aware of this, Vollard loaded the artist with so many projects that Rouault has said: ". . . it would have taken three centuries to bring to perfection the various works. . . ."

Nevertheless, the greatest single body of work produced by Rouault is his series for "Miserere"—an album, rather than a book, of fifty-eight powerful and compassionate etchings and aquatints indicting war and man's inhumanity to man. This magnificent volume is without text save for a brief foreword and captions by Rouault. He worked on this series and other prints, lithographs, monotypes, and etchings for twenty years, during the first decade of which he did little painting. (Pl. XV)

In 1924 Rouault received the ribbon of the Legion of Honor for his service as Curator of the Gustave Moreau Museum.

In 1929 he designed the sets and costumes for Diaghilev's ballet "The Prodigal Son." Early in his acquaintance with Vollard, before the latter had become his agent, he had painted some ceramics and glazed earthenware at the suggestion of the dealer. In 1937 he designed several tapestries.

Since 1932 Rouault has refused to date his canvases, as he often works and reworks them over a period of years before he considers them finished. This stood him in good stead when, in 1947, he brought suit against the heirs of Vollard, who had died in 1939, to recover the 800 unsigned and unsold paintings still in the physical possession of the Vollard estate. The suit was decided in Rouault's favor and the paintings returned to him as his property.

After long and careful consideration of each of these works, Rouault called in the bailiff to witness the burning of 315 of the paintings. There were murmurs from certain quarters of the art world that he had done this to reduce the number of his works and thus make the remainder more valuable. This the artist indignantly and rightly denied; he had destroyed the paintings purely on esthetic grounds. He is not a worldly man, but a deeply religious one whose art has more and more become an instrument and expression of his love for God and man. Since 1940 he has devoted himself almost entirely to religious subjects, which include exalted paintings of the Maid of Orleans. In 1948 he designed stained-glass windows for the village church at Assy, Upper Savoy.

During the past quarter-century Rouault has had one-man exhibitions in Europe and in the United States. In 1951 he was made a Commander of the Legion of Honor. Now in his mid-eighties he continues to work daily, the greatest religious painter of our time.

13 FORM DISINTEGRATES, OBJECT AND SUBJECT DISAPPEAR

HERE WE APPROACH THE BEGINNING OF THE end of an enormous cycle in art—a cycle that, before history was recorded in words, told with crude pictures on caveman walls the story of a hunt or, with ingeniously simple pictographs symbolizing objects or actions, conveyed an idea or a message. Through long years, as each pictograph became more and more identified with a specific idea or object and was therefore quickly recognizable as its symbol, the pictograph grew less and less realistic, finally resolving itself into the hieroglyph and at last into the letter and the word—the word, which is the final *abstraction* of idea or object and bears no visible relation to it even though, millenniums ago, it started from a visual base.

So much for the man of letters, the first abstractionist. But the artist, with caveman ruggedness, stayed with the picture, considering the representation of the actual form of an object worth ten thousand abstract symbols of it—until the expanding and exploding twentieth century dawned and artists began to dissect forms, chop them up, slice them, and then use the component parts as building blocks to put together again the original form—sometimes in almost unrecognizable shape—or else to scramble the dismembered parts into a painting that resembled nothing so much as chaos and old night.

Paradoxically, the movement toward disintegration of form began as a return *to* form and architectonic order. Probably the first indication of this was in the art of Georges Braque. Though he had not shown in the 1905 *Salon d'Automne,* he was early associated with the Fauves. His color was rich and unconventional but not exuberantly wild. Moreover, even at his most colorful, he had from the beginning retained a surer hold on form.

Born near Paris, May 13, 1881, Georges Braque is the son of a house painter and decorator who did landscape-painting on Sundays, sometimes showing his canvases in minor exhibitions.

The Braques moved to Le Havre when Georges was eight and there he spent his boyhood and youth. He knew Dufy and Friesz, and the three future Fauves grew up in an atmosphere of Impressionism. Le Havre was a favorite resort of the leaders of that movement, and the ever-changing scenes of the busy Channel port, its brilliant colors broken into bright facets by choppy waves and brisk dartings-about of big and little boats, were like so many Impressionist paintings waiting to be put on canvas.

With this boyhood legacy of color, Braque also took with him into Fauvism a firmly related sense of form. The new movement did not hold him long; he had too strong a sense of the *logic* of form. Reinforcing it was an instinct for the restraint that results in style. He once said: "I like the rule that corrects emotion." He liked the discipline of working within an area of self-imposed limits, feeling that too much artistic freedom sets a painter adrift in aimless motion like a rudderless ship that never makes it back to port.

He therefore soon decided to limit himself to a very restricted color scale. While still a Fauve he produced two or three canvases in almost a single brilliant color. At the same time, he was delving more and more deeply into the principles that underlie the later paintings of Cézanne. In 1908, in the seven canvases he submitted to the *Salon d'Automne*—chiefly in shades of browns, grays, and subdued greens, with occasional touches of black and white—the Cézanne influence in their "breaking up of nature into cylinders, cones, and spheres" was plainly apparent in emerging geometric forms. Five of the canvases were rejected, and it is legend that Matisse, on the jury, scornfully labeled them "Cubist!"

Braque withdrew the entire seven and put them with other canvases on exhibition at his dealer's. Again they received the new label; in *Gil Blas* of November 14, 1908, the critic complained that Braque had reduced all form to "little cubes." Six months later, reviewing Braque's paintings at the *Indépendants*, the same critic referred to them as "jumbles of cubes." And so the name for the most important art movement of the twentieth century came into being. (Pl. XV)

Important in and of itself as a separate art movement, Cubism's transcendant importance lies in the train of art development it set in motion and of which it was the immediate or the underlying cause. Whether these new movements—Futurism, Suprematism, Abstractionism, etc.—came as action or reaction, Cubism was their catapulting force, and their effects have visually permeated twentieth-century living in the form of architecture, furniture, industrial, typographical, and many other fields of design such as jewelry, textiles, and chinaware. Everything that has modern shape or pattern in the world we live in today has the roots of its design in the original Cubist determination to discover and *uncover*, to rearrange or even to disarrange the essential form that underlies outward appearance.

Cubism had two originators. In the autumn of 1907 Braque met a young Spaniard, Pablo Picasso, who had first visited Paris in 1900 and had settled there in 1904. Although the big world of patrons and established art dealers was still unaware of him, Picasso had a wide acquaintance among other young struggling artists of Paris and with avant-garde poets, writers, and musicians. In 1906 he had met Matisse and although Picasso denies that it was the older artist who introduced him to African Negro sculpture—stating that he suddenly discovered it for himself a year later—it was due to the enthusiasm of Matisse and, to a lesser extent, of Derain, that the primitive distortions and simplifications of African sculpture during this period were beginning to impinge on the general consciousness of all the young and progressive artists in Paris.

Three years earlier, on one of his periodic returns to Spain, Picasso had made a self-discovery of El Greco, whose impact on him became apparent in a slight elongation and attenuation in the figure painting of his "Blue Period." These two influences—El Greco angularity and African sculpture distortion—plus his familarity with the archaic stiffness of early Iberian sculpture and his analytical study of Cézanne's later works, combined to produce one of the most important paintings of modern art: *Les Demoiselles d'Avignon,* which is now referred to (with a certain amount of artistic license) as "the first Cubist picture." (Pl. XVI)

Picasso began *Les Demoiselles* (it was not named until a dozen or more years after it was finished, when a friend titled it in ironic reference to a "street of joy" in Barcelona) in 1906, making many preliminary sketches and studies. He finished the huge canvas in 1907 and although it was not publicly exhibited until thirty years later, it was known and studied not only by the artists of Picasso's generation but also for three decades by many younger ones arriving in Paris from all over the world, for whom Picasso's studio was a mecca.

It was not until after Picasso had finished *Les Demoiselles* that he met Braque. They became the leaders of a group of artists and writers who used a small Montmartre restaurant as a rendezvous where by two o'clock in the morn-

ing the air would be blue with tobacco smoke and charged
with the electric vitality of new ideas. "It was in this room,"
states Vlaminck, "that Cubism was born." At least it was
nurtured there by the exchange of ideas, arguments, ponti-
fications on what was old and avid interest in what was new
on the art scene, and particularly by analytical discussions
of the primitive art of many different cultures and races. The
first decade and a half of the new century was the seedtime
of new expression in the arts, and Paris was the hotbed for
their rapid early growth.

These artists and writers were not dilettantes blowing soap
bubbles of thinly iridescent sophistry. Many of them were
brilliant—some of them profound—thinkers and accomplish-
ers. Through their thinking, their discussions, and their experimentation they projected their aim and their ideal in
words: "Creation, not imitation," and in works that "create
new combinations of known elements," as Juan Gris, who
was to become with Picasso and Braque one of the three
great Cubists, expressed it.

The new art movement finally accepted the title bestowed
in scorn and exasperation and, in 1911, began to exhibit under the name of Cubism. In its first phase, later called Analytical Cubism, the painter broke up any recognizable object—a face, a violin, a table—into cubes which he then
reassembled like building blocks in pseudo three-dimensional
sculptural form. There are no *cubes* either in Cézanne's paintings or in his famous statement about resolving nature into
its basic forms of "cylinders, cones, and spheres"—for the
very good reason that nature does not come in squared-off
blocks. But once on the scent of the geometry that underlies appearance, the analytical Braque and the inventive Picasso followed it far afield. (Pl. XVII)

After their initial sculpturesque method of rebuilding forms
with cubes, Braque and Picasso became absorbed in juggling
their cubes in arrangements of the basic interior *structure* of

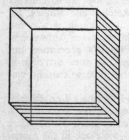

a figure or an object. The next step
came when their "building blocks"
or cubes began to flatten into two-
dimensional shapes arranged in
overlapping planes that appear to
move back or forward or sideways
through the artist's manipulation of
subtly juxtaposed light and dark
facets. In its simplest form—as
many a child studying drawing
learns to his delight—this illusory
movement can be approximated by

Picasso:
The Three Musicians,
1921

PHILADELPHIA
MUSEUM OF ART

Picasso:
The Frugal Repast,
1904

MUSEUM OF MODERN ART

Picasso:
Variation on
"Les Femmes
d'Alger"
by Delacroix,
1955

PLATE XVII

PHILADELPHIA MUSEUM OF ART
Duchamp:
Nude Descending a Staircase,
No. II, *1912*

COURTESY FRENCH EMBASSY
PRESS AND INFORMATION
Modigliani: Nude, *1917*

PLATE XVIII

Leger:
Composition,
1944

COURTESY FRENCH
EMBASSY PRESS
AND INFORMATION

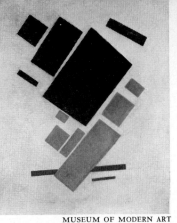

Malevitch:
Suprematist Composition, *1914*

Mondrian:
Composition, *1925*

Malevitch:
Suprematist Composition:
White on White, *c. 1918*

PLATE XIX

Kandinsky:
Light Form No. 166,
1913

Burchfield:
The Interurban
Line,
1920

MUSEUM
OF MODERN ART

Benton:
Homestead,
1934

MUSEUM
OF MODERN ART

Hopper:
New York Movie,
1939

MUSEUM OF
MODERN ART

PLATE XX

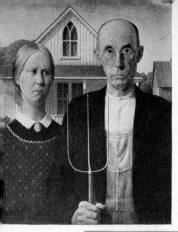

Wood: American Gothic, *1930*

Sheeler:
Architectural
Cadences,
1954

Marin:
Off Cape Split,
Maine, *1938*

PLATE XXI

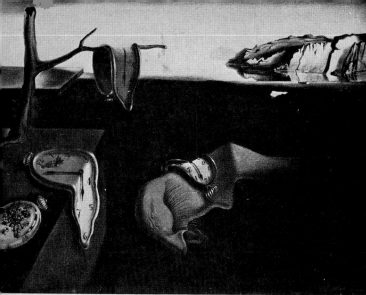

Dali: The Persistence of Memory, *1931*   MUSEUM OF MODERN ART

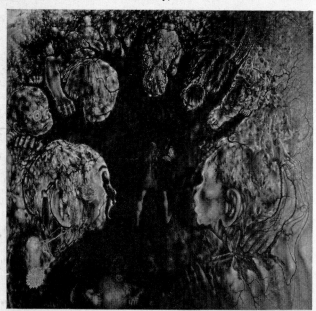

Tchelitchew: Hide-and-Seek, *1940-42*   MUSEUM OF MODERN ART

PLATE XXII

Chagall: Birthday, *1915-23*

Klee: Letter Ghost, *1937*

PLATE XXIII

Tamayo: Women of Tehuantepec, *1939*

Siqueiros: Echo of a
Scream, *1937*

Rivera: Flower Festival—
Feast of Santa Anita, *1931*

PLATE XXIV

Orozco: Prometheus, *1930*

Orozco: Five Heads—The Scientist

PLATE XXV

Bacon: Painting, *1946*

Austin: The Tiger,
1941

PLATE XXVI

Rousseau: The Sleeping Gypsy, *1897*

Hicks: The Peaceable Kingdom

PLATE XXVII

Rothko: No. 10, *1950*

PLATE XXVIII

Pollock: No. 1, *1948*

Kline: The Chief, *1950*

PLATE XXIX

De Kooning: Woman I, *1950-1952*

Vickrey: Conversation, *1955*

Beckmann: Departure, *1932-35*

PLATE XXX

Grosz: The Grey Man Dances,
1949

Shahn: Epoch, *1950*

Salemme: Caught in the Equinox, *1953*

PLATE XXXI

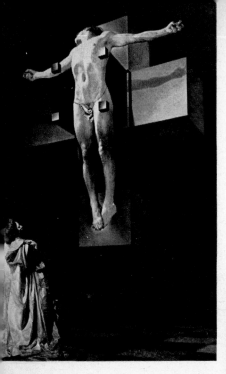

Dali: The Crucifixion,
1955

METROPOLITAN MUSEUM
OF ART

Albright:
That Which I Should Have Done,
I Did Not Do,
1942

COLLECTION, MRS. IVAN L. ALBRIGHT

PLATE XXXII

the shaded drawing of a cube which, as the eye fixes on it, seems to shift its planes from top to bottom or from side to side, advancing to and receding from the viewer.

Although Braque introduced angles and blocks into his earliest Cubist landscapes, both he and Picasso soon turned chiefly toward man-made objects such as tables, musical instruments, chairs, dice, bottles, etc. Nevertheless, they constantly played cubistically with the human face and figure. And they worked so closely together—interchanging ideas, trading techniques, catching fire from each other's inspirations—that it is not always easy to distinguish between the paintings of one and the other.

In their determination to force form to speak for itself—no matter how they shattered or distorted it—they largely abandoned color, adopting a monochromatic palette of pale tans shading into browns, or variations of gray. At the same time, they abandoned the picture-frame or proscenium-arch presentation and invited the viewer to step *inside* the painting —or at least walk around it, as in the arena theatre—and look at it from all angles *simultaneously*. Thus, on the *frontal* representation of a face, they would impose the *profile* of the nose; on a profile they might show the eye, full view. Years later this simultaneity of vision was developed by Picasso into his double-image faces. (Pl. XVI)

After a few years of tearing down an object to its basic forms and extracting or abstracting some of those forms to rebuild in a different pattern a structure that might or might not bear a faint resemblance to the original object, a reversal of method slowly developed into what came to be called Synthetic Cubism. It began as an unconscious or subconscious reaction to the disintegrating process of Analytical Cubism, which finally reached its austere end when nothing was left of the object with which the artist had started except a fragment of its form—a curve or two resembling perhaps the partial outline of a guitar, its frets indicated by check marks one above the other, its strings by parallel lines beginning and ending in blank space. One day the Cubist—it may have been Braque, it may have been Picasso—decided to *begin* all over again at the end of Analytical Cubism, as it obviously could go no further along the road of disintegration. Arbitrarily selecting or *abstracting* one or more recognizable fragments of an object—violin strings, part of a chair, a few bars of printed music, etc.—he painted them on his canvas as the nucleus around which he wove a two-dimensional composition around and over and through the fragments somewhat as a pianist will take a musical phrase and improvise on it. Thus the object—or clearly recognizable parts of it—came back into the picture, painted very realistically. Suddenly pleased with this reverse trend, Braque went a step further and exceeded realism by using *trompe l'oeil* or fool-the-eye technique. He began painting into the composition parts of headlines that looked as though they had been torn from newspapers; he cunningly introduced imitative wood grainings, nails, and other bits and pieces that appeared so real that those who looked at the paintings could not resist testing them with fingertips.

At this point Braque asked himself: Why *paint* a representation of an object? Why not use the object itself or a portion of it? Whereupon, he and Picasso began to paste bits of objects on a canvas or board—a scrap of newspaper, part of a playing card, a torn matchbox cover, even a rag—surrounding them with painted compositions, sometimes only a snatch of color or a few lines. Thus *collage* or paper-pasting was born, and the Cubist circle fetched full around. First the actual object, then the representational or realistic painting of it, the breaking up—in paint—of the realistic form into cubes and planes, the reassembling of the cubes into an approximate form of the object, the flattening out of the cubes into overlapping planes through which it is almost impossible to trace even an approximate form of the object, the extracting or abstracting of a faintly recognizable fragment of the object, and at last a return to the actual object or fragment of it pasted smack on the canvas—and we're right back one step *behind* where we started!

It might be well to quote here a pertinent observation made by Picasso more than twenty years ago:

> The fact that for a long time Cubism has not been understood and that even today there are people who cannot see anything in it means nothing. I do not read English, an English book is a blank book to me. This does not mean that the English language does not exist. Why should I blame anyone but myself if I cannot understand what I know nothing about?

That is profoundly true and very much to the point. But to be able to read a book in the language in which it is written does not necessarily imply the obligation to agree with what one reads or even the capacity to enjoy it. That is up to the individual and his responses. The understanding reader —or viewer—is free to accept or reject as words or picture create individual response.

The period of Analytical, sometimes referred to as "high" Cubism was roughly from 1908 to about 1912. Then Synthetic Cubism began to dominate and, with it, a strong interest in textures, either painted in simulation or actually pasted on the composition. Picasso, who in his early Cubist experiments had used sculpture as one of his mediums, now began to play with constructions of colored paper folded or cut to resemble parts of objects. Assembling these paper pieces, he glued them to board or cardboard to form three-dimensional compositions, a new phase of the paper-pasting or *collages* he and Braque had originated.

All of this would seem rather childish were it not that from such creative play came important developments. But first World War I intervened.

Artists are not prophets. Sometimes their works are curiously prophetic. One day at the beginning of the war, Picasso was walking along the Boulevard Raspail with Gertrude Stein, American expatriate whose home in Paris was a center of hospitality for so many struggling, unrecognized young artists destined to become the "greats" of modern art. Suddenly a strangely painted truck rumbled by—the first of a camouflaged fleet. Picasso stared in amazement, relates Miss Stein, then cried out: "Yes! It is *we* who made it! That is Cubism!"

José Victoriano González, who adopted the pseudonym "Juan Gris," has been termed "the most Cubist of the Cubists." Born in Madrid in 1887, he settled in Paris in 1906, in the same building where Picasso had his studio. His art had its foundation in his study of the Old Masters and the paintings of Cézanne and Seurat, the work of the two modern masters becoming the point of departure for his own painting. Instead of digging down through nature or an object to its architectonic base, he deliberately built up from that base, his forms taking shape as he organized space on his canvas. He said: "Cézanne goes *toward* architecture. I start out from it." Instead of Cézanne's painted implication that a bottle pictured on his canvas has basically a cylindrical shape, Gris painted a bottle where his basic design demanded a cylinder.

Gris did not fully accept the limited palette of Analytical Cubism. His colors were always rich, although more subdued in his earliest Cubist canvases. Because of their exquisitely ordered arrangement—no matter how unorthodox the shapes and juxtapositions there is never a sense of jumbled disorder —and their satisfying harmonies of color—never cloying, never commonplace, but always rich or delicate—Gris's canvases are the jewels of Cubist painting.

Between 1914 and 1917 color returned to Picasso's Cubist canvases. In 1921 he painted the masterpiece of his Cubist period, *The Three Musicians* (he did two very similar versions of it), which is generally considered the peak of Cubism. (Pl. XVII)

Braque served with courageous distinction in World War I. He was wounded and had to undergo a head operation. After the War he seemed to lose for a period his tight grasp on form, painting instead in large flat areas of color. Then his work entered a somewhat Classic phase and in 1927 he introduced bright colors. For several years he moved between real objects (though never realistic painting) and near-abstraction; these were side paths in his progress toward the color orchestration and masterful organization of form that constitute his mature style. He designed sets for several ballets and in 1939 experimented in sculpture. He has had many exhibitions and, still living and working in Paris, is today one of the elder statesmen of modern art.

Fernand Léger, a big, genial Norman born at Argentan February 4, 1881, was apprenticed at sixteen to an architect in Brittany. Between 1900 and 1902 he was a draftsman in a Paris architect's office. After a year's military service in the Engineer Corps, he studied under a *Beaux-Arts* Academician and in two or three independent studios, meanwhile earning his living as a photo-retoucher. During the next few years his art developed under various influences—Matisse and Cézanne being the strongest. His architectural training made him particularly responsive to Cézanne. But he was a man and an artist of such strong individuality that he never adapted to an influence; rather he adapted the influence to his own artistic ends. (Pl. XVIII)

By association, he was accounted one of the Cubists and in 1910 and later exhibited with members of that group. He was never dominated by Cubist techniques or theories, though his early expert handling of form in geometric shapes bore a surface resemblance to Cubism.

Serving at the front in World War I, he was gassed near Verdun and was invalided out. The following year (1917) his painting entered the mechanistic phase—perhaps as a result of his service in the Transport Corps with its big war machines—that was largely to characterize it from then on. Even when he had been most closely associated with the Cubists, Léger's forms had never been superimposed one upon another, nor had they ever overlapped in Cubist fashion. And he had never accepted the Cubist monochrome palette although, like Gris, his early cubelike (rather than Cubist) paintings had been more subdued in color than his later ones. Now, as mechanistic elements began to dominate, his colors became bright and clear and his forms disjointed. He painted even human beings, their backgrounds and the articles of their daily life, in terms of machines and machine parts—cylinders, crank shafts, steel coils, casings. When he brought nature into his compositions, a tree trunk became a curving chimney pipe, flowers stiffened into wrought iron, clouds resembled metal balls. In later years, as his painting became more abstract, he permitted plant life slightly more freedom. He has also painted in purely abstract forms—notably, his huge decorations for the auditorium of the General Assembly of the United Nations.

In 1923-24, Léger was one of the creators of the famous short film *Ballet Mécanique* in which man-made objects—chiefly metal kitchenware and occasional machine parts—are mobilized in mechanical jazz movements. Saucepan tops, tea kettles, dishpans, springs, tin spoons, knives and forks, whirl, spin, bob up and down, march in formation, tumble and bounce in crazy dance rhythms. It is a delightfully artistic performance, a demonstration of the exciting possibilities of abstract form in motion, for even a tumbling tea kettle takes on an abstract quality.

Léger first visited the United States in 1931 and, as would be expected, was highly pleased with the architecture, the mechanistic forms, and above all, the dynamic quality of New York City, where he spent most of his time. On his return to France, he created designs for a ballet at the Paris Opera and did a large mural painting for the Paris World's Fair of 1937. From December 1940 to December 1945 he lived in the United States where, in addition to other paintings, he produced a series of acrobats and bicyclists.

After his return to Paris he worked in mosaic, created designs for opera and ballet décor and costumes, produced ceramics, and designed stained glass windows—at the same time not neglecting his easel painting. In his seventy-fifth year, still working vigorously in Paris, he was producing large canvases of giant machine forms and their human equivalents when suddenly, in August 1955, he died of a heart attack.

"We will sing the love of danger, the habit of energy and boldness . . . courage, audacity, and rebellion. . . . We will extol aggressive movement, feverish insomnia, the double-quick step, the somersault, the box on the ear, fisticuffs. We will declare that the splendor of the world has been enriched by a new beauty—the beauty of speed. A racing motor-car, its frame adorned with great pipes like snakes with explosive breath—a roaring motor-car that seems to run on shrapnel is more beautiful than the Victory of Samothrace. . . . We will glorify War, the only Health-Giver of the world, Militarism, Patriotism, the Destructive Art of the Anarchist, Ideas that Kill, Contempt for Women. . . . On then, Good Incendiaries! Fire the libraries! Turn the floods into the museums —let the famous pictures float! We cast our Challenge to the Stars!"

That voice out of Italy is not Mussolini's. It preceded by more than a decade the public assault of Il Duce's vocal cords on the air waves. The bombastic—and prophetically sinister —declaration issued from the Italian poet F. T. Marinetti in the form of the "Futurist Manifesto" published in Paris in *Le Figaro*, February 22, 1909. At the time Mussolini was only twenty-six and as yet unheard of.

The Manifesto was given to the editor of *Le Figaro* by Gino Severini, one of five Italian artists whose new aim in art Marinetti formulated in words—glorification of the future (hence the name), derogation of the past, and deification of the dynamic present. The following year, in Turin, the artists proclaimed their own "Manifesto of Futurist Painters" which echoed the Marinetti Manifesto but was more specific in detail: "All the truth learned in the schools and studios are abolished for us. Our hands are free and pure, to start everything afresh. We declare that there can be no modern painting except from the starting point of an absolutely modern sensation—'painting' and 'sensation' are two inseparable words. . . . The gesture we seek to represent on canvas will no longer be an arrested movement . . . all is in a state of flux, of headlong change . . . objects in movement multiply themselves endlessly and become distorted as they overflow each other like vibrations launched into space and weaving through it. Thus a trotting horse has not four legs but twenty and their movements are triangular. . . ."

The artists who signed this Manifesto were Giacomo Balla, Umberto Boccioni, Carlo D. Carra, Luigi Russolo, and Gino Severini. Although they denounced Cubism as static they were under a somewhat similar compulsion to take objects apart and put them together again. But with this difference: the Cubist broke down objects to get at structural (but not realistic) form; the Futurists to uncover "lines of force" and then, as they rebuilt the object, to extend it in the direction of the force-lines. In the most fully realized Futurist paintings these force-lines converge upon the sensation of the spectator, driving him into the center of action where a simultaneity of movement overwhelms him—or is supposed to. At least that was the theory. And it is true that these paintings achieve frenetic motion from repetitive series of forms progressively changing as they plunge forward.

Except for Carra, whose work both in geometrical shapes and subdued color more nearly resembled early Cubism than did that of his fellow-artists, the Futurists embodied the kinetic shapes on their canvases in magnificently rich and varied, but completely controlled color. In its most elementary form, Futurism depicts simple forward motion by a multiplicity of nearly similar, slightly overlapping images— very like a series of stroboscopic camera shots of a person walking or running. Or like a strip of motion picture film. An amusing example of this simple form of Futurism is Balla's *Running Dog*, owned by A. Conger Goodyear of New York. Just as clear, but somewhat more complex because of its Cubist elements, is Marcel Duchamp's *Nude Descending a Staircase;* the Futurists' statement that the forward motion of a leg takes a triangular shape is plainly demonstrated in this painting.

Far more complex is Boccioni's *States of Mind I: The Farewells,* in which numerous objects such as a steam engine, signal towers, bridges, railroad lamps, tunnels, curving roads, and many other pictorial elements rush forward, in and around, above and below, one another. Although these elements press toward one another and sometimes overlap, the forcelines are clear indications of directional impulses no matter how complex the movement; and the colors of each element, however dazzlingly juxtaposed, have—unlike many Cubist paintings—lineal boundaries and never slop over these boundaries as in bad color-printing.

As a movement, Futurism did not make many converts. But it indirectly enriched certain aspects of Cubism, and some of its effects were seized upon by the Dadaists and Surrealists. It had a rather feeble offshoot in Vorticism, an art manifestation too slight to be called a movement, which was confined to England for its short and unimportant life.

Stressing as it did the accelerated speed, electric vitality, and machine dynamism of the new century, Futurism was an expression of its time. And it was certainly the world's most striking example of the occasional prophetic role played by art. By more than a decade it unknowingly forecast—in specific detail in its Manifestos—the Fascist movement that was to overwhelm the land from which Futurism sprang.

As applied particularly to painting, the word abstract has two meanings. The lesser one employs abstract as a verb in the sense that the Cubists, for example, *abstracted* or took from an object some element or part of its form as a theme around which to build a composition, or to enrich one. The other use of the word is adjectival, describing a work of art that bears no relation to any real object. It is chiefly in the latter sense that the term Abstract or Abstractionism is here used. An alternate term is Non-Objective Art.

Abstract or Non-Objective Art has two major divisions (and many subdivisions) which may be designated Abstract Expressionism and Geometric Abstractionism. There have been two great leaders of these divisions: Wassily Kandinsky and Piet Mondrian. (Pl. XIX)

Kandinsky (Moscow 1866-Paris 1944) lived for a time as a child in Rome and in Florence. Returning to Moscow, he studied political economy and law. When he was twenty-three he visited Paris for the first time. Seven years later he gave up his career to go to Munich to study painting. He became so proficient that he opened a school, but from 1903 to 1907 he traveled a good deal—Tunis, Holland, Italy—and in 1904 exhibited in the *Salon d'Automne*. By 1908 a change —a looseness of form, a trend away from even the realism of Expressionism—was evident in his painting. In 1910 he produced his first purely abstract canvas—a vivid explosion of disjointed, unrelated, and entirely nonrealistic color-shapes.

He had arrived at this, he said, in two ways: One day the variegated colored spots of a woman's dress suddenly suggested the esthetic possibilities of color alone creating form without help from any realistic shapes; about this time, also, he entered his studio one morning and was astonished to see leaning against the wall a canvas that had no recognizable meaning or shapes but was beautiful in color-form alone. He soon realized that when he had left the studio the night before, he had inadvertently set the canvas—a landscape— upside down against the wall. From then on, he improvised in color and abstract form, likening his art to music and developing the theory that by abandoning all imitation of visual nature and material reality, painting could come nearer to expressing the inner reality of the soul.

With mystical fervor he both painted and spoke his new doctrine. He had been founder and co-leader, with the magnificent German painter Franz Marc, of the Munich group of artists called the Blue Knights or Blue Riders (*Blaue Reiter*), which published an art periodical. Although not many other members adopted his new method of painting, the group wholeheartedly supported him, publishing his articles and exhibiting his paintings. In a remarkably short time he attained international fame. His book "The Art of Spiritual Harmony" was translated into English by Sir Michael Sadler, who wrote in his foreword: "Kandinsky is painting music . . . he has broken down the barrier between music and painting and has isolated the pure emotion."

This was—and is—the effect of Kandinsky's paintings not

alone on the esthetically aware but on people with no knowledge of art and little appreciation of it. They are not confused or angered by the breaking up, distortion, or falsifying of things they know as real. Entirely free from reality, Kandinsky's painting did not take liberties with it. And there was no need to search for—and be baffled by not finding—its *meaning*. It obviously had no more meaning than a summer's day or the trill of a meadow lark, though Kandinsky's painting is always much more dynamic than either. It falls upon the eye like stirring sound and magnificent chords upon the ear.

World War I cut short the development of art in Germany. Kandinsky returned to Russia where in 1918 he was made a member of the Arts Section for Popular Culture and taught in the Moscow Academy of Fine Arts. In 1919 he was appointed director of the Museum of Pictorial Culture. Two years later he founded the Academy of Arts and Sciences of All the Russias. In the three-year period between 1918 and 1921, progressive modern art was not only permitted but encouraged to flourish in Russia. Then the cultural climate changed abruptly. Only the dullest traditional art was tolerated. Modern art—as a dozen years later was to happen in Germany—was denounced as tainted with the degeneracy of the democracies. Kandinsky returned to Germany.

There in 1922 he was elected a professor of art at the Weimar Bauhaus, fountainhead of the great modern art movement in Germany until Hitler came to power. Kandinsky was very active in Germany for eight years, then began to travel widely—Egypt, Turkey, Greece, Italy, France. He had a one-man exhibition in Paris and settled there near the end of 1933. The fifty-seven works he had left in Germany were labeled degenerate and in 1937 were confiscated by the Hitler government. Kandinsky died in France in 1944. Fortunately for Americans, the richest collection of his works is owned by New York's Guggenheim Museum where they are often on exhibition. (Pl. XIX)

While Kandinsky was developing Abstract Expressionism, a fellow-countryman, Kasimir Malevich (Russia 1878-France 1935), was working toward Geometric Abstractionism. Since 1910 he had been painting with the Cubists. Earlier, he had been influenced by Fauvism. He was tending somewhat in the direction of Léger, in so far as form and color were concerned, although he was not so fascinated by machinery. He showed Léger-influenced paintings in the 1912 Blue Rider Exhibition in Munich. Suddenly, the following year, he decided to discard all reference to reality, meaning, and emotion, to purge his canvases of all but geometry and, at least in the beginning, to have done with color, too. (Pl. XIX)

He called his new art "Suprematism—the supremacy of pure sensitivity or perception." He placed black squares on a white background, went a step further and put black circles on white. He reached a peak of purgation and purity in painting a white square on a white background, appropriately calling the composition *White on White*. He later worked out more complicated arrangements of squares, circles and rectangles, using some color. But all his compositions are austere. He said, "Suprematism compresses all of painting into a black square on a white canvas. I did not have to invent anything. It was the absolute night I felt in me; in that, I perceived creation and I called it Suprematism. It expresses itself in the black plane in the form of a square."

Crazy? The words attempting to define his art are perhaps a trifle overwrought. But the far-reaching effect of his painting we see around us daily in the typography of newspapers and magazines—the editorial and particularly the advertising layout—we see it in modern architecture, poster design, in the proportions of iceless refrigerators and electric stoves. The influence stems not alone from Malevich, but he was the first artist to put on canvas those abstract relationships that have since been absorbed into modern design.

In 1917 two Dutch artists, Piet Mondrian and Theo van Doesburg, were the principal organizers of a group of artists who set themselves the task of using geometrical proportions, particularly the rectangle, as the design basis for painting, sculpture, and architecture. They published a magazine called *De Stijl* and the group came to be known by that name. Van Doesburg was a many-sided artist—painter, sculptor, architect, writer. His method in working out an abstract composition was to start with a natural object—say a cow—and, without changing the basic shape, subtract (rather than abstract) realistic details in a step-by-step process until he reached the pure geometrical form; in the case of a cow, a rectangle.

Mondrian, who since 1910 had worked in Paris in close association with Picasso and the Cubists, began in 1913— the year of the Malevich revelation—to reduce Cubism to pure geometrical forms. During World War I he was in Holland, but in 1918 returned to Paris, where he had an immediate influence on two French painters, Ozenfant and Jeanneret. (The latter, far more famous as an architect than as a painter, adopted the name of Le Corbusier for his work in architecture.) These two were already at work developing a theory to "purify" Cubism of what they considered its disorganized, decorative impulses. Their theory, which they named "Purism," became part of the general movement toward geometry and extended into the fields of architecture, industrial design, etc. Actually, the three movements—Suprematism, De Stijl, and Purism—with minor differences and ramifications, all rested on the common base of geometry and had a combined and powerful effect on the entire range of twentieth-century design. (Pl. XIX)

In France Le Corbusier through his architecture became the leader of the new esthetic. In Germany a great art school spread its influence on an international scale—the famous Bauhaus established in Weimar in 1919 by a consolidation of the Art Academy with the Arts and Crafts School. This was accomplished under the leadership of Walter Gropius, young German architect who had conceived the plan while serving at the front in World War I. The basic idea of the Bauhaus was the amalgamation of the esthetics of the visual arts with the needs of mass production. It was a complete art and industrial design school—architecture, painting, theatre, typography, photography, and all fields of industrial design. News of the Bauhaus spread over Europe with amazing rapidity and drew to it teachers—such as Kandinsky—of international repute. The school outgrew its combination quarters at Weimar and moved to Dessau into a magnificently modern building designed for its multiple uses by Walter Gropius.

Its influence and reputation mounted until Hitler came to power. Modern art and modern architecture were anathema to him; he designated them bolshevistic and degenerate. Teachers and students fled, not all of them escaping. Hitler crowned his victory over modern architecture by turning the Bauhaus into a school for Nazi propaganda, while his local cohorts did their bit by perching a peaked roof atop the highest section of its functionally flat roof. But Der Fuehrer was unable to conquer the Bauhaus spirit or kill its influence. The dispersal of its teachers and students was the scattering of its seed to take root and flourish in distant lands.

In addition to the tremendous influence of Geometric Abstract painting, which had its roots in Cubism, another growth from that prolific plant came through collage, the paper-pasting technique originated by Braque and Picasso. Called Constructivism, the new movement developed between 1918 and 1921 in Russia where, in addition to its other forms of expression, it brought in an entirely new concept of stage design—also called Constructivism—which spread from Russia to Germany and thence to other countries.

Although far more allied to sculpture, Constructivism had its origin in Cubist painting and particularly in the three-dimensional collages produced by Picasso. Carried much further, it was the creation of entirely abstract, nonrepresentational objects (mere language gives up with a sputter when confronted with the necessity of supplying a word for an object that is *not* an object!) concocted of a wide range of materials—wood, celluloid, wire, glass, string, various plastics, and different metals. Tatlin, Gabo and Pevsner—all of Russia and the latter two brothers—were the originators, about 1918, of Constructivism as a movement separate from collage which, although obviously the origin of Constructivism, was just as obviously only an adjunct to Cubist painting. Gabo, now working in Paris, and Pevsner, in London, are today still the leaders of the movement and are very great artists. In fact, it is in their creations, far more than in any painting, that Geometric Abstractionism reaches its greatest beauty and the purest expression of forms in space.

All these bewildering varieties of art, this avalanche of isms—excepting only the paintings of Kandinsky and his lesser followers—sprang from the womb of Cubism, mother of many twentieth-century art forms. In its finest painting, Abstract Expressionism conveys emotion to the spectator. Geometric Abstract painting, however, conveys nothing except possibly the sense of order one finds in the diagrams illustrating a textbook on geometry. But those diagrams mean something, whereas Geometric Abstractionism sets out to rob painting of all reference to reality, meaning and emotion. It succeeded in superlative degree, although no one questions its immense value to all modern design.

Geometric Abstract painting brought to a close the enormous art cycle curving back to the crudest cave drawings and the earliest pictographs. Art began with those first attempts at communication through visual symbols. Through ages of development, it reached in Geometric Abstractionism the point of complete non-communication. Also the point of no return? A possible answer will be indicated about midway of the twentieth century, when Abstractionism, particularly in the United States, almost snowed under all other forms of modern painting.

In its early phases, however, Abstractionism by no means dominated modern art. There were many other movements and submovements.

14 PICASSO, GIANT OF MODERN ART

> *A creator is not in advance of his generation but he is the first of his contemporaries to be conscious of what is happening to his generation.*
>
> Gertrude Stein: *Picasso*

THE MOST FAMOUS LIVING ARTIST, THE MAN who in himself encompasses almost the entire range of modern art in this century, in 1956 rounded out six decades as a professional artist. Pablo Picasso is already a legend. He was born October 25, 1881, in Málaga, on the Mediterranean coast of Spain. His father's family was from the Basque country in the Pyrenees of northern Spain. His mother was of Genoese descent. As a boy, Picasso was known as Pablo Ruiz but early in his painting career he added his mother's name to his signature—"P. Ruiz Picasso"—then shortened it by dropping his father's name. (Pls. I, XVI, XVII)

From a very early age the boy showed extraordinary talent. His father, an art teacher, guided his studies until in 1896 he passed the entrance tests for the Barcelona Academy, taking a single day for an examination so difficult that a whole month was ordinarily allowed for its completion. A few months later he repeated this prodigious performance at Madrid. But he soon grew bored with the sterile atmosphere of the Madrid Academy and returned to Barcelona to set himself up as an independent artist at the age of sixteen. His work was somewhat influenced by the prevailing wind from Paris—Impressionism—though earlier, in his even more youthful art student days, it had shown remarkable realistic vigor and amazing maturity. He had his first exhibition in Barcelona in 1897, when he was sixteen. That same year the first article about his work was published in an art magazine.

A few days before he was nineteen he went for the first time to Paris, where he stayed for about two months during the World's Fair. While there, he sold three sketches to the owner of a small but eventually important gallery. As a result of the young artist's first flight from his native land, his work took on a temporary tinge—both in color and in subject matter—of Toulouse-Lautrec, the current Paris talk-of-the-town.

For three years Picasso alternated between Spain and France, his output prolific. In the spring of 1904 he settled in Paris, taking a studio in a battered Montmartre tenement known to its inhabitants—poets, painters, laundresses, actors, underpaid clerks, etc.—as "The Floating Laundry" (*Le Bateau Lavoir*). There for five years Picasso lived the life of the complete Bohemian, usually hungry though never quite starving. But life was full and vivid, for he was part of that circle of vigorous newcomers in the arts—painting, music, writing—which was to have such an effect, funneling out through Paris, on the cultural life of the world during the next half-century.

In 1901 Vollard had given him a small exhibition, his first in Paris. It was not a success, the critics coldly regarding him as an imitator of other artists. But he was not imitating. He was assimilating. At intervals during the next few years there were many artists—old and modern masters, archaic and primitive sculpture—he tasted and tried. Most of them he rejected. A few he assimilated so rapidly that they were lost in the blood-stream of his own art. But in his first Paris exhibition, when he was only twenty, there were traces of those whom, like Lautrec, he had not quite digested. It was these traces that the critics pounced upon. They had no sooner pounced, however, than Picasso slid out from under their disdain in the beginning of that series of amazingly differentiated forms of art that came to be known as his famous "periods."

1901-1904: *Blue Period.* Shuttling about wherever he could find lodging—Paris, Barcelona, Málaga, Madrid—Picasso produced a stream of paintings of the poor, the dejected, the rejected: acrobats, street musicians, underfed children, cripples, work-weary women, sad harlequins, blind beggars, poverty-stricken family groups. Omitting almost all background detail, he painted the pictures of this period in a grayish-blue monochrome shading from light to dark. (Pl. XVII Center)

1905-1906: *Harlequin or Rose Period.* Early in 1905 Picasso's palette began to take on brighter, more rosy hues, as did his life. His interest in circus people—particularly the *saltimbanques,* or acrobats—continued, but they were not the dejected creatures of his previous canvases. And instead of the array of poor souls who fill his "Blue" canvases, subjects of more cheerful, though hardly jolly, aspect people his paintings—a boy leading a horse, women combing their hair, a little nude girl with a basket of flowers. They appear to have more flesh on their bones, too, than the frail, sadly ethereal earlier ones, and are painted with more classic roundness and solidity, instead of with the faintly El Greco elongations of the Blue Period. It must be admitted, however, that many of the "Blue" paintings—though damned as sentimental—are among the most appealing and popular of all Picasso's work. But life was growing brighter—and better provisioned —and his canvases reflected it. Perceptive collectors—among them the expatriate Americans, Gertrude Stein and her brother Leo—began to notice his work and toward the end of 1905 a wealthy Russian merchant started slowly to buy, remaining his patron until the outbreak of World War I. In 1905 Vollard cast a series of Picasso's sculptures in bronze.

1907-1908: *Iberian-African Negro Period*. This was a decisive year in Picasso's art. He departed from the rather loose realist-naturalism, stamped of course with his strong individuality, that had characterized his work through its various developments up to now. He was never to return to it. The influence of archaic Iberian sculpture (which Picasso studied in the Louvre rather than in Spain) shows not only in his major canvas of the period, *Les Demoiselles d'Avignon*, but is reflected in his portrait of Gertrude Stein. In *Les Demoiselles* an equally noticeable influence is that of African Negro sculpture. It is even more apparent in the distortions, the barbaric interplay of angles, and the hatched shadings of the masklike faces of the smaller canvases and studies that followed the big painting. The great importance of this year, however, lies in the fact that during it the artist came of age. Through the many widely varying periods of the next four decades, he is to demonstrate an ability to turn at will momentarily from the style on which he has currently been concentrating, perhaps for years, and produce a work in a previous style. Or he will several times pick up and lay aside a long-continuing style—such as Cubism—while successive new styles engage his attention. Yet it is noticeable that he never goes back beyond this decisive year of 1907-08 when he attained full maturity as an artist, although he had not yet passed his twenty-seventh birthday as a man. (Pl. XVI Bottom)

1909-1913: *Analytical Cubism*, with collage, or paper-pasting, 1912-14.

1914: *Synthetic Cubism* began and, at intervals for more than a decade, reappeared with variations and along with other styles.

1915: Pencil Portraits.   Along with his productivity in other mediums, Picasso this year seemed to take special delight in exercising his superb draftsmanship. He did a meticulously realistic pencil portrait of Vollard much in the style of Ingres, whose work Picasso had long admired. Also this year—and often throughout the next decade—he produced realistic line drawings remarkable in their economy and grace. Occasionally, in some of these figure drawings, he played with a Cubistic overblocking of lines.

1917: Ballet Period.   His meeting with Cocteau led to his designing sets and décor, including the curtain, for Cocteau's ballet *Parade,* which had music by Satie, another friend of the artist. He went with Cocteau to Rome to work on his designs for the ballet. There he met Diaghilev and the dancers of his Ballet Russe, Massine becoming a particular friend. In Rome he also became acquainted with Stravinsky, who was then at work on the *Fire* music. He made many superb line drawings of these people. His ballet curtain—which he not only designed but painted with help from assistants—was his largest and most complex composition up to this time. In every aspect the production of *Parade* was joyously avant-garde and highly successful. Not only his work in it, which was acclaimed, but his association with the many brilliant talents connected with the entire enterprise gave Picasso international standing.

1918-1924: Classic Period.   While in Rome Picasso met Olga Koklova, one of the ballerinas, whom he married in 1918. Before his marriage he had taken trips with Cocteau to Naples and Pompeii and had of course explored the treasures of Rome itself. The two influences—new wife and ancient art—plus the effect the success of the ballet had on his reputation and subsequently rising fortunes, induced a sense of security and calm that was almost immediately reflected in the art of his Classic Period. In many of these paintings the sense of relaxed calm is so great that the figures are heavy and at times, as in *The Race,* seem to be afflicted with elephantiasis. Other paintings of this period are gently serene, like his *Woman in White* owned by the Metropolitan Museum of Art, and his tender and palely tinted *Mother and Child* in the Baltimore Museum of Art. Or they are genuinely monumental like his 1921 sculpturesque oil, *Mother and Child.* (Pl. I Center R.)

1925: Grotesque and Double Image Period. The serenely Classic Period was interwoven with the production of evolving Cubist developments which became richer in color and occasionally introduced a delicate calligraphy. At times the Cubistic forms were greatly simplified and stronger decorative elements were added. Suddenly, in 1925, Picasso plunged into a long period of grotesque distortions and displacements of human features and forms. The Surrealists, who were much to the fore at the time, tried to claim him as their own, but Picasso's art was far too dominant and individual ever to become part of a movement. He himself was many successive movements. His distortions, which at first had taken the form of interweaving arabesques and linear designs in which an approximation of the human form can be discerned, became in 1927 violently antihuman with almost no recognizable elements, and with a three-dimensional, sculptural quality. Spending the summer of 1928 at Cannes, he began to "metamorphoze" figures on the beach into these strange, dehumanized forms. The following summer, at Dinard, they became large, bonelike structures placed on the yellow sands and against the blue of sky and sea. Calmly resting on the seashore, these bone-groupings bear not the slightest resemblance to the human skeleton yet in some wildly improbable fashion remind one of sun bathers at play or at ease.

Again and again, in the midst of these grotesqueries, Picasso reverted to previous styles, particularly the Classic. He also continued his magnificent line drawings in several series for book illustration. Beginning in 1932 he produced several stylized arabesques of women and then went into his "double image" period, one of the largest of these canvases being the richly colored, complex-patterned *Girl Before a Mirror,* owned by New York's Museum of Modern Art. This painting, the artist claims, shows the girl "simultaneously clothed, nude, and x-rayed." (Pl. XVI Center L.)

The double-image portrait in which at times the artist seemed only trying to present simultaneously the full face and the profile of the subject—actually the way we constantly see the faces of those around us—is in some of his paintings angrily distorted, with the features dislocated or even jumbled. Some of those with the jumbled features are so psychologically powerful (as *La Femme Qui Pleure,* 1938) that the viewer is impelled to believe that here Picasso was not painting a face but a state of mind and a condition of the soul.

And that is what he painted when, in a white heat of anger and revulsion, he produced his masterpiece of distortion, his enormous mural *Guernica*. He began the 26-foot canvas three days after Hitler's bombing planes, flying for Franco, destroyed the open town and defenseless population of Guernica, capital of the Basque province of Spain. It is useless to try to translate *Guernica*—painted entirely in black and white and shades of gray—into realistic meaning or to sort it into symbols. It is enough to perceive that its distortions of natural forms reflect the moral dislocation of Fascism and a world in which brutality and terrorism were unleashed. That world was an entirely different one from any known before —a world in which man no longer looked up to the sky as a symbol of hope, however distant, but as an assurance of death, imminent and inescapable. War had changed since Goya's day, when one could see—and paint—a firing squad at the moment of execution. But how can one see—or paint —the moment of obliteration from a rain of bombs? Who knows what a horse or a human looks like at the instant of being blown to pieces? What painted nightmare can compete in horror with the dehumanized corpses of Buchenwald, stiffened into their final grotesqueries? Never has painting been unconsciously so prophetic as Picasso's. (Pl. XVI Top)

Throughout World War II Picasso painted grimly on in Paris, alternating between a series of realistic portraits and the distorted form and double-image face. He also produced a good deal of sculpture. The German occupation command forbade public exhibitions of his work, but he was so famous they hesitated to molest him. Despite the fact that he headed the list of those artists whose work Hitler denounced as degenerate, a number of high-ranking Nazis of cultural pretensions dared visit his studio. There is a story that he presented each with a postcard reproduction of *Guernica*. One day Hitler's agent in Paris, Otto Abetz, called with an offer of some alleviation in the way of food and fuel. Picasso coldly refused his aid, showing him the door. As he left, Abetz noticed a photograph of *Guernica* and remarked: "Ah, so you did this, M. Picasso?" "No," replied the artist, "you did."

For a number of years now, Picasso has lived in the south of France. He has developed a new process of lithography, and continues to paint and to create new designs in ceramics and sculpture. In June 1955 a huge double-retrospective exhibition of his works opened in Paris, the Louvre showing his paintings, the National Library his drawings and prints. The feature of the Louvre show that drew the greatest attention was a series of fourteen variations—painted between December 12, 1954 and February 14, 1955—on the famous Delacroix painting *The Women of Algiers*. The variations afford not only a review of numerous Picasso styles, but occasionally offer a slyly satirical comment on Delacroix's exotic Persian phase and the lush *odalisque* period of Matisse.

Picasso may review but he never repeats himself. He may turn back to paint again in one of the many styles he either originated or made essentially his own, but in each of these "returns" he moves on into new phases. To Picasso, the various separations of his art into periods and styles are so much nonsense. For the ordinary mortal, however, they are convenient and almost necessary guidelines through the bewildering richness and variety of the enormous production of his genius. (Pl. XVII Bottom)

Picasso is still the most modern of all modern artists today, unquestionably the leader of the entire movement that began half a century ago. Much of his art is far from pleasing to the eye. As he has said, "Painting is not done to decorate apartments." Certainly his is not and should not be considered from that basis. The sacrosanctification of Picasso has done much harm; instead of enlightening, it has baffled and confused the general public and caused justifiable indignation instead of perceptive appreciation. All that Picasso produces is not art. Some of it is light-hearted, inventive foolery; much of it is inspired experimentation toward an art as yet unimagined. In her book, "Picasso" (published by B. T. Batsford, Ltd., London, 1938), Gertrude Stein acutely points out:

> *The things that Picasso could see were the things which had their own reality, reality not of things seen but of things that exist. . . . One must never forget that the reality of the twentieth century is not the reality of the nineteenth century, not at all, and Picasso was the only one in painting who felt it, the only one. More and more the struggle to express it intensified. Matisse and all the others saw the twentieth century with their eyes but they saw the reality of the nineteenth century. Picasso was the only one in painting who saw the twentieth century with his eyes and saw its reality, and consequently his struggle was terrifying, terrifying, for himself and for others, because he had nothing to help him, the past did not help him, nor the present, he had to do it all alone.*

It is remarkable that this little book was written early in 1938 and that Miss Stein added the further prophetic comment that ". . . the twentieth century is . . . a time when everything cracks, where everything is destroyed, everything isolates itself." She continues:

The automobile is the end of progress on the earth, it goes quicker but essentially the landscapes seen from an automobile are the same as the landscapes seen from a carriage, a train, a wagon, or in walking. But the earth seen from an airplane is something else. So the twentieth century is not the same as the nineteenth century and it is very interesting knowing that Picasso has never seen the earth from an airplane, that being of the twentieth century he inevitably knew that the earth is not the same as in the nineteenth century, he knew it, he made it, inevitably he made it different and what he made is a thing that now all the world can see. When I was in America I for the first time travelled pretty much all the time in an airplane and when I looked at the earth I saw all the lines of cubism made at a time when not any painter had ever gone up in an airplane. I saw there on the earth the mingling lines of Picasso, coming and going, developing and destroying themselves, I saw the simple solutions of Braque, I saw the wandering lines of Masson, yes I saw and once more I knew that a creator is contemporary, he understands what is contemporary when the contemporaries do not yet know it, but he is contemporary and as the twentieth century is a century which sees the earth as no one has ever seen it, the earth has a splendor that it never has had, and as everything destroys itself in the twentieth century and nothing continues, so then the twentieth century has a splendor which is its own and Picasso is of this century, he has that strange quality of an earth that one has never seen and of things destroyed as they have never been destroyed. So then Picasso has his splendor.

Picasso's impact on art, his importance to modern art, can never be overestimated; some of his works are. But he has his splendor—perhaps the splendor of some "future continent of the mind." It will not diminish.

15 THE LAST BOHEMIANS

THE PHRASE "SCHOOL OF PARIS" IS A TERM loosely embracing all leading modern artists—except the Abstractionists and Surrealists—who were active in Paris from about the turn of the century until, roughly, World War II. Of whatever School, or of no School at all, they were not in any sense a definite group, as were the Impressionists, the Nabis, the Fauves, etc. Although most of the artists were French, some of the most prominent of the School of Paris have been of other nationalities, as were many of their more obscure followers. But all of them at one time or another, and some of them permanently, found in Paris their artistic home.

Four painters of Paris and of the so-called School of Paris may well be called "the last Bohemians." All of them lived in that cradle of modern art, Montmartre. Three fought a losing battle with dissipation and poverty and despair. The fourth was precariously rescued, though hardly restored. He was the only Frenchman of the four, Maurice Utrillo.

Born in Paris in 1883, Utrillo was literally a child of Montmartre. His mother, a teen-age artist's model of peasant stock, was an illegitimate child, as was her son. His father, thought to be an alcoholic amateur painter, played no part in the boy's life and may indeed not have been the instigator of it. Neglected by his mother, the handsome little boy grew up on the streets, in the cafés and studios of Montmartre, where the denizens probably thought it amusing to see a young child stagger blind drunk from their parties.

When Maurice was eight, a compassionate friend of his mother, Miguel Utrillo, Spanish writer and art critic, legally gave the child his name. He went to school intermittently, where he was understandably a poor scholar. When he was seventeen or so, he held a clerical job in a bank for a very short time. By his mid-teens he had become a confirmed alcoholic and in 1901, when he was only eighteen, he had to be committed to an institution.

In the meantime, his mother had become a protégée of

165

Toulouse-Lautrec, who persuaded her to change her name from Marie-Clementine to Suzanne. Through Lautrec she met Degas. He recognized a spark of talent in the young model and under his tutelage she became a surprisingly good painter. Despite her early deficiencies as a mother—she herself was scarcely fortune's child—Suzanne Valadon must have been a woman of spirit and character, as well as of talent. When her eighteen-year-old son had to be committed not only for alcoholism but because of a mental breakdown, she realized the seriousness of the situation and tried her utmost to repair it. For three-and-a-half decades, until her death, she devoted her life and her considerable intelligence to his rehabilitation, which had to be a continual process. Again and again Utrillo had relapses into alcoholism, tinged with madness and sometimes with suicidal tendencies.

As a form of what today we would call occupational therapy, Suzanne, acting upon the advice of a physician, gave her son paintbrushes, canvas, and colors to brighten the boredom of convalescence after his first confinement in a sanitarium. She began to teach him to paint—but only began, for a miracle happened. He did not become, but suddenly *was,* a painter! Painting became an obsession second only to drink, the one formidable rival for Utrillo's attention.

In his early days as an artist, when taken home drunk by some passing friend, he would often sit down at his easel and by the light of a kerosene lamp dash off one of his delightful street scenes. His hand may not have been steady but, miraculously, none of his paintings has a hint of disorder or confusion. Often—on the prowl for a drink and without money in his pocket—he would stop in at some tavern and paint a small scene in exchange for a glass of cognac. Sometimes a canny tavern keeper would lock him into a room furnished on the instant with paint, brushes, and canvas. A steady supply of alcohol would produce several paintings which the tavernkeeper claimed, and kept, by right of possession. As Utrillo gained recognition, certain dealers resorted to similar tactics.

In 1910 two prominent French artists saw Utrillo's work in an obscure, small gallery. They immediately acclaimed him. As his paintings have appeal both for the sophisticated art lover and the man in the street, they began to sell briskly from the time he was "discovered" and given critical attention.

In 1923 he and his mother had a large exhibition at the Bernheim-Jeune Gallery in Paris, which then guaranteed the two of them a joint annual income of one million francs—at that time about $40,000. The following year, however, Utrillo made his most serious attempt at suicide. His valiant mother brought him back to comparative health and sanity, and for the next five years the two painted industriously. In 1929, he received the Cross of the Legion of Honor.

For fifty years, drunk or sober, confined or free, Utrillo has painted unceasingly, turning out thousands of oils, gouaches, watercolors, sketches. He paints almost entirely from memory or from postcards or snapshots, infusing each picture or remembered scene with his own artistic concept. Many of his paintings are of Montmartre. Not the gay or dissipated life of its bistros, dance halls, or café concerts which were captured on canvas by Degas, Lautrec, and so many others, but the Montmartre as it was before the artists took possession —the little town on the edge of Paris, its windmills and winding byways, its white-washed houses, its steep and narrow streets leading to church dome or spire. Utrillo's street scenes are usually without human figures. In the few paintings where they appear, they are mere specks in the distance moving away from rather than toward the spectator This absence or withdrawal of life lends the scene an atmosphere of gentle, but not depressing, melancholy.

Never playing with light as effect, but often making use of an instinct for geometric design, Utrillo produces pictures more structurally solid than those of the Impressionists. Yet in a number of his finest paintings there is a kinship with Pissarro's strongest canvases. The quality of Utrillo's work is uneven, and his very recognizable style is rather easily imitated. In fact, the painter himself has been reported as sometimes unable to distinguish whether a painting is his own or the work of a forger. There is a story to the effect that on one such occasion, involving a lawsuit, Utrillo mercifully signed the disputed canvas to save the defendant from a jail sentence.

Two years before his mother died, in 1938, Utrillo married a widow who not only took over the job of protecting him— chiefly from himself—but who manages his affairs so wisely that he reaps a fortune from his art. They live on a handsome estate near Paris where Utrillo, guarded against relapses and protected in them, still paints remembered scenes of the Montmartre he no longer visits.

Quite different is the end of the story for three of Utrillo's fellow artists. Of these, Jules Pascin, born 1885, in Bulgaria of mixed Jewish-Serbian-Italian ancestry, was endowed with great talent but wasted it in dissipation. He studied art in Vienna, Munich, and Paris, and visited Mexico and the United States, where he lived long enough to become a citizen. But he was exceedingly restless in his life and in his work, throwing both away in trivialities. He delighted in making quick, satirical, amusing sketches of street scenes, prostitutes and other bits of vagrant life. In his few serious canvases—chiefly portraits—there is evident a clear grasp of the principles embodied in Cézanne's work, but enlivened by a rhythmic animation and vitality. Seemingly from lack of purpose, he lived a vaguely sensual life. Just as purposelessly, he committed suicide in Paris in 1930.

Far more weighted from the beginning with tragedy, Chaim Soutine fought more valiantly against its downward drag than did the other three artists to escape their internal demons of destruction. He was tenth in a Lithuanian ghetto family of eleven children, their father a tailor. Born in 1894, near Minsk, he longed from early boyhood to become a painter instead of the tailor his father insisted he must learn to be. Before he was sixteen he ran away from home and enrolled at the School of Fine Arts in Vilna, earning his way as a photographer's assistant. In 1913, with a little financial help from a kindly doctor, he managed to make his way to Paris where he eagerly expected a better life.

But he only landed in another form of ghetto, the ghetto of the desperately poor. What little money he was able to earn he spent chiefly on instruction in Cormon's studio at the *Beaux-Arts*. He lived in a miserable tenement called "The Hive" (*La Ruche*), swarming with destitute strugglers and with political refugees, many of them in terror for their lives. Next door was a huge slaughterhouse, where he made friends with the butchers, who occasionally lent him quarters of meat to serve as models for his paintings or let him make sketch notes of carcasses in the slaughterhouse itself. Revolting as such subjects for pictures seem, they gave the young artist strangely rich opportunity in both form and in color. He did not use it in grisly or macabre fashion but let it develop for him a palette of the intense and vivid hues of decomposition—beautiful if one is able to consider the colors apart from their cause.

Although Soutine made friends with many artists as young and poor as himself, and as destined to become great, the depressing surroundings of daily existence, the omnipresent sight and smell of slaughterhouse death, the apparently hopeless future, one day overwhelmed him with despair. He hanged himself—but just at the moment of extinction was cut down by a friend who opportunely happened in.

Soon after this he became acquainted with Modigliani, the young Italian artist who was the fourth of this sorry quartet of last Bohemians. Through Modigliani he met his dealer,

Zborowski, who bought a few pictures and advised Soutine to leave Paris.

The artist acted upon this advice and in 1919 moved to Céret, returning to Paris three years later with more than 200 paintings. Abruptly, on January 1, 1923, Soutine's fortunes changed. Dr. Albert Barnes, the crusty Philadelphian with the argyrol fortune and the amazing instinct for art, was in Paris starting his fabulous collection. He bought nearly 100 paintings from Soutine.

Darkly colorful landscapes, portraits and figure pieces, still lifes of hunks of meat and animal carcasses, all of Soutine's paintings are characterized by an irregular running-together of richly somber rainbow hues, a breaking up of surfaces, a slight distortion of forms.

From the beginning of 1923, when Dr. Barnes bought so many of his paintings in one grand swoop, the circumstances of Soutine's life naturally improved in every way. He found a calm affection in two or three close friendships and his paintings became less expressive of wild and disordered despair. But despair, however tranquilized, remained in them and in him. He withdrew into almost complete solitude, refusing even to exhibit his paintings. In 1943 he died in Paris.

He belonged to the lost company of the beautiful and the damned. He was the Crown Prince of the Bohemia of Paris —Montmartre, the Left Bank, Montparnasse, the Latin Quarter. He was the artist-starving-in-the-garret—when he had a garret. He was Amedeo Modigliani. (Pl. XVIII)

Women adored him, the adoration coming first from his mother. Of Jewish-Italian parents—he insisted proudly upon the Jew, his mother claiming descent from the great philosopher, Spinoza—he was born in Leghorn, Italy, July 12, 1884. A beautiful child and an extraordinarily handsome man, he was an innate aristocrat: proud in rags, prodigal with his talents—he gravely charged five francs "and a little alcohol" for a single-portrait sitting—gallant and tender with women, and always capable of the grand gesture. He had a passionate love of poetry and a prodigious memory which enabled him, drunk or sober, to declaim entire cantos of Dante, often at inconvenient times.

In early adolescence, Modigliani was seized with a pulmonary affliction so severe that it put an end to formal schooling. In his convalescence he showed an interest in art, so his doting mother put him under the guidance of a local landscape painter. But recurrent indications of tuberculosis began to plague him a year or so later, and his mother took him to the south of Italy to recuperate. During the next few years he studied intermittently in Rome, Florence, and Venice. Although his parents were in very moderate circumstances, his mother managed to provide him with the funds necessary for his study of art and its attendant adventures.

But Paris was his goal, and to Paris he went in 1906 on money supplied by a small but opportune family inheritance. When he arrived, he set himself up in style even though, with the instinct of a homing pigeon, he had headed straight for Montmartre where an artist could live cheaply. The money, of course, did not last long. Drink, dissipation, and recurring attacks of tubercular weakness dragged him down, and his life became one of destitute disorder. His early work was somewhat influenced by Toulouse-Lautrec, and in 1908 he exhibited in the *Indépendants,* receiving no attention at all.

But his personal charm—never consciously exerted—was so great, and the brilliance and beauty and doom of his youth and talent so apparent that throughout the artists' colony hands were stretched out to help and, if possible, to save him from himself. Artists as poor, but not as reckless, shared what they had with him, gave him a floor to sleep on if they had no bed to offer. Sometimes he slept literally on the streets, sometimes in the back room of a café. One of his closest, most faithful friends was Soutine, whose miserable room in The Hive was always open to him.

Racked with illness, he spent the winter of 1909 in Italy but returned in the spring to Paris. He had become friendly with Brancusi, the Rumanian sculptor whose drive toward essence simplified his forms almost to Abstractionism. Occasionally the sculptor let Modi—as he was known throughout the artists' colony—work beside him, encouraging him to carve direct from stone.

Somehow Modigliani had acquired an African mask, which he had not yet exchanged for drink. This he hung in a studio he managed to keep for a while. With him, admiration for African sculpture was not a pose or a novelty. He seemed to feel a deep affinity for the simplified, distorted forms of this primitive art—an affinity that went far deeper than Picasso's conscious assimilation of the influence, which always showed itself in his work for what it was. Its effect on Modigliani's work was far more individualized and delicate—in his paintings sometimes scarcely discernible although the elongation so characteristic of African sculpture is usually present. His expression of the influence, made over into the image and likeness of his own talent, is most striking in one of his few sculptures, *Head,* which he designed for architectural use. In a life-size piece, *Caryatid,* he simplifies and individualizes the classic form. He might have become a great sculptor—all his drawings indicate this—had it not been for the three factors of money, health, and temperament. He was too poor ever to buy stone or other malleable material. He would hover around a half-completed building until some workman gave him a stone to cart away in his wheelbarrow; sometimes he would find one left behind when a building was finished or razed. But no working sculptor could depend for long on such pick-ups.

What really put an end to his three-year career as a sculptor was, inevitably, his health; the dust from direct carving was too much for his already damaged lungs. But even if lack of money and health had not so decisively interfered, it is doubtful if Modigliani's volatile temperament would have stood the continuing strain of the day-in, day-out drudgery necessary to draw forth from the stone the conceived image. In 1913 he turned from sculpture back to painting, which he had largely neglected since 1909. (Pl. XVIII)

The artists had begun in 1908 to desert Montmartre for Montparnasse, on the Left Bank, and that became Modigliani's peripatetic home and wandering place from 1913 until his death seven years later. In 1914 three events occurred that greatly influenced his life. He met the first of the two women who managed to achieve some sort of deranged domesticity with him. All the other women—and there were many of high and low estate—were passing loves for a night, a week, at most a month of intermittent intimacy. But Beatrice Hastings, an English girl of some pretensions as a poet, decided to enjoy and support Modi for a longer period. She managed it for two years, and he painted her many times. During this period alcoholism really took hold, never to let go its grip. He also began experimenting with drugs.

The third event that occurred during 1914 was his meeting with an unsuccessful Polish poet of Montparnasse, Leopold Zborowski, who became his eagerly helpful friend—whenever he could squeeze out a centime from his own straitened circumstances—and eventually his dealer. Zborowski's love for art was as great as his means for acquiring it were small. He made a precarious living buying and selling books. When there was a little to spare he purchased a painting. One of the struggling artists, whose works he sometimes bought, generously interested him in Modigliani. Before long, Zborowski became a passionate advocate, trying with desperate enthusiasm to sell Modi's paintings and drawings. Failing, he bought them now and again himself or from his own impoverishment advanced the artist a pittance to save him from utter starvation.

From time to time, any hour of day or night, Modigliani

might leave at Zborowski's door a painting or drawing in return for the small sums given him. Unceasingly, Zborowski
besieged dealers, collectors, the man on the street, to buy at
any price the works of the artist he was sure would some day
be accounted great. Meanwhile, as his craving for drink and
drugs grew more insistent, Modi himself would take his port-
folios to small dealers and offer sheaves of drawings for in-
finitesimal sums Punctiliously true to his own code of honor,
he never failed to leave drawings or paintings behind to com-
pensate for the back rent of the succession of poor studios
or barren rooms from which he would unfailingly be evicted.

In 1917 Zborowski, despairing of interesting any dealer
in his friend's work, arranged a small exhibition in the Berthe
Weill Gallery. Hoping to attract attention to the show, he
put in the window four of Modigliani's paintings of nude
women. They attracted attention—the attention of the police,
who ordered them removed. As a last resort, Zborowski offered all four nudes to a friend at 500 francs for the lot. The
offer was, understandably, refused. What could anyone do
with four nudes by a totally unrecognized artist? A few years
later a single nude by Modigliani—it may well have been one
of the four—went for nearly a million francs.

It is not strange that so few of Modigliani's works could
be sold during his lifetime. Unlike Utrillo's paintings, which
are instantly appealing to a wide range of tastes, a liking
for Modigliani is an acquired taste. With few exceptions his
work, either single figures or portraits, is characterized by
elongated ovals of face and body. The throats are either
sturdily columnar or have a swanlike length and sinuousness.
Many of his portraits are drawn with almost caricature distortion, the very distortion individualizing the subject and
impressing the spectator with the reality of the person behind
the face. The two-dimensional faces have little modeling, with
color often applied like makeup. On face and body—in the
case of nudes—are an over-all terra cotta, a warm tonality
which the artist uses again and again, sometimes lightening
it to a pinkish-ivory, or darkening it almost to brick red or a
deep reddish-brown. As contrast, he frequently uses a soft
but intense blue or a pale lavender.

Modigliani's nudes are frankly sensuous—the exaggerated
elongation of the torso Freudian in its implication—but
strangely dispassionate. The exquisite variations of subtle
tonalities, merging and blending, deepening and rising to
muted highlights—are very beautiful. Now and again there
is a fleeting resemblance—gone on the instant—to the ethe-
really decorative nudes of Botticelli.

In the late fall of 1918, when Modi was very ill, Zborowski managed to sell fifteen of his paintings for 500 francs. With this, he sent the artist to the south of France to recuperate. In the spring Modi returned to Paris and to Jeanne Hebuterne, the strange young girl he had lived with since 1917. She was the runaway daughter of stodgily respectable and prosperous grocers, who promptly disowned her when, for better or for worse (it grew progressively worse), in sickness or in health (the artist was a physical wreck), until death failed to part them, she joined her life to his without benefit of clergy. Not a pretty girl, she has been described by those who knew her as pale and thin, with a sad oval face and lank, light braids. She lived only for her artist, roaming the streets beside him when they were evicted, sleeping in hallways, bars, on the bare ground. While he tried to sell his pictures on the street, she would go into restaurants to beg crusts for them.

A daughter was born and when Modigliani returned in the spring of 1919, mother and child were housed, through the charity of friends, in a tiny apartment. Modi joined them there. For a short time, as his pictures began slowly to sell for very small sums, his friends hoped he might at last settle down. But he was too far gone. The wild look almost never left his eyes as he drank and drugged—he used hashish now —more and more. One day toward the end of January 1920, he had such a high fever that he could not crawl out of bed. He was taken in delirium to a hospital. Next morning, January 25, he died in a charity ward, at the age of thirty-five. He had decided, long before, on the life he wanted— "brief and intense"—and he had achieved it. That night Jeanne, wild with grief and nearly nine months pregnant, went home to her parents. No one will ever know how they greeted her but later, in the dark, she went up to the roof and flung herself down to instant death.

The news that Modi, the dissolute but beloved, was gone flashed through the sections of Paris. Artists were beginning to gather in groups to raise money for the funeral when from his brother, a prominent politician of Leghorn, came an ample money order and wired instructions to provide a funeral befitting a prince.

As the cortege, the coffin banked high with flowers, passed slowly across Paris from Montparnasse, past Montmartre and at last to the little cemetery of Pére Lachaise, the crowds stood in respectful silence, the artists bowed their heads in sorrow and in silent farewell. They did not know it then, nor did the world, but they were saying goodbye not only to Modi but to Paris as the vital center of living art. This was the end of the School of Paris, last of the successive movements in painting that for two centuries had dominated the art of the western world. The leading practitioners would continue to dominate well into the second half of the twentieth century and their works will probably hold the commanding position almost to the end of the century.

But it is significant that since the School of Paris—Matisse, Derain, Dufy, Vlaminck, Rouault, de Segonzac, Braque, Gris, Léger, Soutine, Utrillo, Delaunay, and so many other great names in modern art, including, of course and foremost, Picasso, who assumed the leadership in 1909—not a single art movement has been generated in the City of Light. True, two new and allied movements—Dada and Surrealism—used Paris as their center, but they did not originate there nor were their chief artists French, as, with the mighty exception of Picasso, had been most of the leading modern artists up to and including the School of Paris.

16 THE NUDE DESCENDS

THE U.S.A. STAIRCASE

"LIKE AN EXPLOSION IN A SHINGLE FACTORY" was the description given Marcel Duchamp's *Nude Descending a Staircase*. And as an explosion she burst upon the sight of the American public in its first view of her in the famed and gigantic Armory Show of 1913. There were many greater and even more arresting paintings in the 2,000 works shown in the exhibition officially titled "The International Exposition of Modern Art." But for press and public the *Nude* became the symbol of the exhibition, which was immediately and forever after called the Armory Show. (Pl. XVIII)

To understand the impact made upon the American public by that 1913 explosion in the Sixty-ninth Regiment Armory, it might be well to review the art activities, attitudes, and accomplishments in this country during the dozen or so years preceding the Armory Show and for the decade and a half following it. Those two periods were characterized by two revolts, both of them anti-Paris and pro-American.

As facilities for travel and communication improved and increased after the Civil War, the influence of Paris on the art and the artists of the United States began its sway. In the last two decades of the nineteenth century it became almost imperative for an artist to study in Paris or with an American teacher who had worked with one of the masters of the *Beaux-Arts*. The only rival for the artistic affections of the United States was the School of Munich, the important art center of Germany where the accent was placed not upon foundational drawing according to the Ingres tradition of the *Beaux-Arts,* but on the direct use of the heavily loaded brush. As the color on the brush was usually black or a dark or muddy brown, this resulted in many murky paintings, some of great technical excellence, that for a time were greatly admired and widely bought in this country because of their superficial resemblance to aged-in-the-varnish old masters. The most popular exponent of this method was Frank Duveneck, originally of Boston but later of Cincinnati, where he taught many students. Another exceedingly influential American teacher, Munich-trained, was William Merritt Chase, who had been somewhat "corrupted"—and his palette lightened—by the French Impressionists.

In the nineties, Impressionism became a strong influence in the work of leading American artists, particularly Twachtman, Hassam, Prendergast, Wier, and Lawson. Theodore Robinson, whose early death prevented full realization of his talent, was the first American to identify himself specifically as an Impressionist of the French School; after study with two *Beaux-Arts* masters, he had worked with Monet at Giverney. Earlier, there had been three noted American landscape painters—Inness, Wyant, and Martin—whose work, taking off from the over-detailed Romantic-Realism of the Hudson River School, felt the Barbizon influence, and eventually approximated Impressionism. This is especially true of Inness, by far the most important of the three.

And of course there were the three great American independents—Homer, Ryder, Eakins—who belonged to no school. They were so strongly individual that except in one instance they had no real followers. That one was a pupil in Eakins' short-lived, ill-fated school—closed by Victorian prudery—who went on to become a teacher, thereby spreading the influence of Eakins' honest Realism. This follower, later assistant to Eakins, was Thomas Anschutz, who in turn became the teacher of Robert Henri at the Pennsylvania Academy of the Fine Arts.

After working under Anschutz, Henri lived abroad for a number of years not only studying art—being influenced chiefly by Manet's pre-Impressionist style—but pondering its potential relation to life. By the time he returned to his native Philadelphia he had made up his mind that art should reflect experience and the painter's reaction to it or emotion about it. This philosophy he passed on to the students and fellow-artists he gathered around him. The ones who were to take his philosophy most to heart were newspaper illustrators: John Sloan (1871-1951), George Luks (1867-1933), the semi-Impressionist William Glackens (1870-1938), and Everett Shinn (1876-1953). Alive to the social changes and political ideas of the turn of the century, these men and the younger ones who were to become associated with them, carried Henri's doctrine of the relation of life to art much further than he did. Henri still retained some of the elegance of Manet. His most successful followers threw elegance and everything that smacked of French suavity out of the window and got happily down to the reality of city backyards with wet clothes flapping on the line and garbage spilling out of lopsided cans, shirt-sleeved beer drinkers in dingy saloons, basement poolrooms, the poor lined up for free handouts—in short, the seamy-sided, shirt-sleeved American scene.

In the early years of the new century most of the group moved to New York where, with Henri and three painters already in the metropolis—Maurice Prendergast, who had developed an Impressionist style somewhat like patches of loosely-woven tapestry, the landscapist Ernest Lawson, and Arther B. Davies—they formed an enlarged group they called "The Eight." With their first New York exhibition in 1908, they were dubbed "The Ashcan School"—a name that became useful in designating loosely all the American painters of the first decade and a half of the twentieth century who turned from second-hand overseas inspiration and influence to draw and paint at first hand street scenes and people of large-city (chiefly New York) life.

Younger painters, attracted by this new American Realism, were drawn into the original Henri group. Among them were Glenn O. Coleman, whose lighter touch indicated that all was not drabness and desperation even among New York's less fortunate citizens; George Overbury ('Pop") Hart, whose superb watercolors and prints found motley crowds enjoying two-bit carnivals and circuses that were less than "the greatest show on earth"; and George Bellows (1882-1925), a younger pupil of Henri's and one of this country's most vigorous and masculine painters. An athlete himself—he had to choose between a career in art and an enticing bid to become a member of a major league baseball team—he delighted in painting full-bodied pictures of sporting events, particularly the boxing matches that became his most popular and famous subject. But he also did lyrical, yet strongly painted, landscapes, and perceptive portrait and figure painting, often placed against backgrounds or in room settings that added interest or a certain dramatic charm.

John Sloan not only was an associate of Henri but also studied at the Pennsylvania Academy of the Fine Arts under Anschutz. Implicit in his down-to-earth depiction of New York scenes and citizens is a wry humor that accents his Realism. Through his teaching he had a wide influence upon two generations of American artists.

Although showing with the group, the Impressionist-inclined Prendergast and Lawson and particularly the eclectic Davies were never allied with the Ashcan School except by association in the opening exhibition of The Eight. The only bond they shared was a common rebellion against current Academism. Sampling many different brands of art and various mediums—oil, watercolor, pastel, sculpture, print-

making, and even tapestry—Davies finally more or less settled down to a weak, sentimental romantic style not nearly
as good as his early work. Certainly the most conventional in
his art, Davies became the hard working leader of the revolt
that brought the big Armory Show to this country. He was
president of an association of painters and sculptors which
organized the show Either members of the association or
collaborators with it were practically all the progressive artists in New York—and as many outside New York as could
manage to lend a hand or raise a voice in support of the project. Davies had many useful friends interested in art—or
at least whom he could persuade to be interested, for he was
very persuasive—and he rallied them all either to give money
or lend prestige to the cause.

Among his many collaborators, in addition to the vigorous and enlarged Ashcan group, their followers and fellow-
travelers, were Walter Pach, Walt Kuhn, Alfred Maurer,
Guy Pène du Bois, Max Weber and Abraham Walkowitz.
The last two, after years of study and painting abroad, had
brought back to New York the most advanced theories of
post-Impressionism and the School of Paris and were putting
these theories into practice before a thoroughly unapprecia-
tive American public; today they are looked upon with respect and admiration as early leaders in the modern art
movement in this country. Pach and Maurer, still in Paris,
were pressed into service to help round up exhibits for the
Show. Maurer starting in the Whistlerian style, did an about-
face and developed a strong individual style after experiments in Fauvism and a study of Cézanne's form. Pach, a
painter eventually to be much better known as an art critic,
historian, and lecturer, became spokesman for the Armory
Show and explainer-in-general of its bewildering array of
avant-garde styles. Walt Kuhn, the young American painter
who had fathered the idea for the show and persuaded Davies
to undertake its direction, went with him to Germany, France,
and Holland to make the selections. He became an important
American figure and landscape painter. Many other American artists whose names are now among the greatest in the
roll-call of American art helped to organize and were exhibitors in the Armory Show. In addition to the big showings of French, German and—to a lesser extent—British
modern art, with works by Russian, Spanish, and Italian artists, there were three groupings of American art: the recently historical, which included Whistler and Ryder; the Ashcan
School and allied Realists of the American Scene; and the
numerous American exponents of the School of Paris.

This was the first time the United States had felt the full

blast of the modern art movement. Earlier, two great American photographers had given their countrymen a sampling of twentieth-century styles that had so vitalized the art scene in Paris. These two pioneers in appreciation were Edward Steichen who, starting out to be a painter, had earned his way as a photographer only to abandon the former art for the latter; and Alfred Stieglitz, at that time America's leading photographer, who had opened a small, one-room gallery at 291 Fifth Avenue for the exhibition of photography as a fine art. From Paris, where he had gone to study painting and remained to make his wonderful series of photographs of Rodin at work, Steichen in 1908 interested Stieglitz in showing avant-garde paintings, drawings, and sculptures by Matisse; and, later, work by other modern artists of Europe. Stieglitz, on a trip abroad, had already seen the work of the post-Impressionists in Paris, and was beginning to champion a few young American artists. Within a few years his small gallery had become the most vital center for the showing of and discussion about modern art in the Western Hemisphere. In the decade 1908-1917 he exhibited works by Matisse, Rousseau, Picasso, Cézanne, Toulouse-Lautrec, Brancusi, Severini, and the Americans: Marin, Maurer, Hartley, Weber, Dove, Walkowitz, and Georgia O'Keeffe. These were the first one-man shows for the American artists, and the first American showings for the European artists. This tiny place, nominally known simply as "291," has rightly been called by Marsden Hartley "probably the largest small room in the world. . . . Everybody in the wide world came there sooner or later—everybody was free to come—it was an open room—and anyone said what he liked . . . this room 291 left a lasting impression in the development of art in America."

But it *was* small, and few except those already interested in avant-garde art—or curious about it—were aware of the room's existence. In 1913 the general public was totally unprepared for the shattering explosion of the Armory Show. In France, for almost a century, one explosion after another had prepared the public to expect the unexpected in art. In fact, they rather enjoyed going into a violent *cri des nerfs* at each big bang—Romanticism, Realism, Impressionism, Fauvism, Cubism. As the nineteenth century yielded to the twentieth, the major explosions were interspersed by so many minor ones going off like strings of small firecrackers that a mild case of chronic indignation sufficed. As the twentieth century moved into its second decade, casual indifference took over. Modern art was seldom news in Paris, except to those who cared about it.

In New York however, when the *Nude* clattered down the *Staircase,* modern art received front-page headlines. It was not only news—it was horrible, disgusting, subversive, insane, perverted, and, above all, hilarious Huge crowds marched into the Armory determined to find some painting that would outrage their sensibilities and make them quiver with delighted revulsion. Newspapers and magazines and letters-to-the-editor proclaimed their conviction that the artists responsible for such filth and imbecility were lewd, unspeakable fellows unfit for decent society Matisse, who in addition was called an imposter asked an American friend in Paris to send word to his countrymen that he was "a normal man . . . a devoted husband and father of three fine children. . . . . I go to the theatre, ride horseback, love flowers, just like any man."

Although with World War I the furor in the public prints diminished, the battle between modern art and the Academic tradition continued unabated, with the conventional artists having the financial edge as people were not afraid to buy their paintings, but with more excitement stirred up by the two branches of modern American art. those who, like the vigorous Ashcan group, "painted American," and the ardent followers of the School of Paris. The latter were gaining adherents; toward the end of the second decade of the century it seemed as though every would-be artist in America was just waiting for the end of the war to take the first boat to Paris and the Left Bank. After one, two, three, or five years —as long as their money could be made to hold out—they streamed back to these shores, many of them adopting New York as their new home. They were all products, or near-products, of the School of Paris, only a few assimilating its various influences in styles of their own.

In addition to this wave of Paris-inspired art, powerful international and French dealers, as well as knowing American dealers, flooded the New York art market with works by the leading painters of Paris. Why buy an American adaptation when you could have a genuine French import at merely ten to twenty times the price? Many American collectors responded to the siren song which, to tell the truth, often hit close to the mark of good sense, good finance, and good art. Many superior modern paintings—now worth from three to ten times the price originally paid for them—came into the possession of American collectors, eventually to go to museums for the benefit of all Americans.

The inundation of Paris-produced art threatened to drown out the individuality of native American talent. It was almost a question of go French or go under. But some rugged souls

—all of the Ashcan group and allied artists, plus a few stubborn individualists—held out against the flood and today have their place in the sun of critical esteem and general acceptance.

There were three artists whose separately developing careers unexpectedly merged—around 1925—into a genuine revolt against the School of Paris and even against the School of New York or Eastern Seaboard painters who next to the foreign imports, got the lion's share of critical attention. This was a "Back to the Farm or Heartland of America" movement and its three apostles were all Middle-Westerners: John Steuart Curry (1897-1946) of Kansas, Grant Wood (1892-1942) of Iowa, and Thomas Hart Benton (1889-) of Missouri. (Pls. XX, XXI)

Curry born on a Kansas farm, was the first person to be appointed "artist-in-residence" by a University—in his case, the College of Agriculture of the University of Wisconsin in Madison.

In this position he had to do no actual teaching. His function was only to inspire—by painting as he liked and what he liked—the student artists of the University and, equally important, to stimulate a general appreciation of art in relation to rural life in the community and through it in the world at large. From easel painting Curry went on to do excellent and at the same time—no small feat—very acceptable mural painting in Westport, Connecticut, in government buildings in Washington, D.C., and in Topeka, state capital of his own Kansas Although his murals—in common with most of those painted by Americans—have too much the quality of enlarged easel paintings, fortunately even his easel paintings have strength and sweep, like the broad Kansas plains and a homely grandeur without mannerisms. They are thoroughly American.

Grant Wood, who worked his way up through poverty by a multiplicity of jobs—carpentry, jewelry-making, country school teaching—yearned for the cultural and artistic opportunities of Paris. Four times he went abroad as an art mendicant, his shoulders bent under the weight of a Middle-Western inferiority complex. On his fourth trip he had an awakening that was practically a revelation. He realized, and acknowledged the fact to himself, that he was no Impressionist and never would be. Instead of depressing him, this self-appraisal released his spirits. He threw off the ill-fitting, ego-bruising yoke of Paris and within a remarkably short time leaped to the front rank of American painters and almost immediate popularity. His original, keenly penetrating—sometimes almost to the point of satire—portrait-pictures can never be mistaken for anything but "American" though they are scarcely in the vein that the jingo-patriot finds inspiring.

Unfortunately, after a few years of rising fame, Wood became so enamored of his individually wrought style that he overdeveloped it. His paintings became highly mannered in the smoothly executed, meticulously detailed tradition of German and Flemish primitives. And he took up the American scene with a vengeance. His *Parson Weems' Fable* of George Washington and the cherry tree shows the young George, mature in all but stature, pointing with exaggerated piety to his little hatchet, while the kindly Colonial parson draws aside a red velvet curtain to reveal this American folk tale. The rich, clear colors are a delight to the eye, while the benign and deadpan humor of the flawlessly executed composition brings an instantly responsive smile from the spectator. And although George and his stern Papa are figures of smooth satire (George's supposedly six year-old face is a miniature Gilbert Stuart portrait) the face of Parson Weems is a fine example of Wood's portraiture at its best.

Even more smoothly stylized, but romantic in feeling rather than humorous, is Wood's *Midnight Ride of Paul Revere*— a miniature village, its curving road a ribbon of moonlight over which tiny horse and rider fly past to spread the alarm through all the painted countryside. These and similar paintings by Wood are clever and delightful, but do not compare in genuine worth with the ones that preceded them by a few years: the portrait of the artist's mother placing a geranium pot on a window sill; the bleakly serious farm couple of *American Gothic*, a masterly composition in which the artist repeats the Gothic pitch of the barn roof in the pointed shape of the window, the upturned pitchfork, the high ovals of the bald head of the farmer and the lank-combed head of his wife; the bland but biting satire of *Daughters of the American Revolution*, Wood's most famous painting. (Pl. XXI)

It is doubtful if Thomas Benton has ever been afflicted with even the shadow of an inferiority complex. His forebears were famous men in the history of his native state of Missouri, he is the namesake of a great-uncle who was a noted senator from that State. His father was a U. S. District Attorney under President Grover Cleveland and had many terms in Washington as a member of Congress. As a counterbalance to the urbane life of the nation's capital, Benton spent his boyhood summers in the Mark Twain Missouri of Tom Sawyer and Huck Finn. From childhood his mind and imagination were packed full with the sight and sound of frontier politics and history-in-the-making; he absorbed the folkways of isolated regions and observed at first hand backwoods crudities. (Pl. XX)

He early began to unload himself of these crowding, varied impressions by constantly sketching them out on paper. Despite his father's disapproval he went to the Chicago Art Institute for a year and a half when he was in his middle teens and was off to Paris at the age of nineteen. Still very young —in more than years—when he returned, he strutted about in what the well-dressed artist in Paris was wearing, spouting undigested ideas about art, and thoroughly out of joint with his American background and intensely American self.

For almost a decade he labored at being an artist without finding his own expression. Then slowly he began to get his artistic footing on his native soil. Technically expert, Benton soon developed a distinctive style that was hailed as indigenously American. Not one to hide his talent under a bushel or his pictures behind a door, Benton—a small, muscular, mustached man with the pounce and combativeness of a fighting cock—became the self-appointed spokesman for Americanism in art, shadow-boxing with dramatic punches all the isms he had originally, fresh from Paris, mistakenly preached and haltingly practiced.

He has executed many historical murals including for his own State Capitol in Jefferson City, Missouri, a folk-history series depicting the James Boys of trigger fame, the melancholy saga of Frankie and Johnny, and the adventures of Huck Finn. These lusty murals were at first received with outcries of indignant horror and Benton was vociferously vituperated from one end of Missouri to the other. But time mellows all things, even Benton's murals—though hardly Benton. His native state is now proud of its son and his works.

Early in 1948 *Look* magazine sent a confidential questionnaire to sixty-eight art critics and museum directors and curators throughout the country, asking each to list in descending order the ten "best" painters then working in the United States. After receiving answers from well over half, *Look* sent the artists most often named the same questionnaire without, however, informing them of the earlier selections. The results of both polls amazingly coincided, the first-named top winner on both polls being John Marin. (Pl. XXI)

John Marin (1870-1953) was trained as an architect and turned from that profession to begin the study of painting when he was thirty years old. When he was thirty-five he went for the first time to Europe where for five years he studied and painted amidst influences from the Fauves, the Cubists, and the German Expressionists. He returned to the United

States in 1911 and from then until his death three months before his eighty-third birthday he divided his time and his art among the skyscrapers and crowded streets of downtown New York, the sunsets of city, country and desert, the White Mountains of New Hampshire, the plains and mesas of New Mexico, and, above all, the Maine seacoast with its little islands. His primary medium was an opaque watercolor. He was sixty before he began to work seriously in oil.

Marin's highly individual art strikes an ever-changing balance between real and abstract forms and thus satisfies a subconscious longing for that perfect expression of our transitional age. He has a quick, slashing, frequently staccato line, often referred to as his "shorthand." But the sense of movement inherent in all his work is far more complete than could be expressed by line alone or even by the multiple "force-lines" employed by the Futurists. The entire picture flows and tumbles with all-encompassing motion like the sea, constantly moving yet always contained, or—in city scenes —like a roughly jolly earthquake that out of sheer earth-vitality shakes and tilts everything in sight but does not destroy. Here again it is the remarkable expression of equilibrium *in motion*, the arrested fall, that makes Marin's art unique.

Among the other artists listed in the *Look* magazine poll were Max Weber, Yasuo Kuniyoshi, Stuart Davis, Ben Shahn, Edward Hopper, Charles Burchfield, George Grosz, Franklin Watkins, Lyonel Feininger and Jack Levine. To that list could easily be added other important names: Reginald Marsh, Georgia, O'Keeffe, Charles Sheeler, and many others.

But there is no strong resemblance between the works of any of these artists. Weber, long our leading representative of the School of Paris, is primarily an Expressionist, his paintings darkly rich in color and emotionally powerful in their distortion of form. Kuniyoshi, born in Japan but educated in California and New York, fused a romantic grace, an Oriental formalism and a deliberately simple folk-naïveté into a personal style that, in his last paintings, emerged as a complex, highly individual form of Expressionism, at times characterized by muted transparencies of color. Stuart Davis, using bright, clear colors that give his paintings an electric vitality, has developed a characteristic style based on the abstracting of recognizable forms.

Ben Shahn paints according to the dictates of his strong social conscience, believing that art is communication. His technique has poster boldness, mural enlargement of the important elements—always the human face and figure—and sometimes an abstract perfection of design without loss or distortion of the realistic components. (Pl. XXXI)

Hopper, Burchfield, and Sheeler, all paint the American scene—but how differently! Hopper projects the essence of reality, the feeling that "This is it; this is the way things really are." He is the great American painter of loneliness. Burchfield's midwestern landscapes and paintings of small towns range from eerie Expressionist fantasy to gentle satire—always with poetic overtones. Painter-photographer Charles Sheeler has a deep instinct for form unadorned which has produced in his paintings a perfect marriage of abstract design with realistic form. (Pls. XX,XXI)

Among all the artists listed in the *Look* poll—and among many others who might well have been included—there is only one common characteristic. They are American—whether by birth or adoption—and they have an innately American quality: individuality.

17 THE GOTHIC AND

THE GROTESQUE

FROM THE LAND OF THE BLACK FOREST, THE Grimm brothers' fairy tales, and the darkling clouds and majestic thunderings of the Götterdammerung, comes art that has the mystic emotionalism of the Gothic spirit. It may lose itself in high-vaulted shadows or, swooping in dizzy descent, perch with macabre playfulness on the grotesque angles of steep-pitched village roofs, dance on the green with Til Eulenspiegel, or run shivering from hobgoblins of its own creating. The brooding emotionalism in modern art known as Expressionism took shape in Germany during the early years of the present century. Its palette is usually heavy and often dark, its distortions unload the artist's emotions on the spectator.

As its name implies, Expressionism is exactly the opposite of unemotional Impressionism, which never goes beneath the surface. Excepting only Daumier and Rouault—the one cloaking his despair and pity in caricature, the other in religion— the French artist looked about him and saw the world a charming and colorful place or a stage set for drama or romance. The German searched his soul and found *Sturm und Drang,* looked outward and saw its shadow darkening the world.

Perhaps temperature has more effect on temperament than we suspect, and climate on character. Anyone knows that continuously gloomy weather is very good for brooding. True, the English and the Vikings had little in the way of sunshine —but they didn't stay home; they set out to sea. People in the heartland of Europe have for centuries remained hemmed in; when they did make the break from their native land, they seldom returned.

Whether the geographical theory is tenable or not, it is a fact that Expressionism had its rise and remained centered in Germany, with four great Expressionists—van Gogh, Munch, Kandinsky, Kokoschka—and one master of the grotesque, James Ensor, coming from countries just across the border. Had van Gogh remained all his artistic life in the low countries bordering Germany, it is indeed doubtful that his palette would have lightened and his spirit lifted. But even in Paris and under the blazing sun of Provence his art remained Expressionist, an outpouring of emotion rather than a recording of impression.

It was Edvard Munch, however, born in Norway in 1863, whose work—early influenced by van Gogh and Gauguin —became the first rallying point for the German artists who as a group developed Expressionism into a movement. Munch studied painting in Oslo for about three years, then in a three-week vis't to Paris when he was twenty-two received his initial impulse from the painting van Gogh and Gauguin were then doing. Four years later he had a one man exhibition in Oslo and was awarded a government grant which enabled him to spend the winter in Paris, going later to Germany. In November 1892 an exhibition in Berlin of fifty-five of his paintings caused such an uproar that it was closed. This of course gave him tremendous public'ty, rallying progressive young German artists to his suppo-t and bringing many under the influence of his painting.

Few of Munch's paintings have been seen in the United States He is known here chiefly through his lithographs and woodcuts, particularly those he did in the 1890's. These are his finest. Like his paintings, his graphic work is expressed in heavy, unbroken lines that may pulse upward on long, sweeping curves but inevitably descend as though pulled downward by their own weight. His composition is uncluttered, the down-curving line giving a heaviness to his figures of people, who often seem to droop in pensive lassitude or wary resignation even in a scene, such as a dance, where one would normally expect gaiety. His colors have a richly dark clarity and, more than most Expressionists, he makes exciting use of areas of high-keyed tones; the pale dresses of several of the women are luminous against the prevailing dark colors of *The Dance of Life* In a similar way, the areas of untouched white where the sky is left bare of the dark strokes, and the staring faces of the people, whose features are but faintly indicated, as in the lithograph *Anxiety*, give an intense, suppressed vitality to his woodcuts.

Munch was a man of moods, most of them melancholy. With brooding intensity he sought the meaning of life, his aim to uncover and express its longings and fears, its hope and its despair—to show living, loving, suffering humanity.

In 1937 Munch—unquestionably Scandinavia's greatest painter—had many carvases in the Paris World's Fair In April 1940, when the Germans moved in on Norway, Munch was invited to join the "Honorary Art Council" set up by the Quisling Government. He refused. In January 1944 he died in Norway of a heart attack.

In 1905, about the time the Fauves emerged as a loosely organized movement in Paris, three young artists joined forces in Dresden to form *Die Brücke* (The Bridge) which was eventually to be recognized as the first group of German Expressionists. (The name—*Expressionismus*—did not come into use until almost six years later.) The young artists were Ernst Ludwig Kirchner, twenty-five, Erich Heckel, twenty-two, and Karl Schmidt-Rottluff, twenty-one. A year or so later Max Pechstein, twenty-five, and Emil Nolde, forty, joined them. Nolde was already known as a rebel artist. He had started his art career at fourteen, with ornamental woodcarving; his first major painting was refused a place in the 1896 Munich Exhibition; three years later he went to Paris, where he found his artistic direction in the work of Daumier, Delacroix, and particularly Millet. He is like a more rugged, more emotional Millet but using the vivid palette of the Fauves.

With these five artists as its core, *Die Brücke* grew in numbers and influence until 1913 when, due to internal differences and the rising forces of World War I, the group fell apart although its leading members went on to individual fame. From the beginning, *Die Brücke* was a revolt against the crushing dullness of German classic painting and the sentimental objectivity of its Romantic-Realistic school. The group had little admiration for their immediate elders, who had done their own rebelling a generation earlier.

The Brücke group showed their kinship with the Fauves in the use of bold, unnatural color and distorted exaggeration of form—the Gauguin influence strengthened by their interest in primitive German woodcuts, a favorite medium with the group. To this combination they added a keen interest in African masks and the primitive arts of the South Seas. The brooding emotionalism basic to Expressionism, however, was their own Teutonic-Gothic inheritance, preceded—rather than inspired—by the paintings of Munch and van Gogh, earlier inheritors of the Gothic spirit.

In Vienna in 1908, the works of a twenty-two-year-old Austrian were first shown in exhibition and were immediately labeled rebellious, shocking, and even subversive. (Actually they were wonderfully prophetic of the art of the new century in their Expressionist tendencies, symbolism, and in certain elements of Surrealism.) They were therefore condemned by the official critics. As a result, young Oskar Kokoschka was expelled from the Vienna School of Arts and Crafts, where he was not only an advanced student but had been employed as an assistant instructor since his second year there, two years earlier. The School, center of the decorative arts in middle Europe, was not only very influential but, for its time and place—in the bureaucratic-authoritarian, highly conservative Vienna of the last days of the Hapsburgs—both progressive and liberal. Athough the young Kokoschka was a rebellious, stubbornly independent student, working out his own methods—with results curiously like the "Blue Period" of the equally unknown Picasso, his Paris contemporary—he had been encouraged in his independence by the school authorities, who were far in advance of their time both in wisdom and tolerance. But even they could not stand up against the onslaught of official circles and their newspaper-mouthpieces, all marching on to their unwitting doom within the next decade.

The newspapers had tagged Kokoschka "Horror of the Citizen," and because of the attendant notoriety, he was unable to get anything but very intermittent, poorly paid employment. He often went hungry and, in desperation, he began to play the role foisted on him. Sometimes he won bets from well-heeled young Americans by drinking them under the table in the Viennese cafés which were striving to acquire reputations for Parisian Bohemianism.

During these early difficult years the young artist was aided—perhaps even enabled to survive—by the great modern architect of Vienna, Adolf Loos, who had an infallible instinct for recognizing talent, an abounding generosity in sustaining it, and the courage of a lion in defending it. Convinced of Kokoschka's superior gifts, Loos introduced him to helpful friends, obtained portrait commissions for him and bought paintings he himself commissioned. Equally important, Loos, whose wisdom equalled his generosity, little by little taught Kokoschka to stand on his own feet financially as well as artistically.

In 1910 Kokoschka went to Berlin, to which the leaders of *Die Brücke* had moved two years earlier. Of their age and artistic heritage—like him, the members of *Die Brücke* were regarded as *enfants terribles*—he was drawn to them but did not join the group. Years later, when he returned to live in Germany, it was apparent that his development into one of the great Expressionists had paralleled theirs, each artist following his individual star.

For four years Kokoschka lived alternately in Berlin and in Vienna. He was severely wounded early in World War I, patched up and returned to the front. After the war he was appointed to a teaching post in Dresden, which he resigned in 1924 for several years of travel. By this time he was recognized throughout Europe as one of its foremost artists. In 1937 a large retrospective exhibition of his works was held in Vienna. The same year, Hitler honored him by confiscating more than 400 of his works owned by German museums and collectors, showing sixteen of them in the famously infamous "Exhibition of Degenerate Art" in Munich.

Just ahead of the Anschluss, Kokoschka left Austria for Czechoslovakia, his father's native land. There he was received with honor and granted immediate full citizenship—only to be obliged to flee to England upon the signing of the Munich Pact by Hitler and Chamberlain. After the war his name was found on the official Gestapo list of 1938 to be "executed without trial upon capture."

Kokoschka still lives and paints in London. He is a profoundly thoughtful man, seeking through painting and writing to uncover the roots of the world's troubles. From the earliest years of his career his love for mankind has emerged in passionately perceptive portraits of psychological insight. During his travels he produced a series of "landscape-portraits" of many of the great cities of the world—London, Paris, Constantinople, Jerusalem, Venice, and others. In London, through the worst years of the blitz, he painted figure compositions—*Anschluss, Alice in Wonderland, Lorelei, What Are We Fighting For?*—depicting allegorically his horror of war and its degenerative effect on men. All of Kokoschka's work expresses his conviction that "The life of the consciousness is boundless. It interpenetrates the world and is woven through all its imagery."

In 1911 the Russian Kandinsky, the German Franz Marc and several other German painters, resigned from an association of Munich artists to launch a new group, *Der Blaue Reiter*—the name taken from a painting by Kandinsky. The Blue Rider group or the League of Blue Knights (as they were sometimes referred to) in quick succession—only three months apart—held two exhibitions in Munich which included the work of French, German, and Russian avant-garde artists. The group was not organized to exploit the work of its members but to encourage and show paintings by artists anywhere who were breaking traditional molds. They brought many such artists to public attention through exhibitions during the next few years and by means of a publication the two leaders established to explain their program and promote its purpose. With vigor they pushed forward the work begun by *Die Brücke* to make Germany aware of and receptive to modern art. The impetus continued after World War I and, until Hitler took over the country, Expressionism was the great modern art of Germany, with acceptance by museums, galleries, and private collectors.

Although the paintings they produced were so dissimilar, Franz Marc, like Kandinsky, was a mystic. His chief subject was animals. His technique was partially derived from the Cubists, but he used the rearrangement of forms and the overlapping of planes for a very different purpose. He felt that by discarding the conventional approach to painting he could penetrate more nearly into the essence—or soul—of nature and nature's animals. He tried to paint out *from* the animal, to express its essential nature—the dynamic grace-in-movement of a horse, the gentleness of a doe, the hunger-tautness of a wolf, the "tigerishness of the tiger." Above all, he sought the understanding, the *in-feeling* with his subject that would enable him to paint its natural surroundings not from the point of view of the artist observing from without, but seeing and feeling *being* the animal enclosed in and part of nature's "oneness."

This poetic-mystical identification of himself with his subject—plus his superb equipment as an artist—brought forth paintings lyrical in color and form. Taming Fauvism to overlay of rich but translucent jeweltones, Marc blended animal forms mysteriously with nature in exquisite camouflage. Then this fine and gentle artist, filled with loving-kindness toward man and nature, went out to be killed in 1916 in the Battle of Verdun.

A forerunner the *Brücke* youngsters did not disdain was the Belgian painter, Baron James Ensor, born of English-Flemish parents in 1860 in Ostend, where he lived out the nine decades of his life—with a two-year interval at the *Académie des Beaux-Arts* in Brussels—and died in 1949. Ensor was a thoroughly independent painter. Familiar with the work of the Impressionists, he ignored their theories and even those of the Post-Impressionists. Lightly tossing them aside, he developed an unclassifiable style uniquely his own. In spirit it is a true descendant of Hieronymus Bosch, as is evident in the painting, *Tribulations of St. Anthony,* owned by the Museum of Modern Art, New York. It is a large canvas crowded with tiny hobgoblins, grotesque faces, gossamer-winged sprites, strange insects, and half-formed squiggles and blotches that are likely to shape themselves suddenly into fantastic little monsters.

Like Turner, Ensor was able to infuse his canvases with light, and all these weird little creatures and bits and pieces of unformed beings float in the pale air, shimmer over translucent pools, or scuttle half-seen through weeds and rocks on the shore, while Hell's fiery breath seems to belch forth others—none of them very horrifying, however In fact, all these small imps and sub-imps appear more mischievous than evil—swarms of supernatural gnats that tease and tantalize but never terrify.

Ensor's most famous picture, *The Entrance of Christ Into Brussels,* is a painted supposition of the welcome the Son of God might receive should He ride into a modern metropolis on Palm Sunday. This is an immense painting which fills a canvas of ten square yards. It shows a vast throng, accompanied by the beating drums and blaring trumpets of the "Belgian Bigots' Band," milling about and marching, each to his own whim, beside, before, and behind the gentle Jesus. The gaily disordered marchers, wearing grotesque and leering masks, carry banners bearing crazily written slogans proclaiming their special interests.

This vast pageant of irony is so full of life, high-keyed color, and an infinitude of fantastic forms and energetic movement that no sense of bitterness comes through. It is as though the viewer is on the sidewalk watching the wild parade, horrified by its inescapable meaning but helplessly laughing and saying to himself with a fatalistic shrug: "There goes humanity, marching to its doom with a brass band." Small wonder *Die Brucke* young men worshipped Ensor for his independence, admired him for his skill, and delighted in his twinkling or sardonic fantasy.

There was one artist o er whose birth the Spirit of Fantasy not only hovered—she claimed him as her own from the cradle Paul Klee wandered at will from the heavy world of the flesh into the dancing, whispering, floating, secret world of grasses written by water in flowing script, of fainting flowers, of a ship-pursuing demon wearing the green sickle-moon and a yellow star in his hair of machines that twitter, of the forlorn ghost of a letter, of a baleful cat gripping a bird-image between hypnotic eyes, of a dream-filled atmosphere pierced by whizzing arrows Klee's pictures are psychocardiograms of the inner senses. (P. XXIII)

For a moment returning to the solid earth, let us examine the bare facts of the artist's mundane life. Paul Klee was born, 1879, near Berne, Switzerland His father was a Bavarian music teacher and conductor, his mother, also musical, was of southern French stock. From birth, Klee was surrounded by music. Throughout his life it was essential to him, and he became a fine violinist When he was eighteen he began the study of drawing in Munich. Two years later he went to Italy and then for the next four years lived with his parents in Berne, taking occasional trips to Paris, Berlin and Munich.

In 1906, he married a musician, a pianist; they settled in Munich, where they lived until 1920.

Klee had his first one-man show in Munich in 1911. The same year he became closely associated with Kandinsky and Franz Marc, forming with them and August Macke, a German artist killed the first year of World War I, the nucleus of the Blue Rider Group. In 1920 Klee joined the faculty of the Bauhaus, living first at Weimar and then at Dessau. In 1929, in honor of his fiftieth birthday, exhibitions of his work were held in many German and Swiss museums. In 1933, revolted by Hitler, he went back to Switzerland, where he died in 1940.

Paul Klee's work has been likened to that of the Japanese, to the art of primitive peoples and drawings by children and the insane. But there has been no artist anywhere, at any time, like Klee. He saw the invisible, he heard the sound of silence, he listened to mute laughter, and he felt the movement of growing things. The miracle of his art communicates all this.

After World War I—despite the constant unheaval of successive short-lived governments, and inflation's terrible destruction of values of all kinds, including human—for a little while and in parts of Germany hope seemed to rise from the ashes of defeat. This was nowhere more evident than in the establishment at Weimar of the famous Bauhaus under the leadership of the young German architect, Walter Gropius. For the faculty of this new kind of industrial school based on the joining of artist and artisan, Gropius brought together artists and designers of international reputation to teach pure and applied esthetics. One of these was Lyonel Feininger.

Born in New York, 1871, of parents who were practicing musicians, Feininger lived chiefly in that city until he was sixteen. When he was eight or nine he began to study the violin with his father and was playing in concerts when he was twelve. Four years later his parents took him to Germany for a year of advanced music study. They had no sooner landed in Hamburg, however, than the youth decided he must become a painter. After studying art in Germany and then in Paris, he became a cartoonist and illustrator, first in Berlin, then in Paris, where he drew cartoons for a leading French publication and turned out every week for the Chicago *Sunday Tribune* two pages of comics: "The Kin-der-Kids" and "Wee Willie Winkie's World."

In 1907, when he was thirty-six, Feininger was able to give up cartooning and illustration to devote full time to painting. He moved back to Berlin, where he lived for the next twenty years, occasionally visiting London and Paris.

From 1919 until Hitler closed the Bauhaus in 1933, Feininger taught there, becoming artist-in-residence when the Bauhaus moved from Weimar to Dessau. In 1924, with Paul Klee, Kandinsky and another Russian, Jawlensky, he formed the Blue Four, which exhibited in several cities of the United States and in Mexico. (In Germany Feininger was considered an American, which was as he always thought of himself even though he had married and raised a family in Germany. Outside of Germany, even in his native land, he was considered a German artist.) In 1931 he was given a large retrospective exhibition in the National Gallery, Berlin. Two years later Hitler honored him by including his work in the exhibition of degenerate art.

Feininger visited his own country for the first time in fifty years when he was invited to teach art in the summer session at Mills College, California, in 1936. The following year he returned to live in this country permanently. He now divides his time between New York City and a small town in Connecticut.

As a child, Feininger had been fascinated by the ships and small boats he saw in the two rivers—the East and the Hudson—that make Manhattan an island. He also carried with him to Germany childish memories of the towering skyscrapers, to which he later added impressions of the crowding old structures of Europe. These motifs show up again and again on his canvases. His paintings have the sensitivity of Whistler —our other expatriate artist who established his reputation abroad—but their design is both more precise and more complex than Whistler's, with strongly accented planes in receding-advancing Cubist technique. His colors are delicate, but never *mingle* as in Impressionist style. Strongly defined, they ray out, cross, meet, parallel each other, combine or coincide, firmly yet delicately poised in architectonic balance. Each color retains its individuality, as do the ordered rays of the spectrum cast by light refracted through a prism. The visitor to a Feininger exhibition feels as though he is walking among rainbows.

For some artists in Germany there were no rainbows. One of these was Max Beckmann, born in 1884 in Leipzig and well known as a painter and graphic artist before World War I. Between the two world wars he developed a strongly individual Expressionism which, as Hitler rose to power, seemed to be squeezed in upon itself in crowded, distorted forms by the unbearable pressure of Germany's anguished upheavals.

As Hitler's power became stabilized, crushing Germany into a new order, Beckmann's canvases took on a stark calmness. No more crowding and distortion—just a methodically mad mutilation of limbs, a binding of body with body, like trussed fowls, a senseless torture. This is shown in the two outer panels of his great triptych *Departure*. In the center panel, however, all is calm. Figures of dignity and peace, one heavily veiled, another clasping a baby, are ready for departure in a boat on serene waters. Beckmann speaks of this as a departure from life's illusions toward hidden realities. (Pl. XXX)

Hitler purged Beckmann's "degenerate" paintings from Germany's museums and in 1937 the artist left the country for Amsterdam, where he lived until he came to make his home in the United States in 1947. He was appointed professor of painting at Washington University, St. Louis. The night before he died, December 27, 1950, he put the last brush stroke on another great triptych, *The Argonauts*.

The artist of our time who has most terrifyingly depicted war, its corruption and destruction of man, is George Grosz. Born in Berlin in 1893 he began the study of art there when he was only nine At the age of sixteen he enrolled in the Fine Arts Academy of Dresden. The following year he sold his first caricature to the *Berliner Tageblatt*.

From the fall of 1914 until early 1916, when he was discharged because of illness, Grosz served in the German infantry. He was drafted back into the army in 1917, hospitalized for illness, and finally demobilized in the fall of 1918, when the army disintegrated. During the next few years, with his savage caricatures of the moral collapse in Germany, he became the world's most famous living satirist, attaining the distinction of being arrested and tried on charges ranging from blasphemy to disrespect for the German army the evidence being his bitterly sardonic and often hideous drawings attacking militarism, officialdom, the greed and sensuality of postwar profiteers, and the decay of moral and human values

Fortunately, just before Hitler came to full power, Grosz was invited to teach at New York's Art Students League in 1932. He wisely decided to remain in this country and in 1938 became a citizen. Here in the climate of freedom his art underwent a profound change. The savage satire that had barbed it in Germany seemed to dissolve in mental peace. He even turned from his accustomed graphic medium to work chiefly in oil, painting tranquil landscapes, still lifes, and figure studies.

But artists are often sensitive barometers of the changing climate of human thought and behavior. The atmosphere of the world began to grow heavy with the precipitation of war. The colors Grosz laid on his canvases became darker and more violent the figures grotesque and gaunt in fear-filled landscapes. There was no satire in his paintings now; only nightmare tragedy weird horror, and haunting lone-liness in the midst of universal destruction. Strange and ter-rifying little "stickmen" roamed the world. Unlike the realism of the war drawings by Goya and Orozco, the paintings by Grosz have a Gothic Romanticism like macabre fairy tales out of Grimm and in the tradition of Bosch and Grünewald. Probably the most compelling anti-war pictures our age will see, these paintings show war's obscene face in the tattered rags of torn and decaying flesh, the walking dead, the final peace of a world torn apart. (Pl. XXXI)

18 DADA AND SURREALISM

Everything is nothing—

—THEREFORE, CONCLUDED DISILLUSIONED AND despairing German artists during World War I, nothing is everything; and they proceeded to demonstrate this. As the war rose to a frenzy of destruction, reducing to rubbish men and all they had worked for and held dear, groups of artists paralleled this awful waste of humanity by creating a wild and sardonic *anti*-art composed of trash—old bus tickets, pieces of string, clockworks, torn lace, crazily cut snapshots and illustrations, bits of wood, broken buttons, and rubbish of all kinds. These they pasted on canvas or set up on pedestals like sculpture, and with mock solemnity presented the conglomerations to the world as exhibitions of art.

Child of despair and destruction, the movement was born in a Zurich café one night in February 1916, the midwives present being artists and writers, some of them war refugees. It was christened by a finger placed at random on the flipped-open page of a dictionary. The christening finger touched the word "Dada"—an infantile double-syllable used, it is said, by French infants to designate a hobby-horse. And so the movement, as a movement, was launched.

A few individual manifestations had preceded it. In 1910 the Cubism of Braque and Picasso had produced such dislocations of natural forms as to foreshadow the nihilism of Dada. In Milan, the Futurists had declared war on the "harmony" and "good taste" that had for centuries been the canons of art. In 1912 Picasso and Braque originated collage by pasting bits of newspapers, calling cards, oilcloth, etc., on canvas as part of painted compositions. The following year Picasso produced his three-dimensional constructions of paper, wood, cloth, etc. In 1914 Marcel Duchamp enhanced a cheap chromo-lithograph of a woodland scene by pasting on the trees tiny red and green drugstore signs. And he gravely "signed" and put on exhibition as a work of art an ordinary metal bottle rack. This was pure Dadaism although neither the name nor the movement had as yet come into being.

Dada did not, however, develop from these individual manifestations nor were the artists concerned a part of the movement when it began in Zurich. Dada was the spontaneous combustion of a state of mind and spread as rapidly as a brush fire among painters and poets and writers in Germany. Long before the war ended it had crossed the border to Paris and the ocean to New York, where Duchamp and Picabia, a Cubist painter, were living. With Man Ray, a Philadelphia painter who later in Paris developed photography as a medium for Dada and Surrealist compositions, they formed a Dada nucleus in New York, exhibiting in "291" under the interested eye of Stieglitz. In 1917 Duchamp was made a member of the executive committee of the first Independents Exhibition in New York. As his contribution to the show he sent a porcelain urinal signed "R. Mutt" and titled *Fontaine*. It was rejected by the committee, from which Duchamp thereupon haughtily resigned.

In Zurich the artist-founders of Dadaism were Tristan Tzara, a Russian poet and painter, and Hans Arp, a French sculptor, painter, and poet. In 1917 a Berlin group emerged under the brief leadership of George Grosz. In 1918 a Cologne group was formed, with Max Ernst its most gifted and inventive member. In 1919 Kurt Schwitters, a German painter and writer of Hanover, founded his own variety of Dadaism, which he called *Merz*. He created Merz pictures and collages, Merz poems, Merz interiors, and constructed at the rear of his house a group of fantastic grottos he called *Merzbau*. Of all the Dadaists, Schwitters took the movement most seriously as a new art form; some of his *Merzbilder* (rubbish pictures) are very fine examples of collage and, in their intricate interrelation of form, line, and color, achieve a genuine artistry.

For several years Dada flourished as an art-and-literature movement in Europe, its brush-fire success due largely to two factors: its anti-rational, paradoxical (an art to end art) aim coincided with post-war world disillusionment; and its mad goings-on—bizarre exhibitions, fantastic balls, and *soirées* of idiotic poetry readings—were widely heralded and minutely described by the newspapers, thus adding to the gaiety of nations long in need of some sort of comic relief.

Fleetingly, a few substantial artists—Picasso, Grosz, etc.—were drawn into the movement but soon left it to continue on their own paths. Lesser artists found in Dada a rare opportunity for exploiting their second-rate talents—it was not difficult to be a Dadaist—but as the movement receded, they were beached on the shores of obscurity. The few of superior gifts, like Ernst and Arp, emerged into more positive forms of art. So the art that was out to destroy art quite logically ended by destroying itself.

Just before its disintegration began, Dada rose to its heights in January 1920 with an exhibition in Paris at which painting and sculpture were shown, poems read, and music performed —all of it Dada, of course. The object that caused the greatest public reaction—chiefly indignation—was Duchamp's exhibit of Mona Lisa with a mustache (he labeled it LH-OOQ), an artistic recreation which has remained to plague us in subways, advertisements, and a recent photograph of Dali posed as *La Gioconda* but garnished with his own stupendous hirsute adornment. In May of the same year a great Dada Festival was held in Paris, followed the next month by a big international exhibition in Berlin.

In June 1922 the last large show took place in Paris, where the movement had been a literary, rather than an art manifestation. Now Tzara, who headed the German groups, and André Breton, poet-leader of the French Dadaists, opposed each other, with Breton emerging the victor. With the support of other prominent French members—writer-poets Louis Aragon, Paul Eluard, and Philippe Soupault—he not only drew many of the German and Swiss Dadaists into his camp but within two years had developed a new movement combining the anti-rationalism of Dada with explorations of the subconscious as material for art and literature. Sigmund Freud's theory and technique of psychoanalysis were very much to the fore in the early 1920's, and Breton's cohorts not only embraced but embellished them. In 1924 Breton issued his First Manifesto of Surrealism, which read in part as follows:

SURREALISM: *Pure psychic automatism, by which it is intended to express verbally, in writing, or by other means, the real process of thought. Thought's dictation in the absence of all control exercised by the reason and outside all esthetic or moral preoccupations.*

Surrealism rests in the belief in the superior reality of certain forms of association neglected heretofore; in the omnipotence of the dream and in the disinterested play of thought. It tends definitely to do away with all other psychic mechanism and to substitute itself for them in the solution of the principal problems of life.

As indicated in this excerpt from the Manifesto, Surrealism was intended not merely as a new form of art and literature but as a way of life. Its more fervent adherents tried to make it just that. Others developed its theories chiefly in painting and writing. One artist, whose sense of nonsense was supreme and whose talent superb, seized on it with joy and (whenever he found it convenient) acted it out in his own life with such fervor that he sometimes endangered that life. Some years ago, when he gave a lecture on Surrealism in London, he nearly smothered in the diver's helmet he insisted on wearing because he planned to "submerge in the subconscious." That of course was Dali who, on his first visit to New York, wore a lamb chop on his head while being interviewed by *The New York Times* (Pl. XXII)

Centuries before Dali made his entrance into the exact center of the Surrealist spotlight, artists were putting on canvas disquieting dream-images and the strange irrationalities that float on the border of consciousness: the double images of Archimboldo the nightmares of Füssli, the heavenly visions of Blake, the Gothic grotesqueries of Bosch, Grünewald, and Breughel. The immediate forerunners of the Surrealist movement, however, are the French Odilon Redon (1840-1916), the Russian Marc Chagall (1889-   ), and the Italian Giorgio de Chirico (1888-   ).

Redon's beautiful graphic work—etchings, charcoal drawings, black-and-white lithographs—have a haunting, mystic quality of great intensity His oil paintings and pastels, chiefly portraits of women and children, religious subjects, and flowers, whisper rather than speak of an unseen more real than the seen, of intangibles nearer to us than our breath.

Marc Chagall is a merry, strongly built little man with a heavy thatch of gray curls. Born in Vitebsk, Russia, the son of a fish merchant, he studied for two years at the Imperial School of Fine Arts at St. Petersburg. There a patron of the arts traded him a trip to Paris for seven paintings. In the French capital Chagall found a corner in the huge warehouse-tenement *La Ruche*, near the slaughterhouse, which sheltered so many future great artists. Chagall soon made friends and became acquainted with avant-garde artistic and literary leaders in Paris. In 1914 he sent 200 canvases to Berlin from which an exhibition was to be selected. A few weeks later he set out for that city with high hopes, on his way to Vitebsk to marry his fiancée. War was declared, but he saw his exhibition and married the beautiful Bella. (Pl. XXIII)

The war, the Revolution, the first years of tremendous hope in the arts for all Russia—then the reversal to the dull mediocrity of dictated bourgeois art. Like Kandinsky and scores of other artists, Chagall left Russia in 1922, returning to Paris.

During the following two decades his reputation mounted. Vollard commissioned him to do several series of illustrations, he had a number of one-man exhibitions in Europe and one in New York. In 1939 he won the Carnegie International. Four years earlier he had been in Poland, where he became deeply apprehensive of war and the spread of large-scale Jewish persecutions, already beginning in Germany. His paintings became somber and dramatic. In 1941 he was invited by the Museum of Modern Art to come to the United States. He lived here and in Mexico until 1947, when he returned to Paris. He now lives in southern France.

Except for the canvases that reflect his deep concern with Europe's impending disaster, Chagall's paintings are wonderfully fantastic depictions of his boyhood in a Russian village, his surrealistic delight in Paris, and his exuberant love for Bella. (When she died in 1944 he was unable to paint for many months.) Never has love of a man for a woman been more joyously celebrated than in the paintings of Chagall: decorated, showered, sometimes cradled in flowers, the two float in blissful happiness above the everyday objects of their home. Upside down with delight, Chagall's dream-image of himself bends over to kiss his Bella from the heights of ecstasy, which have wafted him to the ceiling. Chagall has never needed Freud to chart his subconscious or Breton to read him into or out of the Surrealist movement. In the gayest, softest, loveliest colors, "life and death, the past and the future, the real and the imaginary" spill out spontaneously on his canvases. This is true "surreality" which Breton calls a merging of "two apparently contradictory states—the dream and reality."

Even more closely allied to Surrealism as defined by Breton was the early work of Giorgio de Chirico. Born of Italian parents in Greece, he studied for two years at the Fine Arts Academy, Athens, then went to Italy where he copied the works of the Renaissance masters. Later he studied at the Munich Academy in Germany. But it was during his lonely penniless years in Paris that he produced the pictures that are the earliest and greatest paintings of Surrealism, forerunners of the movement that was not to be born for a dozen years: paintings of empty, sunlit squares with tiny human figures lost in the ominously quiet space; high-shadowed arches stretching out of the picture into infinity; broken pieces of sculpture on a road rising to nowhere. His nostalgia-evoking *Melancholy and Mystery of a Street* with its shadowy little girl rolling a hoop down a lonely sunlit street is one of the important paintings of the twentieth century. And his strangely graceful wooden figures with bald, featureless egg-heads and jointed bodies, inhabiting silent ancient squares and classical landscapes, say something disturbing about modern man.

De Chirico called these "metaphysical paintings," and for a number of years they were ignored by art critics and collectors and scorned by the Paris intelligentsia as too "literary" to be art. They began to be appreciated after World War I, and in 1924 de Chirico worked with Breton and others in the launching of Surrealism. Later he disassociated himself from the movement. During the past quarter-century his work has had little of its early dream quality; he has produced neo-classical paintings, many of them using the horse —the classic white Greek steed—as motif.

Salvador Dali, born near Barcelona, Spain, in 1904, is the most widely known Surrealist in the world and his painting of melting watches being devoured by insects—which he explains as merely "the tender, extravagant and arbitrary paranoiac-critical camembert of time and space"—is certainly the world's most famous Surrealist painting. Despite his exhibitionist antics, which cause many people to underrate his brilliance not only as an artist but as a man, Dali is one of the most skillful painters of our time. His drawings are exquisite and his painting technique, with its miniature precision and control, equals that of the finest of the little Dutch Masters. But he goes far beyond that school of painting in his handling of mass and volume, clearly evident in his beautiful *Crucifixion,* recently presented to the Metropolitan Museum of Art by that perceptive collector of painting, Chester Dale. (Pl. XXXII)

Surpassed only by Dali in fame as a Surrealist is Max Ernst, once head of the Cologne Dadaists. An extraordinarily skilled painter, he is even more noted for his variety of subject matter, his mastery of different techniques, and the wide range of his inventiveness. He developed a technique known as *frottage* by means of which the outlines of strange shapes and combinations of shapes are filled in by rubbing pencil, charcoal, or pastel stick over paper laid on the rough surface of planks, bricks, leaves, stone, etc. Another technique he invented is a form of collage in which he used a quantity of Victorian wood engravings from popular magazines of sixty and seventy years ago. These he cut up and pasted together in unnatural and startling forms, endowing human beings with animal heads and claws, wings and beaks of birds, and reptilian tails. There is no apparent joining of disparate elements. Each picture seems organically complete—an effect Ernst obtained by merging animal and human elements with pencil strokes so closely imitating the original technique of the engravings that they blend indiscernibly. This is the essence of Surrealism, the blending of the real with the unreal. He has worked in many mediums and combinations of mediums. For the past decade and a half, however, his chief work has been paintings, superb in technique and fascinating in content.

There are two basic types of Surrealism· the photographic and the amorphic In the first, every object in the picture is painted with photographic clarity even though—as in the work of Yves Tanguy, for example—such objects may never have existed· or, as with Dali, real objects are pulled out of shape (though still clearly recognizable, like the limp watches) or are rendered in new combinations such as spiders' legs on elephants. In this branch of Surrealism every element of the painting—no matter how phantasmagoric—is rendered with photographic realism, thus achieving one of the two principal aims of Surrealism: the marrying of the unreal with the real.

The other important aim of Surrealism is to yield to "the omnipotence of the dream" through "the disinterested play of thought." This is exemplified in the near-abstract work of the French André Masson, whose paintings appear to be produced like automatic writing, in which the hand is allowed its own freedom without conscious dictation of thought, and in the work of the Spaniard, Joan Miró, who has created some of Surrealism's most delightful canvases. In Miró's *Composition*, 1933, certain viewers profess to see suggestions of animal silhouettes; others frankly see nothing at all except meaningless abstract shapes in a handsome composition of subtly combined dark colors and solid or delicately outlined forms. This difference in optical reaction is similar to that of a man who sees a face, an animal, or a castle in cloud or mountain formations, in cracks in a plastered wall or discolorations on wallpaper, while his companion can see nothing but the mountains, clouds, cracks, and spots. But Miró has produced far more than these debatable canvases. He has a genius for delicate absurdity, creating endearing yet comical representations of man's—or dog's—puny efforts to challenge the universe by barking at the moon, or his elaborate preparations to perform a simple act.

Pierre Roy, a French artist who also studied architecture, uses the photographic Surrealist technique in exquisite paintings of objects that, taken singly, have no connection with one another but, combined, suggest the theme of the painting. *Daylight Saving*, for example, is represented by a watch—its hands pointing at five minutes to four—suspended by its heavy chain from a bow of satin ribbon to which are also tied two heads of ripe wheat and a chain of robins' eggs. These are all hung against a sheet of paper (on which a cardiogram is recorded) nailed to a wooden fence.

A somewhat similar art of suggestion is employed by

Arthur G. Dove, the American painter who before World War I gave up a good living as a commercial artist to endure the privation and ridicule which was the lot of the abstract painter of those days His rendering of the invisible—for example, the *sound* of a fog horn instead of its appearance —is highly imaginative yet immediately understandable, adding a new dimension to the world of the senses.

Pavel Tchelitchew, another Surrealist painter of note, has been particularly inventive in working out extremely subtle and complex metamorphic relationships His *Hide-and-Seek,* a very large painting of inter-related multiple forms, is owned by the Museum of Modern Art, New York. Viewed from a distance, the painting appears to picture a huge tree trunk, its wide-spreading lower branches thick with leaves in autumn colors. As one approaches the painting, all but the trunk itself is metamorphosed into a multitude of child forms and faces, the eye of one a blossom, the ear of another a leaf, the veinings of leaves becoming the veins of the children's faces. The heavy, above-ground roots of the tree are seen to be the toes of a giant foot, at the base of which lies a large-headed, tiny-bodied human embryo. At the center of the dark tree trunk is a long-haired little girl running into its hidden depths. The picture is a fascinating and superbly painted study in illusion and mystery. (Pl. XXII)

Surrealism has been one of the important movements in twentieth-century painting. During the period of its greatest activity, 1924-1939, it fanned out from its center in Paris to cities throughout the world—London, New York, Brussels, Warsaw, Copenhagen, Prague, Barcelona, Belgrade, Stockholm, Teneriffe, Tokyo—where groups were formed. As a movement, however, it scarcely exists any longer, although the most brilliant artists once associated with it still paint wholly or partly in the Surrealist tradition.

For some years André Breton, author of its Manifesto and its perpetual leader, has been "reading out" or excommunicating from Surrealist ranks those poets and painters he feels have fallen away from its theory and practice—an idle gesture, as most of them during the last decade and a half have voluntarily gone their own way. It would seem that the only logical retort to Breton's illogical—and therefore thoroughly Surrealistic—action might be found in the "ready-made, assisted" object created by Duchamp in 1921, at the height of Dadaism It is a birdcage filled with lumps of marble sugar, a thermometer, a cancelled postage stamp, and a desiccated hunk of parrot food.

Its title is: *Why Not Sneeze?*

19 THE INNOCENTS OF ART

How blest are they whose hearts are pure;
From guile their thoughts are free,
To them shall God reveal Himself,
They shall His glory see.

THAT VERSE FROM THE OLD HYMN IS PROBably the clearest definition of those who produce paintings (occasionally wood or stone sculpture) loosely termed folk or primitive art, art of the people, art of the common man, art of the untaught or self-taught artist. Each of these terms is inadequate, if not actually misleading. Genuine folk art, for example, is usually found only in a country where a large section of the population has had roots in the land for centuries and clings to the old customs, cultures, songs, and attitudes. These people are often very artistic, but their feeling for color and form is chiefly expressed through gay needlework and carved or painted objects of wood.

The term "primitive art" is sometimes used as a substitute or synonym for "folk art" but there is little or no connection or similarity between the two. They are distinctly different types of art, separated by centuries and civilizations. The word primitive can properly be applied only to the esthetic instinct that shaped and colored and decorated the objects of use or magic made by authentically primitive peoples: the Aztecs, Mayans, Indians and other races and tribes of the Americas, the drawings of the cave dwellers of Europe, the African Negroes, the aborigines of the various continents. Residual traces of ancient primitive art can be seen in the startlingly beautiful color designs of the hand-woven cloth still produced by almost primitive methods in Guatemala; it is only in such rare instances that primitive and folk art show their kinship.

The designation "self-taught artist" would be the most accurate were it not for the fact that many artists teach themselves by copying the works of other artists—and their output ranges all the way from the banal and obviously imitative to great examples of painting; many of the finest artists of the nineteenth century substantially taught themselves by studying and *copying* old masters in the Louvre. True, these artists copied master paintings only to get at secrets underlying the techniques; these they developed, adapted, and dis-

205

carded at will. Nevertheless, they *taught themselves,* as all genuine artists must—Michelangelo and Rembrandt, for example.

Although the phrase "naïve art" indicates the innocence of those who, untrained and unafraid, take brush in hand to put on canvas what they see with the outward or inward eye, perhaps the adjective "untaught" most aptly describes the heart-warming form of art characterized by an ingenuous love and awareness of beauty, or a desire to record or communicate so strong that it unaffectedly spills out on canvas. It should not be assumed, however, that mere ignorance, obvious lack of any esthetic instinct, or unqualified clumsiness constitutes naïve or untaught art. Unfortunately much American "folk art" has had no basis for exploitation other than those negative qualities, which add up to nothing more than "quaintness" if even to that. There must be a spark!

There are perhaps a dozen untaught artists of the United States who might well engage our attention, most prominent among them: Edward Hicks, Joseph Pickett, John Kane, Grandma Moses. The greatest is Edward Hicks. (Pl. XXVII)

Born in Bucks County Pennsylvania, in 1870, Hicks was orphaned when very young and was adopted by a devout Quaker couple Elizabeth and David Twining. They brought the child up in their faith and at thirteen apprenticed him to a coachmaker During his seven-year apprenticeship the boy learned to build a sound coach and to paint it well. In the hurly-burly of the shop, however, he lost much of his early piety and "instead of weeping and praying I soon got to laughing and swearing," having, as he adds, "a natural fund of nonsense."

Engaged on his first job after leaving the shop—he was hired to paint a local doctor's house and build him a coach —a serious illness laid him low and gave him time to consider the state of his soul. He turned more deeply to religion and when he was about thirty became a Quaker preacher. To provide a living for himself and the family he was acquiring year by year, he continued with his trade of building and painting coaches, to which he added the business of sign-painting. In the years between his apprenticeship and his Quaker ministry, the "lighter" side of his nature had begun to find expression in the painting not of useful things like coaches and houses and signs but of mere fripperies—pictures that served no purpose but to hang idly on the wall. Intermittently—and unsuccessfully—Hicks wrestled with his soul in an effort "to sacrifice all my fondness for painting."

His Quaker friends, approving the subjects of his paintings—chiefly *The Peaceable Kingdom, Penn's Treaty with the*

Indians, and *The Grave of William Penn*—were not disturbed. One of them gently said to him: "Edward, thee has now a source of independence within thyself, in thy peculiar talent for painting. Keep to it within the bonds of innocence and usefulness, and thee can always be comfortable."

In the painting of signs, Hicks could let himself go a bit. Usually one who ordered a sign wanted it enhanced by a picture, and Hicks was always happy to oblige. The proprietor of an inn commissioned a sign to include a picture of himself driving his coach-and-four. When Hicks delivered it to him, he protested that the man on the box appeared to be drunk. Hicks replied: "Thee is usually that way, and I wanted it to look natural." On the innkeeper's promise to reform, Hicks repainted the sign.

Traveling about to towns and villages to witness to the Inner Light, preaching at Quaker meetings even in the cities of Philadelphia and Baltimore, Hicks found it difficult to keep up his trade. He tried farming for a while but when that failed he turned back to painting, for he could always sell a sign or a picture. His paintings have a sureness of structure and a skill with materials that rest on the solid foundation of good craftsmanship—like his coaches, they are soundly built and well painted. It is Hicks' sense of composition, however, and his unerring eye for arrangement of pictorial elements in space, that make him a true artist. Often his spatial arrangements are complex—he is not afraid to handle varying depths of perspective—but they have remarkable clarity and firmly controlled design.

This basic soundness, subconsciously satisfying the viewer, releases him to enjoy to the full the naïvely painted figures: those good, *good* animals, the wistful lion, the alertly dignified leopard, the lamb cuddling down under the paw of the wolf, and the little child always there to lead them. Hicks is thought to have painted forty versions of *The Peaceable Kingdom,* his favorite subject. Its beaming, beautiful innocence gently nullifies the grim warning he wrote in his Memoirs: (Pl. XXVII)

> *If the Christian world was in the real spirit of Christ, I do not believe there would be such a fine thing as a painter in Christendom. It appears to me to be one of those trifling, insignificant arts, which has never been of any substantial advantage to mankind. But as the inseparable companion of voluptuousness and pride, it has presaged the downfall of empires and kingdoms, and in my view stands now enrolled among the premonitory symptoms of the rapid decline of the American Republic.*

Full of grace, Edward Hicks died in 1849.

Europe has numerous naïve artists—no doubt some still to be discovered—who are worthy of mention, but in the short space of this chapter we must confine ourselves to France, and from the score or more of noteworthy French *naifs* we shall select one, Henri Rousseau.

The greatest of all untaught painters, and one of the very great artists of the last decade of the nineteenth and the first decade of the twentieth centuries—and there were many great ones in those twenty years—was Henri Rousseau. He was born in Laval, France, of parents whose poverty, he said, was all that kept him from preparing for an art career from the beginning. He has written of himself: "It was only in 1885, after long vexation, that he started to paint, all alone, with nature for his only teacher—and a little advice from Gérôme and Clément." (The two artists he mentions were noted Academicians.) (Pl. XXVII)

In his brief account of himself Rousseau says nothing about having served with the French army in Mexico—as many believe he did—and he does not mention even his service in the War of 1870. Yet from official records we know he emerged from that war a sergeant and was a little later appointed to a minor position in a customs toll house. Although French army records of the Mexican engagement were burned, and Rousseau left no written or directly quoted reference to such experience, it seems reasonable to assume that he served as a military musician with the army in Mexico (1864-1867), as is often stated.

It is certain that he never had any formal art training. In 1886, the year after he says he began to paint, he showed two pictures in the second exhibition put on by the *Indépendants*. That same year he retired, at the age of forty-four, on a small pension to which he added tiny fees charged for teaching drawing and music—he could play violin, clarinet, flute, and mandolin—to neighborhood children. He was able, however, to devote much time to painting, straight from the heart, everything that interested him: local weddings, portraits of friends, landscapes, still lifes. His portraits and his pictures of wedding groups have an engaging stiffness that seems to accent rather than obscure the character of both the person and the event. His landscapes range from meticulously painted detail to a broad free use of the brush to achieve mass and volume that is very impressive. His flower paintings show the tiny separate spike-petals of asters, the delicate patternings of fern leaves, and every pansy has its child-face brushed in with loving care.

But it is in his exotic scenes that Rousseau reaches the

height of his genius—the wonderful jungle paintings where from richly green tangles of branches and bushes monkeys with wistful eyes or grinning mouths peer out, lions and leopards skulk, and from trees with filigree leaves oranges hang like lighted globes. It is difficult to believe, on seeing these pictures, that Rousseau had not spent some time in Mexico for although the lions, leopards, elephants and monkeys he puts in his jungles are habitants of several other continents— and can, moreover, be seen in any large-city zoo—the luxuriance of tropical vegetation, the darkly glistening colors, the atmosphere of light-filled air that filters through even the densest growth, could not have been merely imagined by a little Frenchman tethered by poverty within narrow, humdrum limits. He could have seen the individual plants in the botanical gardens, of course, as he saw the exotic animals in the zoo, but the massing of the growth and the mysterious shadow-filtered light of the jungle could scarcely have been visually experienced in a Paris conservatory. In his single— and magnificent—painting of a desert it is plain to see that it is his imagination rather than his memory that is at work, for he places a river between stretches of desert sand. This is a dream picture, one entirely outside his experience. Rousseau thought of himself as a realist; in fact, he describes himself as "on the way to becoming one of our best realistic painters." When he paints a dream, he states it is a dream.

That is the title he has given to his greatest painting, *The Dream*. Into the magnificent jungle scene of this huge canvas Rousseau brought the fondest image of his heart. On a red plush sofa set down in the midst of giant plants with wide, spiked leaves, a nude woman with long braids of hair half reclines. Around and above her wave tall blue and purple lilies. Behind trees decked with oranges and tropical birds, an elephant lifts his trunk. Two bemused and sad-eyed lions stand half-hidden among the bushes, and a mysterious black figure, with skirt of blue and red and yellow bands, lifts a golden trumpet to his lips.

This was Rousseau's last painting. The lady on the couch was his first and—although he had twice married and would have taken a third wife had the lady not hardened her heart against him—his lasting love, the Polish sweetheart of his youth, Yadwigha. He completed the painting the year of his death, and when he sent the canvas to the 1910 *Indépendants* he attached a poem to Yadwigha, fallen asleep on the red plush couch (which, incidentally, was the chief and most resplendent article of furniture in Rousseau's shabby sitting room) and dreaming of the jungle to which the artist has transported her.

Faithfully exhibiting year after year in the *Indépendants,* Rousseau's paintings—too forceful and genuinely beautiful to be ignored—were at first objects of ridicule. Then here and there a perceptive writer—or an artist who had been laughed at in his time—really *looked* at Rousseau's paintings and was surprised into approval. The gentle and highly intelligent Pissarro was one of the first to perceive and admire; Gauguin, too, discovered certain original techniques which he could—and some think he did—adopt into his own work. Around 1905 Derain, Vlaminck, Delaunay, Picasso, and the poet Apollinaire began to be impressed.

Rousseau, so long either ignored or ridiculed, took this sudden, flattering attention with childlike, dignified pleasure but with no surprise. He loved his paintings, he thought them good—they were the very best he could do, and he toiled over them day and night. Now, slowly and still for very little money, he began to sell paintings to others than his immediate neighbors, for whom he had often done portraits for a few francs. And he began to invite his new friends to the *soirées* it had long been his custom to hold in his crowded studio. The invitations to these music and art "evenings" were always formally written: "Monsieur Rousseau requests the honor of your presence. . . ." His new friends came and were amused and, let us hope, a little touched by the old-world manners and gracious dignity of this shabby, elderly little man who was a far greater artist than probably even they suspected.

The *soirées* opened with "Marseillaise," as was proper, then Rousseau played violin solos, sometimes of his own composition, and sang old songs either alone or with pupils he had invited to take part. Sometimes he recited poetry, his own or another's. He had written a three-act comedy in 1889 and no doubt he sometimes read excerpts from it or from the drama "A Russian Orphan's Revenge," on which he had collaborated with a Russian friend.

In 1908 Picasso gave a banquet for him, and Rousseau was in danger of becoming the pet of the sophisticates, who thought it piquant to refer to him as *le douanier* although he had not been a customs collector since the year after he had begun to paint, twenty years before. But he had time to do no more than savor his mild success, when a cruel and undeserved misfortune overtook him. In January 1909 he was arrested for innocent involvement with a swindler. He was tried and technically convicted, but the judge suspended sentence, as Rousseau had so plainly been victim rather than accomplice. In making his decision, the judge took the artist's paintings into consideration; upon their evidence he adjudged the painter both simple-minded and incompetent.

As though that had not been trouble enough for an old man, Rousseau had the further misfortune to fall desperately in love with a flinty widow who accepted the presents he made himself poor by lavishing upon her—and then laughed at the giver and the paintings that made his gifts possible. So his life ended, as it had begun, in poverty. He died of pneumonia October 2, 1910.

Sincere or not, the interest taken in Rousseau by the avant-garde group centered around Picasso and Apollinaire served to bring his great paintings to the attention of those who were beginning to be aware of the modern art of the new century. Rousseau's paintings had a beguiling directness of vision and intuitive control of the technique necessary to place that vision before the viewer. And their simple, natural beauty must certainly have been a relief from the convoluted and involuted intellectualism of the Cubists and their followers.

At this distance of time it would appear that the American painter Max Weber took Rousseau most seriously as a friend and an artist. A few months before the death of the weary old man, Weber arranged with Stieglitz for an exhibition of his works at "291." It was held two months after Rousseau died, his first one-man exhibition anywhere in the world.

Where Rousseau acquired the amazing technique required to paint his pictures, the exquisite color sense, the superlative knowledge of pattern and design, is as mysterious as one of his own jungle paintings. One can only conclude that it was a gift from heaven to the guileless of heart. He saw the glory, and he straightway transferred it to canvas.

20 SOUTH OF THE BORDER

ART, LIKE VEGETATION, SEEMS TO FLOURISH more luxuriantly in the Western Hemisphere the nearer the land lies to the equator. Colors become bolder and richer, forms more dynamic. Even when colors are limited to the earth pigments—brown, dusty yellow, dull red—they take on a vitality and strength not found in paintings by Northerners. And the stolid figure of the Indian in Latin-American paintings has the strength of a monolith. Art south of the border flowers, too, in gaiety and a sardonic or macabre humor that makes even the skeletons dance with glee.

Unfortunately, distances are so great and transportation so costly and difficult, that in the United States and in Europe the art of Latin America can be seen only seldom in big representative exhibitions or, more often but still infrequently, in the work of a single artist such as Tamayo, who divides his time between New York and Mexico, with trips to Europe, or of Matta, who left his native Chile in 1933 and has since lived in New York, Italy and France. Other artists of Central or South America sometimes spend several months in the United States, where on rare occasions they or their stay-at-home compatriots are given one-man shows. Yet people living in the large cities of this country can become almost as familiar as Frenchmen with the art of the leading French painters of the nineteenth and twentieth centuries, much of whose work is either owned by our big museums or exhibited by them in frequent loan shows sent over from Europe. To become really acquainted with the art of our hemisphere neighbors, however, it is essential to spend time in their own countries.

Cuba's exciting, colorful canvases are sometimes seen in New York and, recently, paintings from Haiti—as colorful but less sophisticated—have been shown here. One of the Cuban painters best known in this country, although only in a few large cities of the Eastern Seaboard, is Cundo Bermudez, whose deep but brilliant colors and semi-cubist patterns trace out musical motifs. Wilfredo Lam, also of Cuba, is internationally known for the closely woven jungle rhythms and Surrealist shapes that cover his canvases, their subtle colors expertly interrelated.

Art in Brazil has recently received impetus through the erection of a museum of modern art in the big industrial city of Sâo Paulo, second in size only to Rio de Janeiro. In 1951 Sâo Paulo held a large exhibition of European and American art, and in 1954 an enormous show in the same city drew 200,000 visitors from Europe and the Americas to see the 4,000 works assembled from all over the world—more than half of them from Latin-American countries. Candido Portinari, however, is the only Brazilian artist whose works have been seen to any extent in the United States.

It is natural that the art and the artists of our nearest neighbor to the south should be best known in this country. But twenty centuries of Mexico's art were no more than sampled in the huge exhibition held at the Museum of Modern Art in 1940 and in the one at the Metropolitan Museum of Art in 1932.

To do even minimum justice to the outstanding Mexican artists of the past three decades would require a large volume. Indeed, we can glance only briefly at the work of the Big Three of Mexico—Orozco, Siquieros, and Rivera—and the fourth, who is, of course, Rufino Tamayo, younger than the triumvirate who made Mexican art so well known in the twenties and thirties. (Pls. XXIV, XXV)

Tamayo was born in 1899 in Oaxaca, son of Zapotec Indians who moved to Mexico City when he was a child. In his teens, Tamayo went for a short time to the official San Carlos Academy, but his imagination was fired by color reproductions in art magazines of School of Paris paintings, particularly those of Picasso and Braque. That was the direction he wanted to take, and he had the inspired wisdom to see that ancient Mexican art was much closer in kinship to advanced modern painting than was the more conventional art offered for study at the San Carlos Academy. In that treasure house of pre-Columbian art, the Museo Nacional in Mexico City, he made a deep study of the art of the Mayans, the Aztecs, Tarascans, Mixtecs, and other archaic cultures including that of his own ancestors, the Zapotecs. At the same time, he took every opportunity to see the work of the avant-garde French painters in color reproduction and, occasionally, in the few originals that reached Mexico.

These two widely separated sources watered the roots of Tamayo's talent which developed into a strongly individualized synthesis, entirely different from either but partaking in essence of both. His forms are semi-abstract and he is a superb colorist, employing in strong but subtle fashion the earth colors of his native land or using a wider palette range more muted but equally rich. Tamayo has painted murals in Mexico and, in this country, at Smith College, Northampton, Massachusetts, and at Arizona State College. But he is chiefly an easel painter of moderate-sized canvases, thus making it possible for the world outside Mexico to enjoy the finest contemporary art by a Mexican painter. (Pl. XXIV)

The name of Diego Rivera probably comes most immediately to mind when there is discussion of Mexican art. Born in a mining district of Mexico in 1886, he was enabled to study at the San Carlos Academy in the capital. When he was twenty-one he went abroad, studying first in Spain, then traveling in France, Belgium, Holland, and England. After a brief return home, he again went to Paris, in 1911, and remained there until 1921, becoming a friend of Picasso, Braque, and Gris. The greatest influence he met with in Paris, however, was the work of Cézanne. He spent the year 1921 in Italy, studying Giotto's wall paintings and Byzantine mosaic. He then returned to Mexico to become one of the leaders in the renaissance of Mexican art and the Mexican mural movement. (Pl. XXIV)

A man of great physical strength and gargantuan powers of enjoyment, Rivera has never been reluctant to make his opinions known even when today's are contradicted by tomorrow's. He has been an on-again, off-again member of the Communist party, often—with much attendant publicity —bouncing into or out of the party. All of his murals are gorgeously decorative; many of them have political implications, such as the huge one he did in the main building of Rockefeller Center in 1933, ordered destroyed because he had inserted into it the head of Lenin. Rivera's genius for large-scale decoration and his very evident love of it take precedence, however, over everything else. He does a good deal of easel work and has painted several murals in the United States and many in Mexico.

The mural and easel painting of David Alfaro Siqueiros, born 1898 in Chihuahua, Mexico, has always been the expression of his deep concern for the sufferings of the people of the world. One of his most powerful paintings is *Echo of a Scream*, an agonized protest against wars that bomb babies and destroy civilizations. The artist experienced the horrors of war at first hand from the age of sixteen when he enlisted as a drummer boy in the Mexican Revolution. He was a staff officer when it ended. Given a year of art study abroad, he returned to Mexico to take part in the beginnings of the great mural movement. He was one of the first to experiment with Duco as a substitute for oil paint and has for many years used it. Art, he insists, instead of being used as the vehicle for a specific ideological message, should rest upon esthetic principles while expressing the temper of the times in which the artist lives and works. Then, whether the subject be history of a thousand years ago or an event only a few hours old, it will be art not just of the past or the present but for all time. (Pl. XXIV)

Admittedly, it would be difficult to select a single artist to epitomize the art of an entire nation—Italy, for example. Yet among all that nation's great and various artists, it might still be possible to say to Michelangelo: Here stands *Italia!* With even more centuries of art behind Mexico and much greater continuing abundance there today, the selection for that country might seem more difficult. Inevitably, however, the choice would fall on José Clemente Orozco not only as the apex of Mexican painting, but as the greatest painter of the Western Hemisphere.

This statement will of course be challenged. Many would concede that Orozco is the greatest *mural* painter of our hemisphere, but would be quick to point out that his easel painting does not approach the mastery of his murals. That is true. And it is equally true that his murals are not all of equal greatness. But no artist of this hemisphere—painting in whatever medium—has touched in grandeur and supreme genius Orozco's great Guadalajara murals, the masterpieces of Western Hemisphere painting.

Incredibly, he needed only one hand! Perched high on a scaffold with paints, brushes, trowels and other paraphernalia spread out on the trestle beside him, he had extraordinary dexterity. Whatever he set his single hand to—whether it was tying his shoelaces or painting in the difficult medium of true fresco on vast walls or in the tremendous arched vaults of high-domed ceilings—he could do more expertly and often more swiftly than most people, including artists, who are equipped with the full complement of hands.

Orozco was born November 23, 1883, in the city of Guzman, state of Jalisco. Two years later the family moved to Guadalajara, which always remained Orozco's spiritual home, as it was the home of both his paternal and maternal ancestors. Orozco was purely Spanish. When he was seven the family moved to Mexico City. On his way to and from primary school the small Clemente watched through the windows of a printing shop the great Mexican caricaturist, Posada, at work. Orozco has said this was his first impetus toward art. Not long after discovering Posada, the embryo artist learned that night classes in drawing were held in the nearby

San Carlos Academy of Fine Arts. After some difficulty, because of his extreme youth, his mother's persuasions won out and he was admitted.

When he was fourteen, Orozco's family sent him for three years to the School of Agriculture at San Jacinto. But he did not want to be a farmer. He returned to Mexico City to spend four years at the National Preparatory School, where he became noted for his skill in mathematics. But he still wanted to be an artist. He attended painting classes at the Academy, supporting himself, after his father died, by working as a draftsman in an architectural office and, later, as a newspaper illustrator.

Orozco was intermittently drawn into the Mexican Revolution as it followed its violent and disordered course. Partly because of the loss of his left hand and partly because of his nature, he did all his fighting with art. A fellow Mexican artist, Covarrubias, has said: ". . . in the period of the Revolution the ferocious caricatures of Orozco made and wrecked political reputations."

In no sense could the Mexican Revolution be called Communist or Communist-inspired. It covered, roughly, a decade of confused and interfactional slaughter Starting in 1909 with the overthrow of the tyrannical and corrupt thirty-year reign of Diaz, it degenerated—after the assassination of Madero in 1913 by the bloodthirsty General Huerta—into a bath of blood for the whole nation, taking a toll of ten million men, women, and even children killed or horribly mutilated. Out of his eye-witness experiences came Orozco's great and terrible series of drawings, *Mexico in Revolution,* executed from sketches made between 1913 and 1917.

During a period when Mexico City was comparatively quiet and not occupied by contending armies, Orozco became a government inspector in the red-light district of the city and began painting, chiefly in watercolor, his poignant *House of Tears* series of underworld women. In 1915 an exhibition of these was held in a book store and received little notice, as the artist was considered a caricaturist. A few discerning fellow artists and intellectuals, however, perceived and remembered the masterful technique and moving tragedy of the paintings. Two years later, when Orozco crossed the border on his first visit to the United States, the customs inspector at Laredo, Texas, tore up half of the 120 paintings as too "immoral" for entrance into this country.

Meantime, the surge toward a national art rose to its crest in Mexico. When Orozco returned in 1922 the Revolution was over except for an occasional sporadic outburst, the air was thick with art manifestos, and the government had set up an extensive program under the Minister of Education, the remarkably liberal José Vasconcelos. It was a genuine renaissance which drew artists from all over Mexico. Those who had been studying for years in Europe—Rivera, Siqueiros, and others—came hurrying home. The art of true fresco, which had been used in Mexico as early as the sixth century A.D. but had been largely forgotten since the sixteenth century, was revived under the leadership of Orozco and Rivera.

Almost overnight the Syndicate of Painters and Sculptors was organized and all the leading artists became members. The Minister of Education gave it his blessing and agreed to pay the artists a small daily wage based on the number of square feet of fresco finished each day. A mural art for the people was launched and artists were given not only miles of walls to paint on but the freedom to paint as they liked. Of course the conservatives raged and, at times in pitched battles with the artists, mutilated, obliterated or covered such murals as they deemed too radical.

The Syndicate, instead of living up to its motto, "One for all and all for one," became chiefly the tool of the politically powerful artists, who almost literally shoved their less aggressive fellows off the walls. Orozco, never able to play politics, found himself with no walls to paint in spite of the fact that he was acknowledged one of the leaders of Mexican art.

The legends, particularly in the United States, that grew up around Orozco gave him considerable sardonic amusement. One of these was that he had lost his hand while engaging in some wild-eyed revolutionary activity or, at the very least, in a hand-to-hand bomb-throwing match between Zapatistas and Villistas. As a matter of fact, he had lost his hand in his teens while working out a chemistry experiment—"just an ordinary accident," he said, "like any other."

Unfortunately, the legend with the least truth, in fact with no truth in it at all, persists to this day—the fantastic claim that Orozco was or ever had been a Communist. This is factually untrue and temperamentally impossible. It is true that Orozco was a member of the Syndicate of Painters and Sculptors. It is also true that when the Syndicate was organized in 1922 it published a belligerent little newspaper which its editors—Guerrero, Rivera, and Siqueiros—illustrated with big, bold woodcuts. When the Syndicate disintegrated—as it rapidly did after it became useful only to the politically smart artists—the Communists took over, or revived, *El Machete* and made it their official organ. But by this time the Syndicate no longer existed and Orozco had for some time been in the United States.

Orozco's nature was in complete opposition to Communism. Above all, he was an individualist. He claimed that right for himself and desired it for every human being on earth. He had a profound and compassionate love of humanity, but little faith in human nature especially as expressed in any political or organizational activity. His deep distrust of organizations was well founded on bitter personal experience and for that reason, as well as because of his nature, he was never a "joiner." With his fierce individualism he was always at odds with mass movements, the mob mind, and the assumption of authority. The double-edged blade of his brilliantly savage caricatures slashed like a machete right and left. He was neither pro- nor anti-Communist. He was pro-humanity and through the powerful medium of his art struck out relentlessly against any force—greed, cruelty lust, superstition, regimentation—that exploited, enslaved, or injured mankind.

At the age of forty-four, Orozco left Mexico to try his fortunes in the metropolis of the country to the north. He arrived in December 1927 and found more than the weather cold. He lived in a basement apartment on Riverside Drive, near Columbia University, and often had to dig himself out through the snow. He knew two American artists, little better off than himself, who did, however, succeed in interesting Juliana Force of the Whitney Museum in buying ten of his powerful *Mexico in Revolution* series—at the even then fantastic price of $35 apiece. (Today each of these drawings would bring $500 or more.) Nevertheless, the money came at a critical moment and served to tide the artist over until June 1928, six months after his unheralded and unnoticed arrival in this country

Here fate, in the person of the extraordinary Alma Reed, took a hand. A San Francisco journalist to whom Mexico was a second home, Mrs. Reed was told of Orozco's difficult situation by a friend who at the same time warned her of the artist's sensitive pride. Mrs. Reed immediately called on him in the small and barren, but excessively neat Chelsea studio on West 23rd Street to which he had moved. Within a few days she had drawn him into her vast and stimulating circle of friends, one of whom bought a small oil from him and commissioned a portrait.

Mrs. Reed interested individuals in his work, then the heads of galleries, museums, and art associations. She arranged exhibitions for him and, in 1929, took the daring and decisive step of opening a gallery of her own on East Fifty-seventh Street, center of New York's art world. The Delphic Studios showed other artists—Benton and Siqueiros, among them—but it was primarily for the exhibition of Orozco's work, with the ultimate object of securing walls anywhere in the United States on which he might be commissioned to paint murals. (Pl. XXV)

First of these was the *Prometheus* at Pomona College, Claremont, California, with its great central figure reaching into the arch of heaven to grasp the forbidden fire for a humanity of little souls indifferent, preoccupied, or even frightened; only a few stretch out their hands to receive the gift bought with such heroic anguish. For this magnificent art treasure, Orozco was paid scarcely enough to cover the cost of his materials and the wages of his mason! For murals he next executed on the walls of the dining room in the New School of Social Research in New York City, he was paid even less.

Orozco's third and by far his largest and most extensive mural in this country was executed for Dartmouth College. It is the only one in which the theme "Epic of Culture of the New World" is at times savagely or sardonically bitter: the rejection by society through the ages of the saviours or the teachers who could make life better and happier. Christ chops down his cross with an axe; Quetzalcoatl, the Mexican god of arts and crafts, turns from the country that refuses to benefit from his gifts; and current civilization is represented by a group of spectacled skeleton professors presiding over the birth of "stillborn education," which is brought forth from another skeleton.

For the Dartmouth mural Orozco was more adequately paid. He received a professor's salary and lived at the college. It was during this period, 1932-34, that he was able for the first time to go to Europe and see the art of France, Italy and Spain, and particularly to study the frescoes of the Renaissance masters.

It was in triumph that Orozco returned to Mexico. From then on he was offered more walls to paint, more commissions to execute than one man could accomplish in a lifetime. In his frescoes for the Bellas Artes, Mexico City's magnificent palace of the fine arts, the fallen woman—though here without compassion—of his early *House of Tears* series became the symbol of exploitation. It is in Guadalajara, however, in his native state of Jalisco, that Orozco touched the summit of his career. In that impassioned series, culminating in the figure of fire surging upward almost to pierce the vault of the dome, the artist soars to the height of his genius.

He returned to New York for a few weeks in 1940 to paint a "portable" fresco—weighing 2,700 pounds—commissioned by the Museum of Modern Art. It is composed of six movable panels on steel frames, each 9 feet by 3 feet, the plaster being held by wire mesh. On this six-part surface Orozco painted in true fresco *The Dive Bomber,* a massed wreck of machinery with the legs of the aviator sticking up out of it. One of the most fascinating and sardonic features of the mural is that the panels can be placed together in any order and either upside down, straight side up, or varied irregularly, and the resulting composition is still what the artist intended it to be—the destruction of man by the machine he has created. For who can say what is top or bottom, left or right, of a wreck?

Thus Orozco warned man against bringing about his own annihilation. And he continued to warn through the murals he painted the remaining years of his life. The last day he worked was the last day he lived. In the afternoon of September 6, 1949, half finished with the first nearly abstract mural he had ever attempted, he laid down his brushes. The next morning he was found peacefully in bed in his last sleep.

The government officially proclaimed him one of Mexico's "Immortals" and he was buried with full state honors. His beautiful Guadalajara studio, four stories high, is now a national monument, and a museum is being built in Mexico City to house his collected paintings. But his real monument for a thousand years will be the great series of frescoes he painted on so many of the walls of his native land for his fellow Mexicans and for all the world.

21 TODAY AND TOMORROW

THE YEAR 1953 SAW THE COMPLETION OF art's tremendous cycle that began with the first attempt of a caveman (the primordial father of art) to communicate fact, idea, emotion, or message through pictorial or symbolic scratches on rocks. After untold centuries of art's development, the cycle curved to its end precisely in position above its beginning, completing its rise on the spiral when the movement inspired by Kandinsky's blaze of abstract lines and swirls and Mondrian's colored geometry dominated Western art at its most Western outpost, the United States of America.

Kandinsky's paintings communicate emotion to the viewer, though it is doubtful if anything but exasperation is evoked by the painted scrawls and amoebas of many of those who think they are his followers. Although to the casual eye it appears as though Kandinsky might be the easiest of all artists to imitate, such feeble or frantic attempts leave the spectator cold; they never reach him, for the painting puts forth nothing.

It is also true that Mondrian cannot be successfully imitated; strangely, no artist has ever tried to do so. A considerable number, however, have set out from their own basis of thinking—which may or may not have been inspired or encouraged by Mondrian's example—to design the "beauty of shapes" which, according to Plato, are not "as most people would suppose, the beauty of living figures or of pictures; but . . . straight lines and circles, and shapes, plane or solid, made from them by lathe, ruler, and square. These are not, like other things, beautiful relatively, but always and absolutely."

But is it art, which started and through the ages developed as the expression of meaning and significance? Is it not, rather, the point at which the great cycle has completed itself. from the first rock scratches made to convey meaning, to this year's lines and shapes and scratches conveying nothing? Mondrian's paintings, for example, give the viewer only the esthetic satisfaction of a well-organized but totally meaningless design. It is significant, however, that in the last composition completed before his death in 1944, Mondrian was moving beyond the great cycle—completion of which his own art had signalled—toward the beginning of the new cycle in the spiral of time. Instead of giving his final composition a number, as was customary with him, he gave it a name: *Broadway Boogie Woogie,* stating that its complex but rigid design was, to him, the form-equivalent of the broken rhythm of jazz. But this was a secret between Mondrian and his canvas, plus the few who read or heard his explanation and knew the title of the composition. Without the title and the name of the artist not even the initiate could have guessed that it was more than a pattern in red, blue, and yellow blocks that would have made a handsome design for a bolt of gingham.

This is not to deny Mondrian's secure and important place in the development of art—above all, in modern design from architecture to iceboxes to textiles, probably including gingham—but his work is the end of the art cycle, where it leaves communication and departs into design. A painting that, minus its title and the name of its artist, conveys nothing, is merely self-communion no matter how its creator may protest that it is only the crass ignorance of the viewer that prevents his response.

Going through gallery after gallery of paintings by artists talking to themselves, the "crass" public may be pardoned if an old legend comes to mind, the legend of *The Emperor's New Clothes,* which tells of a couple of distinguished weavers from the next town who sell the Emperor—could he also have been a museum director?—on the proposition that they will weave for him a wonderful collection of clothes so fine, so delicate, of such surpassing beauty that they will be invisible to the crass and the gross; in fact, the clothes may be used as a touchstone to distinguish the sheep of esthetic sensibilities from the uncultured goats. The weavers then go through all the motions of weaving and making the clothes of nothing. The result is, of course, nothing, in which, with due ceremony, they clothe the Emperor. Even he dare not confess that he sees and feels nothing—for not even an Emperor wants to be considered an esthetic boob—while the courtiers murmur in great admiration of "plastic values," "tragic implications," "organic tensions." Then the Emperor marches out to exhibit his new clothes. So strong is the fear of being caught with your culture down that the public humbly repeats the phrases of the courtiers until an astonished child, seeing nothing, reports that fact in shrill tones: "But the Emperor is wearing no clothes!"

Fortunately, the artists-who-talk-to-themselves—painting

"sound and fury signifying nothing"—are few in number. Unfortunately, because of museum purchase and exhibition, they are great in influence They have been in high favor in the United States during the past several years and reached their zenith in attention and financial rewards in 1955—never in popularity for the public does not like their empty and often unbeautiful scrawls. But museum officials, in their endless search for something novel, have bought—with much attendant publicity—strange items such as a canvas so large (9 feet by 12 feet) that its load of paint must be dripped or dribbled on it from above (often from a ladder) with the canvas flat on the floor, the result appearing to be an extraordinarily tangled weave of homespun tweed. Or a canvas even larger, the upper half tinted an uncertain pink which fades off toward the center to a ragged magenta untidily dripping into the lower half of the canvas, which is tinted a fade-away yellow. Or a stark white canvas on which a few irregularly thick chunks or swatches of dull black are thrown. And then there are those splotch-paintings like Rorschach ink-blot tests or old-fashioned batik designs made three or four decades ago by dipping knotted cloth into dyes. (Pls. XXVIII, XXIX)

Paintings such as these have during the past few years entered museum collections with much fanfare, thereby influencing many private collectors to buy similar canvases at the highest prices being paid for the current work of any contemporary artist. What the upcoming generation of the year 2000 will say of grandfather's taste in art when they come upon these paintings hidden in attic and cellar—if there are any attics or cellars—staggers the imagination. The museums that own such canvases will blush to drag them out of their basement stacks even as curiosities. Now they keep the bucolic romantic realism of Rosa Bonheur, the sentimentalities of Greuze, the curvaceous ladies of Bouguereau and his imitators there. But when museums grew ashamed of luscious ladies painted nearly a century ago, they were used to dress the finest saloons of the Old West. Can you see the drip-and-dribble canvases and the Rorschach tests today performing as decorative a function fifty years from now?

But, says the apologist for the talk-to-themselves boys, this is art in flux, as is the whole world; these artists are finding their way, they are developing toward something. That may be true, but a musician is not handed Carnegie Hall in which to practice Czerny before an audience, so why not keep these five-finger exercises in art in the painter's studio until he reaches that point of development where his efforts more nearly resemble a painting than does a tinted book-jacket of enormous size, a scrambled design for tweed, or a group of ink blots? Instead, these canvases are exhibited in leading museums not as a *process toward art*—in which museums may legitimately concern themselves—but as the most advanced art of today This is a strange reversal of the Academy position in France of fifty and a hundred years ago—the too-rigid exclusion of anything new somersaulted into the wide-open acceptance of anything novel—and just as harmful

It is possible, of course, that these strange manifestations on canvas may be just a gigantic joke played by the artists—not in concert but, one becoming successful, others may quietly have compounded the joke—on a too-willing art world, the cream of the jest naturally being the good prices they get, prices very much higher than those they received for pictures they had such difficulty selling before they adopted their present nihilistic styles. The earlier paintings of certain of these artists were very good; some of their canvases were even disciplined and superior examples of genuine abstract art. It is possible to suspect that at least one artist, wrathful at so seldom selling what he knew were excellent paintings, took the largest canvas he could find and in despairing rage flung paint at it. One can scarcely blame him for repeating and elaborating the performance and gathering in the financial rewards when, no doubt at first to his stupefaction, museum purchasing committees and docile collectors began buying the things.

Highly placed museum officials and erudite writers on art take the manifestations very seriously, writing involved and intimidating articles, essays, books, and catalog forewords on them. One author has even applauded a certain painter's peak of artistic performance in dropping cigarette stubs and paint-tube tops on his masterpieces-in-process. As the paint dries, the trash is solidly imbedded as an integral part of the composition. The applauding author interprets this as a manly gesture of the artist's contempt for "the true and the beautiful" so long innocently considered an aim of art. But perhaps the cigarette butts and empty paint tubes could equally well be interpreted as the outward and visible sign of the artist's inner opinion of the worth of his paintings and his estimate of those who buy them.

Whether you call these highly touted wielders of disintegrator paint pistols "space cadets" as does the mordant Jack Levine, himself an artist of no mean reputation, or believe them to be "masters of the new baroque" producing "the most perfect beauty imaginable," it is certain that they have almost pushed off the current art stage a considerable body of artists painting today in either abstract expressionism or geometric abstractionism whose work in individual statement conveys something of the emotional power of Kandinsky or the design perfection of Mondrian.

Abstractionism in its various phases has been the major art movement in the United States during the past decade. After the Armory Show, in 1913, the work of Kandinsky and Mondrian gradually became known in this country and a few artists began painting along similar lines. By 1940 there was a small but fervent group—the American Abstract Artists—who felt they were not receiving even the minimum attention due them They were ignored, seldom exhibited, and practically never purchased by museums. In April 1940, soon after the Museum of Modern Art moved into its new home on New York's 53rd Street, they "picketed" the place, handing out an amusingly sarcastic manifesto setting forth their grievances in jumbled varieties of old-fashioned type (to indicate, of course, how unmodern the Modern Museum was) and demanding recognition. The Museum pointed out that in 1936 it had shown an exhibition entitled *Cubism and Abstract Art*. The embattled abstractionists outside the Museum quickly pointed back that *that* exhibition had included only European artists. The counter-reply of the Museum was that in 1935 the Whitney Museum had held a large showing of American abstractionists. At that point World War II began to absorb everyone's attention.

Suddenly, after the war, it became apparent that not only the American Abstract Artists group but a considerable number of other artists were "painting abstract," some with beautiful and important canvases to show for it. For several years previous to World War II various artists had been turning to abstractionism—or starting with it—as the art expression that best suited them. The most influential teacher of it in this country was Hans Hofmann, himself a well-known abstractionist who seems able to impart to his students a rich color sense and a feeling for form apparently based on Cézanne. Abstractionism was, however, only one branch of painting among the many being taught and practiced throughout the country (Pls XXVIII, XXIX, XXXI)

After the war the abstract movement seemed to hit the United States as a delayed reaction and with accelerating force. In 1950 the Metropolitan Museum of Art held a huge national competitive exhibition, *American Painting Today*, in which wall after wall was hung with abstract paintings. In 1951 the Museum of Modern Art came forth with a large show entitled *Abstract Painting and Sculpture in America*. To cap it all—and silently to signal the beginning of the end—the English abstractionist, Ben Nicholson, won the 1952 Carnegie International. By that time it was not at all unusual to hear that this or that artist, known before as an Expressionist or even a Realist, had "gone abstract." Some artists explained this as a natural development. Others shrugged and said: "Economic necessity. Nobody's buying anything today but abstractions." A few artists spoke of it as a catharsis—a means of sweeping the slate of their talent clean of all the old familiar forms and fashions.

This last reason seems to hit nearest the mark, especially in general application. The century started with explosion of color, went on to disintegration of form and at mid-century reached chaos on the canvases of the leaders of the dominant art movement in the United States. Finally, in September 1953, absolute nihilism was achieved a New York's Stable Gallery in an exhibition of abstract paintings by Rauschenberg which included several framed empty canvases—there was nothing at all on them, not even a tint. Rauschenberg had done the seemingly impossible; he had advanced art beyond Malevich's *White on White* by putting nothing on nothing. These canvases were not presented as a joke; and at least some well-trained members of the New York public gave them serious attention, anxiously telephoning art critics for an explanation of their significance. But the gallery had thoughtfully provided, in lieu of a catalog foreword, a statement by John Cage, noted percussion musician and composer whose music is characterized by long intervals of silence. Here is the statement:

> ' To whom,
>   No subject
>   No image
>   No taste
>   No object
>   No beauty
>   No message
>   No talent
>   No technique (no why)
>   N idea
>   No in ention
>   N art
>   No object
>   No f el'ng
>   No black
>   N wh e (o and)
> ' After car ul con deration, I have
> come to the conclusion hat there is
> nothing in these paintings that could

> not be changed, that they can be seen
> in every light and are not destroyed by
> the action of shadows.
>
> John Cage

It was in the United States, beginning about 1945, that the latest and largest abstract movement took place. Could it have been that the seismograph of art in this country felt the preliminary quiver of nuclear fission and was already recording chaos and nothingness on canvas before and as the atom bomb ushered them in? Art has a way of being unwittingly prophetic, of foreshadowing large events and world directions. If that is true, a faint ray of hope is dawning. Here and there chaos on canvas is beginning to shape itself into resemblance of the human form; for two or three years one of our most noted abstractionists has been fighting either to get into or get out of his paintings the figure of a terrifying woman. What will be the outcome of the battle—which has outlasted a dozen canvases and, it is reported, greatly interests the younger artists—no one knows, but at least the lady has already achieved the distinction of being the most fearsome female in the history of art. (Pl. XXIX)

Of course there will always be abstract art. In spite of temporary aberrations, each year will bring forth a considerable body of excellent work, with some outstandingly fine and interesting examples Before we leave the subject, one unique development of it should be mentioned—the "Lumia" created in 1941 by Thomas Wilfred inventor of the Clavilux color organ. The Lumia is a constantly dissolving succession of remarkably beautiful abstract forms projected in color and motion on the ground-glass face of a cabinet (in size and shape not unlike that of a television receiving set) which houses the light source and motor The designs are formed by moving lenses, colored glass, and mirrors intercepting the light beams. The Museum of Modern Art acquired a Lumia in 1942 and has it on exhibition from time to time. The composition-sequence takes seven minutes to complete; the color cycle seven minutes, seventeen seconds. The two cycles coincide every 245 hours or every ten days and five hours; therefore it can be run for that length of time without repeating one of its design compositions. Certainly a strange—and emphatically a twentieth-century—variant in art!

But to return to the more human varieties. In 1913 the public interest in modern art generated by the Armory Show was composed chiefly of ridicule and censure. In the fall of 1929 the Museum of Modern Art opened its doors and for the first time in this country the public had continuous access to a place where modern art in various phases was always on view. Through the Museum publications and traveling exhibitions genuine interest in such art began to be stimulated throughout the country. But it was not until the middle of 1935 that art—chiefly modern, because most of those concerned with it were young and forward-looking—got down to the grass roots of the country, and it became apparent that the grass roots had been thirsty for it.

In August 1935, under the direction of Holger Cahill, the Federal Art Project was organized as part of the Government's anti-depression Works Project Administration. When the Project was discontinued in 1943, nearly 1,000 murals had been completed for public buildings, the number of prints produced was prodigious, and several hundred sculptures and easel paintings numbering tens of thousands had been allocated to museums, schools, and other tax-supported institutions.

"For the first time in art history," Mr. Cahill pointed out, *"a direct and sound relationship has been established between the American public and the artist. Community organizations of all kinds have asked for his work. In the discussions and interchange between the artist and the public concerning murals, easel paintings, prints, and sculptures for public buildings an active relationship has been established. The artist has become aware of every type of community demand for art and has had the prospect of increasingly larger audiences, of greatly extended public interest American artists have discovered that they have work to do in the world.*

"The organization of the Project has proceeded on the principle that it is not the solitary genius but a sound general movement which maintains art as a vital, functioning part of any cultural scheme. Art is not a matter of rare occasional masterpieces. it is not merely decorative, a sort of unrelated accompaniment to life. In a genuine sense it should have use, it should be interwoven with the very stuff and texture of human experience, intensifying that experience, making it more profound, richer, clearer, more coherent. This can be accomplished only if the artist is functioning freely in relation to society, and if society wants what he is able to offer."

Nearly all of those employed on the Project were paid a bare subsistence wage The works of art they produced did not belong to them but to the Government. Some of these were of the highest quality, some were of little or no market value. Some of them—particularly the murals, as is their common fate whether they are Government projected or not —caused violent controversy. Yet one of the most bitterly denounced (later destroyed) murals—by Arshile Gorky in the Newark, New Jersey, airport—was a fine example of the work of an abstractionist now considered one of the best American artists of the past quarter-century, whose highly prized easel paintings today bring as much as $5,000 apiece. Canvases by many of the young artists whose weekly wage on the Project averaged a little over $20.00 now sell for $2,000 and upwards, a considerable number being purchased by our leading museums. And no one can compute the value of the Index of American Design, now in the National Gallery in Washington, a selection from which was published a few years ago in a handsome book selling for $15.00.

There, in hard dollars and cents, are a few examples that must be multiplied a thousand times to give even a slight indication of the economic gain to this country of its short-lived Federal Art Project. The really big financial profit it turned in, however, came from the nation-wide interest in art so powerfully engendered through 103 community art centers organized by the Project. This was soon apparent all over the country in the rising participation in and sales of everything connected with art—color reproductions, books, art materials, museum memberships and attendance, and even the purchase of works of art by those who could afford them but had never before been interested in acquiring a painting or a piece of sculpture. Most of these people—especially the purchasers of art works—had had no connection with and not much knowledge of the Federal Art Project. They were swept along on the wave of enthusiasm and interest which started as a ground swell in the grass roots. This country has never known such a tremendous appetite for art as has been increasingly apparent the past twelve or fifteen years.

There are no figures available on the annual purchase of painting and sculpture in the United States—much of it still imported, yet a healthy amount also paid out for the home product—but the sales taxes, the corporation and income taxes alone must contribute a sizeable sum to the United States Treasury. Statistics are at hand, however, for the enormous sales in art materials: more than $150,000,000 in retail sales for the year 1953 and substantially larger in 1954.

By far the largest part of this sum is paid out by amateur painters, from the President of the United States down to the humblest citizen, an estimated total of three and a half million color-happy adults, painting busily away at home, in the fields, on the seashore, from the tops of mountains, and many of them eagerly going to art classes—usually at night —all over the land. Lessons are also sold by mail, in kits, and even through instruction talked off on records mailed to the learner. Many groups of professionals in other lines—doctors, dentists, lawyers, photoengravers, chemical engineers, etc.— have their own amateur art associations and give exhibitions of members' work. The U.S.A. has waked up to art.

And what about the professional artist? There are at the very least 10,000 (exclusive of commercial artists) in this country, who because of the excellence of their work, deserve that classification even though they may be able to take little time from the business of earning a living or running a household to devote to the art they are capable of creating. Some of these artists paint year after year in comparative obscurity, unable or unwilling to put their work to the test of a New York exhibition. One of the latter is Fannie Blumberg of Indianapolis and Miami, who did not begin to paint until her family was raised and she herself was past the half-century mark. Largely self-taught through her acquaintance with and keen observation of the work of leading modern artists in this country and abroad, she is far from being a so-called "primitive" or naïve artist. She knows what she is doing and produces canvases, chiefly Expressionist in style, of superb color, boldly handled form, and frequent emotional power. Throughout the United States—particularly in the Midwest—artists never heard of in New York are steadily and without fanfare raising the standard of art in this country.

Yet it is doubtful if more than thirty or so artists in the United States make their living today solely from their art. Perhaps one thousand manage to carry on their creative work, selling a few paintings or sculptures annually, while relying on occasional commercial work and on teaching art for most of their income. Every year a total of about 1,000 art shows opens in New York City during the ten months of the art season, each one demanding, requesting, silently or vocally pleading for reviews from the deluged art critics.

In a book which attempts to trace the modern movement in art from its rise soon after the French Revolution, it is impossible to list the names even of outstanding painters working just in the United States today. And there is no room at all for comment on the current European art scene except to say that no new movement has taken place there since the School of Paris. A few individual artists are making names for themselves. Paris, however, seems to be lagging behind both Rome and London in this respect, possibly because many of the giants of the past half-century of modern art have been active on the scene there until very recently. Picasso still is the world's most famous living artist and no abatement in his productivity is apparent. One artist of the new generation in Europe must be mentioned—England's Francis Bacon, whose powerful and horrifying canvas, entitled simply *Painting,* grimly indicates the artist's significance to our age. (Pl. XXVI)

As for the United States, only the most random sampling can be given. There is Abraham Rattner, master of form, whose canvases have magnificent richness of color. Loren McIver, the Emily Dickinson of American painting, reveals through delicate veils of color the artistic significance of the familiar, the unique in the commonplace. From the miasma of Darrel Austin's poetic swamps ethereal ladies rise and great and wonderful tigers regard one with soul-searching green eyes. Ivan Le Lorraine Albright, one of the world's most skillful living painters, invests his marvelously meticulous—and often repulsive—realism with philosophic overtones. During World War I he made surgical drawings and has carried over into his art its detailed exactitude. He paints decay and dissolution: withered flowers, shriveled fruit, rotting wood, raddled flesh. Yet the suggestion comes through that as the worn-out shell drops away the essential flower and fruit will emerge, the rotting wood will be renewed, the spirit freed from its crumbling chrysalis of flesh. (Pl. XXVI)

A decade and a half ago Jacob Lawrence was simplifying and flattening realistic forms into two-dimensional patterns, chiefly in three or four primary or solid colors, so that his paintings had an abstract design force (strangely reminiscent of Malevich) which strengthened rather than diminished their actuality. His recent work has grown far richer in color and more complex in form but it still has the basic strength of firm design.

Jack Levine, boy prodigy of the Federal Art Project, has more than fulfilled his early promise. His paintings, dark in tone and loosely expressionist in technique, satirize the social and political scene. He has been called the Daumier of our day, but his sardonic intelligence largely rules out the compassion that made Daumier great. His longtime friend, Hyman Bloom, was an equally promising prodigy of the WPA Project. Though not so early successful, Bloom is today, like Levine, one of this country's leading artists. From the beginning a Byzantine richness of mosaic pattern in deep-toned jewel-color was apparent in the crowded detail of his religious paintings, in the shimmer of his crystal chandelier series and Christmas tree lights, in the iridescent decay of

Buried Treasure and *The Bride,* interred in all her wedding finery. For several years this painter seems to have had a corpse-obsession, with resultant morbidly powerful paintings of the human (occasionally the animal) cadaver in all stages of decay and dissection. His 1955 exhibition at the Whitney Museum was like an excursion through a morgue. There is no compassion in these paintings, no social or humanistic comment. Carrying the theme of death one step beyond the body, two of his most impressive canvases—*The Medium* and *Apparition of Danger*—dealt in sweeping, swirling forms with psychic and ectoplasmic manifestation. Although markedly different in technique, *The Medium* brings to mind Redon's canvases of mystery and ghostliness.

To turn from gruesome particularity to the cleanly abstract, the thought occurs that Charles Howard's handsome designs might more satisfyingly have decorated the big Assembly Hall of the United Nations than do the present Léger murals. The intricately abstract patterns of George L. K. Morris, a leading practitioner of that form of art long before it became fashionable and popular, have a disciplined freedom unknown to the current blob-and-spatter artists. The rounded forms of Carl Holty's abstractions, entirely unlike the work of Morris, are similarly directed by artistic intelligence and a firm grasp of design. Uniquely beautiful, the abstract compositions of Rice Pereira capture through layers of glass, each with its painted geometric design, the light which is the goal of art. Balcomb Greene, most abstract of artists, achieves an effect of light, mysterious in origin, in paintings that never confine form to reality yet suggest an infinity of visual experience. Sue Fuller's remarkable compositions of string appear rugged as suspension cables or delicate as a very modern spider's web. And there is John Hultberg, winner of first prize in the 1955 Corcoran Biennial, whose abstract paintings have the curious quality of *seeming* to represent reality—a prophetic signpost, perhaps, that points to the direction his fellow abstractionists may take tomorrow.

But the youngest generation to arrive on the art scene has not been waiting around for a signpost. As was inevitable—and clearly to be foreseen two years ago when abstract art in this country reached its apogee—the pendulum has begun its swing back from the farthest edge of nothingness. The first curve of the new cycle has started its ascent on the spiral of art. And as in the beginning, when our prehistoric ancestors used art to communicate meaning, so our newest painters—pioneers of the future—now step from the same basis but on a rising level. Again art becomes communication, pictures are beginning to talk to us again. This time, however, it is not the flat statement of objective representation. Perhaps this newest movement in modern art can most exactly be labeled Subjective Realism. This is not to be confused with the tricky and somewhat mannered form of painting which for the past dozen years has been called Magic Realism, akin to Surrealism.

The Magic Realist (we have several who are imaginatively original and technically skillful—George Tooker is one) usually paints into his picture a specific though unstated meaning. At once more subtle and more forthright, Subjective Realism, going much deeper, does not communicate specific meanings; the reality it portrays may convey as many different meanings as there are different viewers of the painting—which, it should be pointed out, is never anecdotal or literary. Robert Vickrey, still a very young artist—he was thirty in 1956—has been painting in this manner for several years. In 1952 the Whitney Museum purchased his *Labyrinth* —a fascinating arrangement of rectangular forms with a frightened and bewildered woman caught in their maze. The artist will tell you that this picture has no meaning at all —yet the painting speaks for itself in the language of each viewer's innermost perception. Vickrey's latest canvas *Conversation* is less complex, but it also makes abstract use of real objects (the torn signs and the nun's headdress) and again the viewer is free to read his own meaning into the relation of the two figures with each other and with their tattered background. (Pl. XXX)

Alton Pickens, in complete command of realistic technique, often uses off-center angles and distorted positions—not distortion itself—with dramatic effect. Some of his paintings, emphatically realistic, are at the same time superb examples of abstract design. Keith Martin's lyric realism, even when it moves into abstraction, still conveys an actuality of meaning. Carlyle Brown, especially in his *Round Table with Fiasco and Landscape*, poetically and subtly expresses the trend toward Subjective Realism.

Margo Hoff reduces reality to essential form, then through exaggeration makes her point—as in *Grownup Party*, where the child is surrounded by gigantic and shadowy enlargements of the other figures. McKie Trotter approximates reality by a painterly astute manipulation of abstract forms, particularly in his adroit interpenetration of light and dark areas. Conversely, he often lets abstract pattern plainly emerge through realistic shapes. The expressive realism of Honoré Sharrer strikes much deeper than surface actuality; it is concerned with "men's predicaments, joys, his relation to the machine and the earth." With this painter, art is communication and has meaning. At the other end of the scale—non-human forms with a curious suggestion of reality, arranged in exquisitely calculated geometric design that with comic gravity imitates human activity—are the paintings of Attilio Salemme. Born in Boston in 1911, he went to New York when he was eighteen. There he had his first one-man exhibition in 1945 and made his first sale to a museum. He died suddenly in 1955. Jan Yoors, a young Dutch artist who has been in this country several years, is a master designer of mural tapestries, which he weaves himself. His work has Gauguin-like simplification of form and bold richness of color, yet there is a suggestion of medievalism at once elusive and satisfying.

The general level of excellence of the art being produced in this country continually rises. We are not now and have never been a nation of creative artists. In large measure our thoughts and energies have been concentrated on other objectives. But a slight shift in the focus of our attention is faintly discernible. We are at least becoming aware of the extraordinary number of vigorous and original artists working in our own country today, with more coming into bloom every year. Who knows what heights may be reached when the peaks begin to shoot up above this ever-rising level of excellence?

In the meantime, have fun! Never enter a museum or an art gallery to kowtow to culture. Take wonder, eagerness—above all, take with you readiness of mind and heart. Look at a picture as through an open window; you may look out on a new country, look into another's mind or heart and discover your own. Take laughter, if you like, but don't be surprised a few years hence if the joke turns out to be on you.

Enjoy yourself!

INDEX